Buddhism
on the
Couch

Buddhism

FROM ANALYSIS

on the

TO AWAKENING

Couch

USING BUDDHIST PSYCHOLOGY

CAROLINE BRAZIER

Ulysses Press

Published by:
Ulysses Press
P.O. Box 3440
Berkeley, CA 94703
www.ulyssespress.com

First published in the United Kingdom by Robinson,
an imprint of Constable & Robinson Ltd 2003

Library of Congress Cataloging-in-Publication Data
Brazier, Caroline.
    Buddhism on the couch : from analysis to awakening using
Buddhist psychology / Caroline Brazier.
        p. cm.
    Includes bibliographical references and index.
    ISBN 1-56975-349-0
    1. Buddhism--Psychology. 2. Change (Psychology)--Religious
aspects--Buddhism. 3. Spiritual life--Buddhism. I. Title.

BQ4570.P76B7 2003
294.3'01'9--dc21   2003042642

Printed in Canada by Transcontinental Printing

10 9 8 7 6 5 4 3 2 1

Distributed in the United States by Publishers Group West
and in Canada by Raincoast Books

Contents

Preface

It was a glorious autumn day. The sky was a deep vivid blue. As I walked along the road toward my school, the golden leaves on the lime trees that overhung the schoolyard were filled with light, forming a shimmering canopy above my head.

It was the early seventies. I was seventeen, and at that age I was finally allowed to escape from the school's confines at times when I did not have lessons. I had probably been into town to buy lunch, or maybe to meet with friends for coffee in one of the cafés where we frequently hung out.

In that moment, sun and dancing leaves seemed to fill me. I thought: *This is as good as it gets*.

It was an ordinary moment. Just sunshine, a gentle breeze, and the bright colors of sky and leaves. Yet in that moment I knew for certain that this experience was perfect. I felt complete joy. There was no room for anything better in my heart. It was full.

Most of us can remember moments of this kind—moments when the world opens its heart to us and we embrace it.

Too often though, our hearts are closed.

Too often we are caught in a prison of our own making.

*

The world is a wonderful place. It is also a place where terrible things happen. This morning, as I write, a golden sun is breaking through the strands of cloud that edge the horizon, bathing the January landscape with warm light and throwing the elegant branches of winter trees into contrasting darkness. From my window, high in the house, I look out over a landscape that could be the Pure Land, the world of the Buddhas, where enlightenment is always available.

At the same time, this world hovers in uncertainty. Talk of war crowds in alongside other potential disasters. We hear from the rural health project that our group supports in Zambia of growing famine. Much farming in the area has gone over to cash crops, so local staples are no longer as plentiful. Now the rains have failed again. Climate seems to be changing. It is doing so in many places across the globe. Next week we will be campaigning on behalf of primates who are due to be subjected to the most terrible treatment in the furtherance of science. Whether the experiments will actually improve people's ability to cure the ravages of the aging process is uncertain, but humans fear such sickness and are willing to go to considerable lengths in an attempt, however vain, to avoid it.

At the same time, the shops are crowded. Christmas glitter has given way to hard-nosed January sales. Cars line up to fill already overcrowded car parks. People jostle and struggle through the crowds, laden with carrier bags and cardboard packages. New acquisitions join the Christmas gifts, and houses are overfilled, so other goods must be discarded, half-used. The refuse collectors are doing overtime. Ads for diet foods assault my computer. Most Westerners are paying the costs of an overindulgent festive season.

Why do humans act this way? Why do we so often not see the beauty in the things that we already have? Why are we always grasping at what we do not have and trying to avoid or destroy what we do not like? Buddhism has always struggled with such questions. The Buddha himself began his spiritual search in response to his realization of the omnipresent afflictions of life. The answers that he found created the basis for a religion that places a high emphasis on understanding the mind's ability to create misery through its attempts to find personal comfort at the expense of facing what is really there. It created a religion in which the understanding of mental process and the creation of methods for working with it became central. For Buddhism, therefore, psychology is not a peripheral interest. It is, rather, embedded in its most important teachings.

In some senses, therefore, it becomes questionable whether it is even possible to treat Buddhist psychology as a separate discipline from Buddhism as a whole. At the same time, of course, presenting the teachings as psychology creates the possibility that the understanding Buddhism offers can be extended to those who might not otherwise engage with the religious aspects of the faith. Also, for those of us who are practicing Buddhists, it challenges us to look at the practical expression of the teachings, always a priority for the Buddha himself, and to avoid falling into abstract metaphysics, divorced from our day-to-day lives. This book, then, presents the Buddhist teachings viewed through the eyes of the therapeutic practitioner. It offers a practical guide for those who engage with others in therapeutic ways, and a source of personal insight for the general reader.

Buddhism teaches that it is because we try to shut out the terrible things that happen in the world that we also shut off the beauty and the wonder that are all around us. Buddhist psychology teaches us how to restore our vision and break out of this imprisonment. Buddhist training provides methods for doing so. This, in a nutshell, is the theory that is unfolded in detail in the work that follows.

*

In 1995 my husband, David Brazier, wrote *Zen Therapy*. That book changed the direction of our work. We had been running a training course in psychotherapy for some years. Based on Western phenomenological approaches, the course was strongly influenced by our Buddhist practice, but it was still framed in Western terminology and ideas.

It was a crisp, bright day in late autumn of that year when we drove to Edinburgh together. The drive from Newcastle, where we then lived, was about three hours. We took the inland route over Carter Bar, a magnificent run across the high moorland of Northumberland, up past Cat Clough reservoir, and on toward that border crossing point where all the southern Scottish plains lie spread out like patchwork as far as the eye can see. How I had grown to love those open northern spaces.

Traveling together is something we greatly enjoy. It is a time when we talk and share ideas, plan and develop our thinking. It is creative time sandwiched between episodes in our busy and varied lives.

We stopped for coffee in a small country inn. It was warm and welcoming, and a wood fire burned in the grate. We were discussing the course.

"Why don't we start to teach Zen Therapy in the course?" I asked.

"Why not?"

"Why not?" was rather our motto. Over the years we have often said "Why not?" and have consequently followed many interesting new strands in our work or welcomed fruitful new relationships with others involved in similar areas. "Why not?" led to the founding of Amida Trust in 1996 and its subsequent growth, which was to become an umbrella for the new training course as well as for the many other engaged Buddhist activities in which we are now involved.

So we began to discuss how the theoretical framework David had written about in *Zen Therapy* might become the grounding for a dedicated Buddhist psychotherapy training program. What would we teach? How would we train students to put into practice the models which Buddhist psychology offers? We decided to relaunch the course, incorporating these new ideas more actively than before under the rubric of a Buddhist psychotherapy training program. New students joined and a new era in our work together began.

Since that time the course has developed, and our understanding of the subtleties of the psychology embedded in the Buddha's teachings has gone on developing with it. David's lifelong studies in Buddhism have borne fruit in two books, *The Feeling Buddha* and *The New Buddhism*. In 1998 we created a Buddhist Psychology Distance Learning Course, which is now offered by Amida Trust, and sets out the core theory for the Buddhist psychotherapy training program. All through this time we were also actively working as psychotherapists, both with individuals and with groups, and reflecting on our therapy practice in terms of the theoretical models that we were developing and applying. We were also moving into other forms of applied Buddhist work in which the same theoretical models could be brought to bear.

Alongside this work, and under the auspices of the Amida Trust, the Order of Amida Buddha came into being. This is a socially engaged religious order in the Pure Land school. Within the order, spiritual training in engaged settings has grown, both through the growth of the Buddhist House community in Narborough, Leicestershire, where we now live, and under the umbrella of a new course program in "fully engaged Buddhism." This new venture, launched in autumn 2002, also drew on an understanding of Buddhist psychology and its analysis of mental conditioning processes.

For guidance in this work, we have returned repeatedly to the original texts, and especially the Buddhist sutras of the Pali Canon, where a great deal of specific material on mental process and its ethical consequences can be found. We have also drawn much inspiration from the Pure Land Sutras, as well as many of the important texts of the Mahayana tradition.

This present book, then, is a synthesis of the new developments that have come about in our work since *Zen Therapy* was written. It reflects our deepening use of the models that Buddhist teaching offers for comprehending the mind and its conditioned nature. In writing this book, I hope to share what has been an exciting journey for me. I also acknowledge deeply my gratitude to David for the knowledge and ideas that he has shared with me, which are at the root of much that is included here, and for his companionship in the path of discovery.

At the same time I must also acknowledge the contribution of students, fellow members of our community, and those I have worked with in various therapy settings. It has been said that a therapist should learn something from every client. Certainly it has often been through my work with people who have come to see me in this capacity that it has become apparent how the processes described here unfold; and it has been in these situations that the possibilities for change suggested in this book have become clear. My gratitude to others who have been involved in the processes that have created this book reaches out in many other directions to many people. Some of them are mentioned in the anecdotes included here as illustrations: my family, parents, children and friends, and those who have taught me over the years in many ways and many places. Sometimes our acquaintances have been longstanding and mutually recognized. At other times they have been simple encounters, perhaps hardly noticed by the other. Inspirational meetings take many forms. To all these bodhisattvas I give thanks.

*

This book provides a sequel to the theoretical material presented in *Zen Therapy* and also in David's 1997 book, *The Feeling Buddha*. It pulls together the main psychological teachings of Buddhism and shows how they all fit into one picture. It describes the processes of self-limitation into which we fall and the ways in which we attempt to avoid the existential pain of life. We create deep-rooted patterns of habit-energy, which we come to identify with and think of as a "self." This self entraps us, leading us into repetition of unhelpful avoidance strategies. It becomes our prison.

Buddhist psychology is broadly applicable. The Buddha taught ordinary people so that they could train in order to develop spiritual maturity. He sent them out into the world to pass on what they learned "for the good of the many." Thus, Buddhist psychology was born in the context of the community. It was always intended as a path lived in the wider society rather than in the isolation of a monastery. As a therapy, Buddhist psychology need not be confined to the therapy room.

Buddhist psychology thus provides a framework that is relevant in many helping settings. Because it is based on an understanding of the way that the mentality is conditioned by actions, it is particularly relevant to lifestyle-based approaches to psychological helping. It is practical and behavioral. At the same time it offers detailed analyses of the psychodynamics of conditioning, thus bridging with wonderful clarity the division Western psychology has erected between, on the one hand, psychodynamic and, on the other, cognitive behavioral schools.

This book is suitable for anyone who works with others in psychological or therapeutic ways. It offers important material for the psychotherapist, but is equally applicable for the community activist, the educator, or the humanitarian aid worker. Also, Buddhist psychology offers a framework for understanding mental process to those who wish to develop their own spiritual training in this direction or to support others in doing so. Its vision is of the engaged Buddhist practitioner. This person, like the early followers of the Buddha, is engaged in working with others in these varied settings, and, in the process of this, is also developing his or her spiritual training.

The path of the engaged practitioner is a path of training. As we help others, our own habit patterns become all too apparent to us, and these can then be tackled. In Buddhist practice, qualities such as compassion and calm can then be developed that support work in difficult settings. Thus going out into situations of engagement and returning to periods of meditative practice provide a balance for one another. At the same time, within each activity, encounter and the development of stillness can co-exist. In both situations we learn to find the still point in the midst of turmoil, whether that turmoil is external or within our own minds. The practitioner develops spiritual training through right action and refining the mind. In doing so, he or she brings benefit to others and creates conditions for a better world.

The world is currently beset by many of the problems that the Buddha saw in his own times. We are bound in situations of conflict and acquisitiveness. The Three Poisons, which the Buddha identified as creating such havoc in our lives—greed, hate and delusion—are as rife in our culture as they ever were in former centuries. Buddhist psychology offers insights that can potentially transform these and bring about a more enlightened culture. Let us work together toward this end.

USE OF SANSKRIT TERMS

This book uses some terms in Sanskrit because these terms are technical and have specific meanings. Although the new terminology does take some getting used to, it prevents the dangers of misunderstanding that arise when an equivalent Western word is chosen. Ultimately it is less confusing to use words in Sanskrit than to use translations, since Western words have their own associations that do not necessarily match the associations of the words they are translating. Many of the misconceptions that have arisen in western Buddhism have come out of poor translations of terms. Even when a word is accurately translated, it is easy to forget that nuances of the original may be lost, or new meanings may be construed that are not faithful to the original term. The use of Sanskrit terms is a reminder to be cautious in these matters. With the key terms we are using, it is important to find the right meanings.

In fact, this book requires the reader to master only around thirty words. These are explained in the text as they are introduced so that the necessary vocabulary can be gradually acquired. A glossary is also provided for reference.

Part 1
Theories and Models

· 1 ·

An Afflicted World

All of us have been born. We have experienced ill-health. Maybe we have experienced declining abilities. We have been separated from, and sometimes lost, those we love. We will grow old and we will die. Many of the events that shape our lives are difficult to bear and cause us sadness and distress. Inevitably, we and our loved ones are caught in forces we cannot control.

Yet the sun shines on a spring morning too, and new leaves break out of the hard buds on the tips of wintry branches. The white dog violets grow along the newly cleared path that cuts across the woods at our retreat center in France, and clouds of cowslips dance on the grassy bank by the old well.

No day passes when we do not switch on the news to see tragedy unfolding in many corners of the world. And yet these few events that make the headlines are nothing compared with the many small and large experiences that shatter lives and leave jagged edges of pain in societies waiting for the next conflict to erupt.

Yet, as I walk across the water meadows dotted with yellow mustard flowers waving among the new green grass, a heron flies overhead, a dark shape against the clear blue sky. Its wings flap slowly, and the sun catches the silver of its back.

Last night one of our community spoke to a Kurdish friend in London. A group of thirty-two of his fellow Kurds have recently died in prison back home. Home? These are a people without country, living on the borders of several countries in the Middle East: Turkey, Iraq, Iran. In all places they are oppressed minorities. More Kurds died in the hunger strike protests that followed the killings. This man's brother will be in the next wave of hunger strikers. He will likely die too. Our friend has lived and worked with these refugee people in London and knows their grief and loneliness. He caught the early bus this morning to be with his Kurdish friend.

"There is nothing I can do, but I have to be there," he told me.

This weekend he will play with his friends in a concert of Kurdish music. This concert will bring together refugees and supporters. It will replenish the spirit of these people. He will share their pain and witness their strength. He will stand by them in their grief.

None of this will reach the headlines. Nor will many of the other sufferings people endure around the world. Suffering is everywhere.

The Roots of a Teaching

In my therapeutic work I see many people caught by suffering. Sometimes people seek support at times of crisis; sometimes they come years later, still struggling to come to terms with painful events from earlier in their lives. Sometimes they fear the future and cannot bear the uncertainty of living with a knowledge that life is transient for them and others. I have no answer that will prevent loss or death or physical discomfort. These are the realities that shape all our lives. They are also the factors that may bring us to look at life more deeply and eventually lead us to live more fully.

The Buddha was affected by the events and sights that he encountered in his early life. These colored the direction of his teaching. Although the historical details of his life are uncertain and no doubt differ in some respects from the traditional stories, these stories are the potent backdrop to all Buddhist teachings.

The Buddha was a prince who grew up in some luxury in a palace in northern India. We know that his family was of the warrior caste, which no doubt influenced his steadfast spirit. Although the Buddha's mother had died seven days after his birth, he was surrounded by family and servants. His early life was comfortable and indulgent, but this did not satisfy him. His heart was full of questions and his mind set on discovering spiritual meaning, so he renounced the palace to embark on a spiritual search, joining the numerous wandering ascetics of his day.

According to the story, the young prince, named Siddhartha, had what we might think of as a sheltered childhood, kept within the confines of the royal palace, where his father attempted to shield him from the view of anything disturbing or unpleasant. A prophecy made at the boy's birth had foretold that when he grew up he would either become a great ruler or a great religious figure, and this had disturbed the old king. He determined that his son should follow the first of these courses and avoid anything that might awaken spiritual interest in him. In this, the king seemed to know that pain and suffering hold the keys to spiritual awakening.

Indulging the young man's senses with every pleasure imaginable, the king tried to deaden Siddhartha's curiosity. Good food, attractive women, dancing and merrymaking, beautifully adorned apartments: these were the distractions on which the young prince was raised. Myth has it that three pleasure gardens were created within the palace walls, one for each season of the Indian year, filled with perfect comforts and insulated from the darker side of life. How could any young man resist?

As he grew older, Siddhartha's status increased. As heir to his father, he was recognized and honored as the future ruler. He settled into palace life and took a wife; together they had a son. It seemed he would indeed become the great leader his father wished. But Siddhartha grew bored and uneasy with the life of the palace. We can imagine the frustration that such limitless pleasure, but limited scope, brought to this bright young man. Even in an idyllic world where he wanted for nothing, he sensed that there was more to life.

The young prince wanted to understand life more deeply. Pleasure and status were not enough. He felt impelled to go out into the world to see its other aspects. He wanted to find out what life outside the palace was like. So, persuading one of his horsemen to accompany him, he planned to visit the town. Together they crept out of the palace by night.

The next part of the story describes the pivotal point in the Buddha's transformation. That night, outside the security of the palace, Prince Siddhartha had an experience that was to confirm him in his later direction as a spiritual leader. At the heart of his story lie the encounters that occurred that night.

The town outside the palace was a different world from anything Siddhartha had seen before. He saw poor people living in hovels, struggling to survive on poor diets and in cramped, insanitary conditions. He saw lean animals and barefoot, ragged children. He saw beggars, the elderly and sick people on the streets, just as one does in India today. Although there would have been laughter and bustle, there would also have been a great deal of pain and suffering apparent everywhere.

Seeing such suffering, Siddhartha knew he had been right to suspect that there was more to life than pleasure palaces and dancing girls. He was confronted with the knowledge that pain, disease and death were inevitable. In contrast with his palace of comforts, here it was impossible to avoid knowing that suffering existed and that life was precarious. With his sensitivity to the pain of others, he found this knowledge almost unbearable.

These encounters with the uncomfortable and unavoidable reality of suffering have been formulated in the traditional Buddhist teachings as *The Four Sights*. They are recounted as a series of meetings on the city streets. No doubt the four encounters described in this teaching are in fact symbolic of the many actual encounters that the young man had. These four sights confirmed Siddhartha in his search for spiritual knowledge and ultimately led him to start out on the path to enlightenment.

The first three sights were, according to tradition, a sick man, an old man, and a corpse. We can imagine that such sights would have been commonplace in the India of his day. These three sights brought him to question his companion in horror:

"What are these things? What do they mean? How can such terrible things be overcome?"

The answer he received brought little comfort. These were not isolated ills. We must all face sickness, old age and death.

In shock and dismay Siddhartha absorbed the news. His ability to live in the world of pleasure was shattered for ever. Siddhartha's father had been right to fear that images of pain and suffering would divert his son onto the path of spiritual enquiry. Siddhartha looked around in desperation for an answer. At this point he saw the fourth sight, a sadhu or holy man who was walking across the town square.

We can imagine the impact of this figure as he walked across the market place. The sight of a holy man, grounded in spiritual practice, both present to his surroundings and not swept away by them, evokes a deep reverence and respect. This man's presence inspired Siddhartha to embark on his spiritual journey. It brought him to a realization that there was a different way to live and a determination to set a new course in his life.

Returning briefly to the palace, Siddhartha prepared for his departure. His spiritual journey had begun. His act of renunciation was final. He left the palace, his father, the aunt who had brought him up, his wife and son, and set out on a course that took him to many of the great teachers of his day.

Siddhartha experimented with many ascetic practices and followed different philosophies, studying with the finest thinkers he could find. He reached many deep understandings, but ultimately these didn't satisfy his searching mind. He moved from teacher to teacher, learning much but never finding quite what he was looking for. Along the way he found others who were also searching for spiritual answers. Particularly, he found a small group of men who followed ascetic practices, but even with these fellow practitioners he did not resolve his questions. Having pushed deprivation to its limit, he knew there had to be another way. His friends moved on, leaving him alone. Finally, he had exhausted all the teachings that were available and found himself, without companions, still searching for an answer to the pain of life, in solitary desperation. Here, at the point when he had all but abandoned hope of finding the goal of his quest, Siddhartha reached a place of breakthrough. This time it was complete. The breakthrough was his enlightenment.

All night Siddhartha sat in torment beneath the bodhi tree. His struggles on that night of his enlightenment are chronicled in the Pali sutras. He struggled against all the forces his mind could summon to distract or tempt him away from his resolution to make sense of the suffering that was inevitable in life—struggled with the forces of fear, longing, and destruction that the knowledge of that suffering provoked, and with the pull of the past. Holding firm to his intention to understand, he sat unmoved. Seeing the morning star rise on the following daybreak, he understood. He was enlightened. It was at this point that he realized the *Four Noble Truths*.

The Four Noble Truths: An Understanding of Suffering

The Buddha understood the inevitability and universality of suffering. His spiritual search began with a direct encounter with suffering. It ended in a new understanding of affliction. This understanding was embodied in his teaching of the Four Noble Truths—a key element in the understanding that came to the Buddha on the night of his enlightenment. The Buddha's understanding of suffering grew out of his own experience. His encounter with the Four Sights and the teaching of the Four Noble Truths mark the beginning and end of a spiritual search.

The teaching of the Four Noble Truths is a cornerstone of Buddhist understanding. It offers an analysis of the basic human process of responding to life's afflictions and a framework for understanding and working with the pain in our own lives and in the world.

In his book *The Feeling Buddha* (Brazier 1997), David Brazier presented his interpretation of the teaching of the Four Noble Truths. This interpretation differs in some respects from the traditional one, and it is on his interpretation that I will draw in the remainder of this chapter. Whether or not this interpretation offers the most accurate understanding of what this particular teaching intends, its broad spirit reflects the essence of Buddhist psychology and practice. It is not my intention to enter into discussion of the merits of the different interpretations in detail here, since David Brazier has already done so at length in his book. His interpretation is grounded in linguistic analysis and, besides being convincing in this respect, offers a perspective that sits well with the other major teachings of the Buddha. For anyone wanting to apply Buddhist psychology, it offers a positive and practical framework of ideas, consistent with traditional Buddhist practice.

Since the analysis of Buddhist psychology presented here depends upon our understanding of the meaning of particular words, there is, for the layperson, a difficulty of language. The words used are technical terms and as such have quite specific meanings. Translating these words makes for easier reading but ultimately creates confusion, since equivalent western terminology never fully covers the meaning of the original and often carries its own set of associations, which may be wholly inappropriate to the real meaning of the term. For this reason I will use Sanskrit terms in this book. Sanskrit is one of the ancient languages of India and has become the language most commonly used in the West for rendering Buddhist terms. I will be quoting extensively from texts, or sutras, that were written in Pali, another ancient Indian language, but for consistency, I will stick to using Sanskrit for technical terminology. It is my hope that the reader will become familiar enough with the terms used (of which there are around thirty), to use them easily. Words such as "karma" and "Buddha" have already become familiar parts of the English language, and there is the possibility that other terms will also cross this usage barrier, just as technical terms from Western psychology have. For quick reference, a glossary is provided at the back of this book.

Let us return, then, to the teaching of the Four Noble Truths, and look in more detail at the elements that make up this teaching. The Sanskrit terms for these are:

- dukkha;
- dukkha samudaya;
- dukkha nirodha;
- marga.

What the Buddha gained on the night of his enlightenment was a deep realization of the inevitability of affliction. The Sanskrit word for affliction is *dukkha*. He further saw how a deep understanding and acceptance of the inevitability of dukkha provides the route for human transformation, just as it had for his own.

Dukkha

Whoever you are, you cannot avoid painful experiences. You will become sick, get disappointed, and lose people you love. You may not get what you want, and you will die. This was the Buddha's first understanding. More than this, though, these things are not shameful. They are inevitable parts of life, and they are noble. As a man of the warrior caste, Siddhartha understood nobility. He understood the need to stand firm in the face of the enemy. He understood endurance. Despite his sheltered lifestyle, he knew how to face pain. This was the truth of dukkha.

> *The noble truth of dukkha, affliction, is this: birth, old age, sickness, death, grief, lamentation, pain, depression, and agitation are dukkha. Dukkha is being associated with what you do not like, being separated from what you do like, and not being able to get what you want. In short, the five skandhas are dukkha.* (Samyutta Nikaya 61.11.5)

In this passage we can see that the Buddha lists as dukkha both the inevitable events of life and the emotional reactions which arise in response to them. In referring to the latter, he picks out in particular the "five skandhas." This term, sometime translated as the *five aggregates of grasping*, is important in understanding Buddhist psychology. We will return to it in some detail in Chapter 5. Suffering is inevitable in the sense that you cannot avoid painful events; but there are also things that cause suffering that may be amenable to change. In particular, it is grasping or attachment that creates inner anguish.

It is important to understand the meaning of the skandha teaching, as it is easy to think that the Buddha advocated detachment from life. Reading that one should not grasp or be attached, some people suppose that the Buddha discouraged close, loving relationships. In fact, the intention of his teaching is the opposite.

For the present, it is enough to know that the skandha teaching concerns the trouble caused by an attachment to maintaining your own position, views, and habitual comforts. Buddhist practice helps you achieve more contact with the world as you encounter it in each moment. This includes encountering your suffering. It also includes encountering those you love. The Buddha often exhorted his followers to "give up the skandhas"—for example, in Majjhima Nikaya 23: the Ant Hill Sutra, discussed in Chapter 7 of this book. (The Majjhima Nikaya [hereafter MN for brevity] is one of the collections within the Pali canon, and there will be many quotations from it in this book.) In doing so, he was exhorting his followers to become fully alive to the world. We inevitably experience losses, but we do not have to compound our suffering by clinging to things we cannot have, by trying to fit the world to our viewpoint so that we can feel safe, or by falling into compulsive patterns of avoidance behavior. These are all aspects of the skandha process that we will deal with later in this book.

Dukkha Samudaya

The Buddha understood that when you encounter dukkha, responses arise in you. This is the second Noble Truth, *dukkha samudaya*. Of this the Buddha said:

> The noble truth of samudaya, response to affliction, is this: it is thirst for self re-creation that is associated with greed. It lights upon whatever pleasures are to be found here and there. It is thirst for sense pleasure, for being and for non-being. (Samyutta Nikaya 56.11.6)

In this description of the second Noble Truth, the Buddha offers an explanation of the way people respond to suffering. You experience dukkha and a feeling response arises in you. This response has emotional energy.

It is easy to recognize the physical surge of emotion that comes in response to a painful situation. You hear of a friend's death, and your chest fills with sensation. You burn with anger or feel torn apart with grief. As my companion heard of his Kurdish friend's plight, he did not simply react with thoughts, he responded with agitation and with a hunger to act. He wanted to go, to be by his friend's side, to move and not to stay still.

The Buddha describes the physicality of this response as a thirst. Often it is a thirst so powerful that you feel overwhelmed. You seek to assuage it through distractions. Although you might use the energy by acting to improve the situation you are in, you may feel powerless and therefore seek to dissipate the feelings through behavior which has no direct relevance to helping the situation, like indulging in eating, drinking, work, or whatever comes to hand most readily. These behaviors quickly become compulsive patterns. It may be noble to stand firm in the face of affliction, but facing dukkha is uncomfortable. People respond by craving for ways to get rid of the uncomfortable feelings.

So a first step in releasing yourself from compulsive patterns of behavior is to master the ability to find stillness in a place of suffering. Although your impulses may all be toward doing something to distract yourself, you need to learn to stop and just be with the feelings of dukkha. Even if the impulse seems good, such as the impulse to help others, it may still contain strong elements of distraction and escape. At this point, you need to stay with the feelings of grief or anguish that arise and honor them. There will be a time to use the energy that we have for action; but first it must be properly harnessed.

When something painful happens, then, the impulse is to escape into distraction and activity. The Buddha speaks of this response as a thirst, and he also speaks of self re-creation. When something really terrible happens, like a sudden tragic death, the experience can threaten you at a level where you feel your whole being is disintegrating. It cuts apart the sense of permanence and identity and leaves you feeling raw and all too aware of your own fragility. You feel the unbearable pain and are overwhelmed with the compulsion to rebuild a secure sense of self. Building identity is one response to dukkha. It is a way in which people attempt to control the uncertainties that surround them and create an illusion of safety. Building a self-structure is seen as a defensive process in Buddhist psychology. In this book we will learn how this self-structure is created and how it may be let go.

Dukkha Nirodha

The third Noble Truth is *nirodha*. Of this, the Buddha taught:

> *The noble truth of nirodha, containment, is this: it is the complete capturing of that thirst. It is to let go of, be liberated from and refuse to dwell in the object of that thirst.*
> (Samyutta Nikaya 61.11.7)

This statement suggests that the way to face dukkha is to let go of the object to which the thirst has become attached. Nirodha is frequently translated as "cessation." It is quite possible to use this translation and interpret dukkha nirodha as the cessation of attachment to our various objects of distraction, but this translation may miss a dimension of the teaching. If cessation is the Buddha's meaning in this teaching, he uses the word nirodha in a way that was unusual for his time. In *The Feeling Buddha*, David Brazier points out that the common meaning of the word nirodha was to confine, originally associated with the creation of an earth bank (rodha). "Ni-' means "down," so we can see an image of sheltering a fire behind a bank or containing it. In using the word nirodha, the Buddha may be alluding to an image of the containment and harnessing of a fire.

The image of the contained fire would be a familiar one in the India of the Buddha's day. A fire that is not contained is a danger in any community, for it may quickly get out of control. On the other hand, a fire may also go out without containment: the wood may be too scattered, so that the heat is insufficient to maintain it; wind or rain may extinguish the flames. With an earth wall around it, the fire can be directed and used. It can be damped down at night, or its heat can be intensified so that it can be used under cooking pots.

The Buddha saw the spiritual path as one in which powerful and potentially dangerous forces could be harnessed and applied beneficially. He used the fire analogy on a number of occasions.

He also expressed similar ideas using the simile of the snake, a potentially dangerous creature which is, nevertheless, a source of healing if caught in the correct way, when its venom can be milked and used as a medicine. The Buddha described his own teachings as like a snake (MN 22).

If you look at the description of nirodha given in the passage above, you will see that there are two main elements:

1 containment or capturing of the arising passion; and
2 unhooking yourself from the object to which your thirst or craving has become attached.

These two elements provide a methodology for working with the responses you experience in situations of acute pain. The two elements operate in a cyclical relationship: feelings arise; you harness and intensify them; this creates more feelings; and so on.

Typically, as a person faces affliction, a feeling response occurs. The person shrinks away from the distress, falling into patterns of distraction or escape. The pain of dukkha feels shameful as well as unpleasant. You try to hide. If you can be supported to face the pain at this point, however, rather than dispersing it, the possibility for transformation occurs. You break out of habitual patterns of behavior that have a limiting or dulling effect, and you free energy to live more fully and usefully.

This energy must be held and not dissipated in distractions. By unhooking yourself from the patterns of distraction, you make more energy available. This is the energy that has previously been used in the compulsion to escape referred to earlier. In particular, it is energy that was caught up in maintaining habitual ways of being that constitute the self-structure. This extra energy now becomes available to be harnessed and used. The unhooking process is itself not an easy one. Not only does it involve facing the immediate pain of the situation, but it also brings you into awareness of the cravings which have led you to build up habit patterns and hold those patterns in place.

Marga

The final element in the Four Noble Truths is *marga*, or the path.

> *The noble truth of marga, the right track, is this: It is the noble eight limb way, namely right view, right thought, right speech, right action, right livelihood, right effort, right mindfulness, right samadhi.* (Samyutta Nikaya 61.11.8)

This final element of the Four Noble Truths teaching describes the spiritual path. The path is outlined in the form of another well-known Buddhist teaching, that of the Eightfold Path: right view, right thought, right speech, right action, right livelihood, right effort, right mindfulness, and right samadhi. This teaching describes the spiritual life, a life that flows in a direction of purposeful action. The teaching is also a description of a process. One element flows from another. If you have the right vision, you think the right way. If you think the right way, you speak the right way; if you speak the right way, you act the right way. If you act the right way, you employ yourself ethically; if you employ yourself ethically, you put in full effort. If you put in full effort, you become mindful. And if you are mindful, you experience samadhi. Samadhi, the state of clear, meditative mind, in turn brings you vision. The eight steps therefore make a complete cycle, and the Buddha called this the Dharma Wheel. They are the natural outcome of a life free from escapist distraction.

The spiritual path can be seen as a description of the spiritual life and also as a method of training. On the one hand, the Eightfold Path can represent a description of the life of faith or spiritual confidence. If one trusts the spiritual teachings, and is oneself trustworthy, one naturally lives this path and finds oneself carried along by it. The path is intrinsically satisfying, and you find yourself gaining faith in it. In this way, faith becomes self-reinforcing. It is thus possible to get on to a good path that continues to grow under its own momentum.

On the other hand, you can train yourself in all the elements of the Eightfold Path, knowing that each will provide the conditions for the arising of all the others. Just as the Buddha and his followers led a disciplined life, following particular codes of behavior and observing and eliminating those mental processes that hindered their work, so too training can be an important aspect for each of us in becoming more fully alive. Training involves harnessing energy and directing it in positive ways rather than frittering it away on distractions. Each element in the Eightfold Path is concerned with positive application. The prefix "right" in each element carries an implication of wholeheartedness.

Symbolic Aspects of the Buddha's Story

The historical facts of the Buddha's early life are difficult to verify. It seems likely that the story of his early years has a historic basis but that the tale has grown in the telling. Whatever the facts, however, the legendary aspect of the story of Siddhartha provides a symbolic reflection of his later teachings.

Stories are often more a product of the times in which they are told than of the original incident that gave rise to them. The stories each of us tells about ourself are often distorted in this way. These self-tales, too, have usually grown in the telling. They are the result of selective memories and elaboration of the past. The Buddha's story, as his followers retold it, has come to reflect elements of his teaching in a symbolic way.

First, we can draw a connection between the teachings that mark the beginning and end of the Buddha's journey to enlightenment. The Buddha reached an understanding in which the Four Sights became transformed into the Four Noble Truths. What connects these teachings? First, the Four Sights included sickness, old age, and death. These are also listed among the things the Buddha describes as dukkha. The fourth Sight was the sadhu, and the fourth Noble Truth was the Eightfold Path. This Eightfold Path describes the lifestyle of the holy man. In this way the Four Sights are transformed into the teaching of the Four Noble Truths. That transformation is represented by the first and last elements in that teaching: dukkha becomes marga. The teaching becomes a description of the transition Siddhartha experienced from encountering the first three distressing sights to the resolution he felt on seeing the sadhu.

Some Buddhist practices involve the practitioner in a struggle with an insoluble problem. An example of this is the Zen practice of working with *koans*. Koans are spiritual questions that do not have straightforward answers. The aim of working with a koan is not so much to reach intellectual understanding as to reach a point of experiential breakthrough. The Four Sights were like a koan for Siddhartha as he set out on his spiritual quest.

There are further parallels between the two teachings. Both teachings describe processes. Disease, aging, and death are stages in a natural process. It is not accidental that the four sights are listed in that order. Events like death and sickness are not isolated incidents. It is only our limited view that makes them seem so. They are part of a bigger picture of the cycle of life and death. Indian philosophy of the Buddha's day was deeply concerned with the processes of life and death and with their cyclical nature. This cyclical view of nature underlies many of the Buddha's teachings.

The Buddha understood that in any situation there are seeds that will give rise to the next situation. One thing provides the conditions for the next. This theory is set out in the teaching of *dependent origination*, one of the key teachings of Buddhism. On the night of his enlightenment, the Buddha understood the process whereby all things are conditioned. It was in this context that he also understood the Four Noble Truths. We will return to this theory later in the book.

Conditions give rise to events that then condition further events. The theory of conditioning is a thread that runs through many of the Buddha's teachings. We can imagine Siddhartha struggling with the images of sickness, old age, and death, and coming to recognize the connections between them. So the Four Sights were the seeds from which the Buddha's greatest teachings grew. Once sown, these seeds stayed with him through his spiritual journey. Like the koan, they defied easy resolution, acting as an irritant that stimulated his search and fed the process of realization. Suffering is not necessarily to be relieved too quickly. Often it holds within it the key to spiritual breakthrough.

The Engaged Path

The teaching of the Four Noble Truths describes the wholehearted application of energy that becomes possible when you contain and use the fire of your passion. It is an active process. Buddhism is not a path of withdrawal from the world, but one of engagement with it. In order to live wholeheartedly, you need to connect with others deeply; and in connecting with others, you cannot help but see and face their experiences of dukkha. Our lives are intertwined and we each provide the conditions for one another's well-being or otherwise. The engaged path is not one of quietism. It is one of constant challenge. It requires the containment and direction of our energies in the creation, not so much of personal improvement, but of the conditions for a better world for all.

In crisis situations we are often faced with people who have much passion. Passion is the other side of depression and despair. Our friend meets with his Kurdish companions to play music. On the weekend I mentioned earlier, they played to two thousand people in London, giving voice to the pain of a people cut off from their land and from loved ones. The music they play is traditional. Like that of many oppressed peoples, it is a powerful combination of pathos and energy. In sharing their music, our friend bears witness to the grief and pain which the Kurdish refugees experience as they hear of the terrible things happening in their homeland and to the powerlessness they feel as they are unable to return to be with those they love. The passions that might become directed into angry reprisals or turned inward in destructive or depressive emotions instead are harnessed in a performance that touches many hearts.

To play music requires training and personal discipline. Although the music is full of passion and spontaneity, it comes to life only if the musicians have trained. They must also be able to play together. Producing good music in a group requires good cooperation. The players must be willing to blend with one another, letting go of individual styles and preferences in favor of the collective sound. They must be willing to place the shared performance higher in their priorities than their personal agendas and to focus energy toward this. At the same time, producing music requires faith. A musician practices in advance of the performance, but on the day he must simply let go of the conscious effort and play. If he is not able to do this, his playing will be stilted, and he may well end up falling into self-conscious mistakes. He must let go and allow the music to play itself through him.

Likewise, being part of a group of players requires trust. The way that sounds blend cannot be entirely predicted. The musicians must allow a process to unfold between them. Thus good music is a blend of hard practice and a willingness to flow with the performance as it emerges.

There are many parallels between the practice of the musician and that of the Buddhist path. Through galvanizing your energies and containing your passions, you can apply your actions wholeheartedly to a higher purpose, bringing many benefits. Nor should you think that you are too hurt or too damaged to be of use. It is often those who have been through most who have most to give. It is from the energy of suffering that transformation becomes possible. All this is not, however, a matter of willpower. It is rather a matter of being willing to flow.

Playing music with his fellow musicians, our friend shares the energy that arises from pain. In his sharing he acts as a witness to their suffering. Together they are able to contain the fire of reaction so that it is not dissipated in destructive ways. Instead, their playing will have many good outcomes. People will become more aware of the Kurdish people's suffering. People will be moved by the courage and beauty embodied in the music. They will be inspired by the cooperation of people of different nationalities working together. Some will feel their own sadness understood as they hear the sadness in the playing. As the music affects the audience, the ripples will move out from the concert in many directions. That is how it is when energy is harnessed to a higher purpose.

So what makes the difference? How does the pain of dukkha become a positive influence in your life rather than a desructive one? First, you need the discipline not to squander energy in distraction or in unfocused reprisals. The energy must be contained. Second, you need to apply the energy in positive ways. You need to have a deep faith that this is possible and, through that faith, to develop vision and purposefulness. Third, you need to transcend your personal agenda so that you can cooperate and so that your vision can be a bigger vision, one that encompasses a wide perspective, rather than one that simply fulfills self-centered ends. If these three conditions are present, you have the potential to bring about real change.

THEORIES EXPLAINED IN THIS CHAPTER

- the Four Sights;
- the Four Noble Truths; and
- the Eightfold Path.

THEORIES BRIEFLY INTRODUCED TO BE ELABORATED LATER

- the five skandhas; and
- dependent origination.

· 2 ·

A Psychology of Addiction and Encounter

Dukkha is an inevitable part of life. This was the Buddha's realization.

In small ways we are constantly experiencing dukkha. My knees are still sore today from a longer than usual period of meditation last week. It's no big deal, but it makes me aware that dukkha is not to be avoided. Sooner or later we experience it in big ways. A loved one dies, or we discover a permanent disablement. This is not shameful. It is life. Dukkha is a noble truth. Nothing has gone wrong. We do not need to hide our suffering. Dukkha happens.

When dukkha happens, we have a choice about what we do. At this point, feelings arise. The Buddha described them as a thirst or craving. We feel impelled to react, and commonly we respond in ways that would broadly be labeled by Buddhist theory as attachment or clinging. If we recall the description of samudaya quoted in the last chapter, we see that the Buddha speaks of a thirst for "self re-creation" arising in response to dukkha. Associated with this arise "greed" and "pleasure-seeking." He also speaks of a *thirst for sense pleasure, for being and for non-being.* This last phrase is important and one we will explore in some depth in this chapter. It basically suggests that there are three levels of response to dukkha. Initially we seek sensory comfort to divert ourselves from the pain. Then we fall back on our role or identity; in other words, being. Finally, when these fail, we seek oblivion or non-being.

Escape, Compulsion, and Addiction

You may recognize the patterns of escape only too well. When things go wrong, people commonly use a whole range of physical distractions. They eat more. They smoke more. They drink. They have sex. They watch television. They exercise to excess. At times of stress the impulse to escape into such behaviors can feel almost overwhelming.

Buddhist psychology is concerned with the way you respond to the inevitable suffering of life with compulsive patterns of escape. These patterns are powerful, particularly because they create cycles, which quickly become self-reinforcing. They develop habit-energy, the basis for what is termed *avidya* or ignorance (literally, not seeing). We all have patterns of behavior that we use to cope with the pressures and difficulties we encounter from day to day; but for some people, these patterns can be particularly strong and concentrated in one or two behaviors. They take on a secondary level of compulsion, where the behavior itself creates a lot of suffering or dukkha. This secondary dukkha then leads to further attempts to escape, through the same behavioral patterns, creating a downward spiral of behavior. Such patterns are commonly thought of as addictions.

Addictions are particularly difficult to break precisely because they are so powerfully entrenched in the mind of the addict. Addictive patterns of behavior represent one end of the spectrum, but they are not substantively different from the processes of compulsive avoidance in which Buddhist psychology suggests we are all caught.

I have spent many years working with women who eat compulsively. Such behavior forms an addictive pattern, which has similarities with the patterns of addiction to alcohol or drugs, though with food addiction there is generally less chemical dependency. The drive to use food in this way can be a very painful experience. It can be so compelling that it feels impossible to resist it, yet it also feels shameful. Understanding the roots of the compulsion can be difficult; breaking it is generally even harder.

Sometimes the cause of stress is, at least in part, obvious. Susan has three small children and is a single parent. Despite her low income, she still often finds herself eating the week's groceries on a Monday night. She feels overcome with remorse afterward, yet she cannot seem to stop herself.

Judy has frequent rows with her partner. Judy's partner is having an affair with someone from work. He says it has ended, but Judy knows otherwise. She dares not confront him. Judy comforts herself by raiding the fridge in the middle of the night.

The roots of these behaviors may be complex. Compulsive eating patterns may symbolize anger, neediness or other unexpressed feelings. At a more immediate level, however, both Judy and Susan are using sensory ways to escape from their painful situations. Rather than confront the difficult feelings, both women take refuge in food.

Both these examples involve a response to a current situation. Habit-energy from past situations contributes to the reaction, making it more likely that the person will use eating as the means of escape, but there is also a trigger in the present situation. There is a source of dukkha currently happening in the person's life. This is not always the case. Sometimes the urge to eat has become such a strong pattern that it seems no longer to require a crisis to provoke a binge. Here the eating has become a habit-pattern and itself creates enough dukkha to be self-perpetuating.

Gemma binges every night at ten o'clock. She plans her binge and shops for it at her local supermarket. She buys those foods that she knows she can easily vomit because she does not wish to become fat. The pain is not always apparent. Gemma seems calm as she talks about her binge eating. One week, Gemma's therapist persuades her to experiment with interrupting the pattern of nightly binges. When she manages to do this, she finds herself weeping uncontrollably. For Gemma, the eating behavior is effectively distracting her from the painful feelings in her life.

As long as she keeps on behaving in this way, there is a kind of equilibrium in which the sadness she feels is kept at a distance by the behavioral patterns she has developed. When these behavioral patterns stop, Gemma becomes aware of the pain caused by both the behavior and its original triggers.

Not everybody eats compulsively, but most people have some pattern of reaction to painful events. Each of us has our preferred distraction. A person may binge-eat or drink or smoke or may prefer phoning friends or burying themselves in their work. They may not necessarily see these as addictions, but if there is an element of compulsion behind them, that is what they are. Look at the patterns of behavior that people suffering with addictions go through, and you'll see a more extreme version of the same attachment behavior that you may think of as normal.

As a person then repeats these patterns of distraction, the behaviors create a cycle that has a life of its own. He or she enacts the behavior just because it is familiar. There is no immediate fear or threat, but they still repeat the pattern. And as they do this, the patterns themselves become painful. Being caught in a compulsive behavior pattern, they long to be free of it, but they fail to break out of the cycle. The individual suffers immensely from the compulsion itself.

What may have originally been a comfort response has long since ceased to be pleasurable. Ironically, one may take refuge from this pain in the very behavior that is the source of his or her misery. As Susan despairs of her weight gain, it is all too easy to try to avert the distress with an extra chocolate bar.

In the description of dukkha quoted in the previous chapter, you saw that dukkha was sickness, old age and death; but it was also the skandhas, or "five aggregates of grasping." The grasping that seems to be an escape from suffering is itself a creator of suffering. It is this form of dukkha that we are talking about here. Dukkha in this case, then, includes:

- the original affliction; and
- the secondary pain of attachment behaviors.

The Three Levels of Samudaya Response

The response to dukkha described in the teachings on samudaya, the second Noble Truth, is an arising of feelings and a displacement of those feelings on to some object or behavior that acts as a distraction. You can look at it as a tendency to respond to pain through compulsive or attachment behaviors. The response has three levels. Let us go back to the Buddha's words.

It is thirst for sense pleasure, for being and for non-being.

This description offers a model of compulsive behavior patterns. It provides a taxonomy for addictive and compulsive behaviors.

The examples we have looked at so far can mostly be seen as craving for sense pleasure. This is a first-level response to difficult events. The Buddha proposed two further levels: being and non-being. How are we to understand these? The Buddha taught a great deal about the delusional nature of self. He taught that all things were non-self. In the first two of the Four Noble Truths he is really teaching how "self" is created. A person experiences affliction (dukkha) and reacts by clinging to distractions (samudaya). This clinging to distractions creates compulsive and habitual patterns of behavior, which are really the birthplace of the self. This book will explain the process behind such self-creation in more detail as we come to look at other teachings of the Buddha. For the present, we can confine ourselves to the references to self re-creation in the Four Noble Truths teaching.

The second level of escape given in the teaching of samudaya is concerned with creating an identity, and the third level with its destruction. Thus, to return to the Buddha's formulation, the three levels of escape are:

- sensory pleasure;
- being (self-creation); and
- non-being (self-destruction).

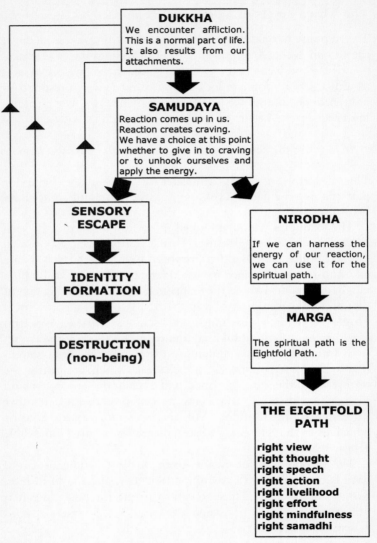

Figure 2.1

The Four Noble Truths, represented as a process model
This model includes the three levels of samudaya, each of which causes secondary dukkha.

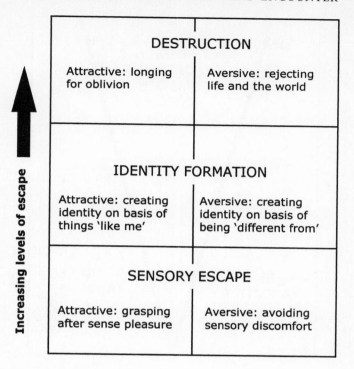

Figure 2.2 (a) Samudaya escape

The three levels of samudaya escape. At each level there may be attractive or aversive responses.

Sensory Pleasure

Sensory pleasure is immediate and can override painful feelings; but, as we have seen, there are two dangers in this kind of escape. First, the strategy gives only short-term benefits. It may give an immediate lift, but the sensation does not last. Quickly one wants the next drink or the next cookie. He or she indulges the senses and sets up a thirst for more.

Second, the strategy tends to be repeated each time the person encounters stress or painful feelings, and so starts to create its own cycle of reinforcement. Habit-energy is generated. One gets

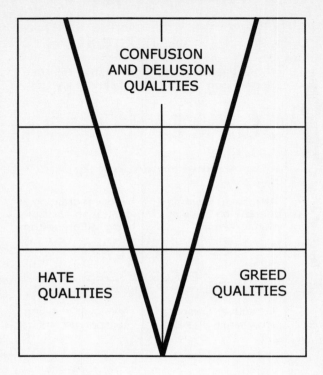

Figure 2.2 (b) Samudaya escape

As a person moves through the three levels, increasing delusion sets in. At the sensory level, greed and hate predominate. At the destructive level, delusion predominates.

used to binge-eating or smoking. When people are not able to do these things, they miss them. This creates a painful situation which in itself generates the desire for more escape. So the behavior becomes self-reinforcing.

Not all sensory escape behaviors are pleasurable. Some of the ways in which people distract themselves from painful experiences are extremely unpleasant. A teenage girl who self-harms, cutting herself with razor blades to alleviate her distress at her abusive family situation, may also be exercising a form of sensory distraction. Her behavior arises in response to the dukkha she is experiencing. Like binge eating or drinking, it involves stimulating the senses in order to avoid feeling the original pain of her situation.

Some sensory responses are avoidance responses. A person may respond to dukkha by rejecting certain sensory experiences. A person may refuse or restrict food. He may avoid sexual arousal. She may choose a lifestyle that lacks sensory stimulation. This can also be seen as a form of sensory escape. It is a manipulation of the sense world in order to create a distraction from painful feelings.

Sensory escape works basically by distraction. You take your mind off the thing that is causing distress by focusing our attention on something that is more compelling, either because it is pleasurable or because the pain it causes is more immediate and specific (and therefore less frightening or overwhelming) than the original pain. The distracting stimulus is, however, impermanent, and this fact sets up the dynamics of a habit cycle.

Identity Formation

As the patterns of escapist behavior repeat, they start to become familiar. Something is being born that seems more permanent. One starts to identify with the behavior. The person says "I am a bulimic;" "I am an alcoholic;" "I am a sports fan." By now, the person has reached the second level in the samudaya response. This is the level of identity creation. The person has started to identify with his or her behavior patterns.

Gemma may have started binge eating as a way to control painful feelings about life, but she is in danger of starting to think of herself as "a bulimic." She reads a lot of books on eating problems and attends several groups for people with eating disorders. Her life centers on her difficulties with food. She is *someone with an eating problem*.

Grasping after identity arises out of seeking sensory comfort. Life is uncertain, and when we face dukkha, we look for certainty. As we come to terms with the reality of dukkha, we struggle with the experience of impermanence. We want to believe that there is something reliable that cannot be taken away from us by the cycle of birth and death. In a changing, uncertain world, there can be comfort in believing that something is permanent and reliable. Initially this may be something that is constantly available, such as food. Judy may feel that whatever else happens she can always rely on having food in the fridge. When all else fails, however, I may end up feeling that the only thing I can rely on is myself. There is a kind of security and satisfaction in "knowing who I am." The feeling that "only I am trustworthy," however, drives a person toward the illusion of self-sufficiency and toward isolationism. To quote the Simon and Garfunkel song: "I am a rock, I am an island."

The song ends: "A rock feels no pain, and an island never cries." But of course, we know the deep loneliness involved in this kind of withdrawal into the self. This knowledge of the futility of isolationism is not lost on the song's audience; indeed, it is from this that the music's pathos arises. There is a kind of bravado in this escape into identity, but ultimately it too is the source of further dukkha.

For most people the process of self-creation is less rigid and isolating than the image in the song, but nevertheless, inasmuch as it is there, it creates a separation between the world and the person. It creates the dichotomy between "me" and "everything else." This is an artificial split, born out of our partial withdrawal from life. It is what is sometimes referred to in Buddhism as dualistic thinking, or *vijnana*—splitting the world falsely into one's personal experience and the rest.

Non-Being

When the first two levels of samudaya response cease to bring relief from painful feelings, a person may move on to a new level of response. This is the level of "non-being." At this stage, hope is finally given up. Despair sets in. The world is experienced as hostile, so that the person withdraws into a world-denying state, no longer making any attempt to connect with others or to actively engage with life at all. At the same time, this withdrawal makes it difficult for others to be heard even if they try to make contact. Any such attempts are likely to be distorted by the person's restricted view and to be dismissed as futile or else treated with

30

suspicion. The self-prison has become well-nigh impermeable. There is very little contact with the world. Isolation is complete.

At this stage, a person has moved from patterns of behavior that create identity to patterns of behavior that are self-destructive. Such destructiveness can take many forms. It may include breaking down those structures of identity that were created in the previous phase, self-harming behaviors and, ultimately, suicide.

This final phase of samudaya is the most distressing. It involves the fighting of pain with pain. It entails a deeper cutting off from life than happens on either of the other levels. It is an attempt at escape from pain that results in a person falling into such negative mental states that it can be hard to return from them.

The Self-Prison: Self as a Defense Structure

Buddhist psychology is sometimes described as a non-self psychology. The self is a defensive structure, built in response to affliction. If you encounter difficulties and retreat into various patterns of avoidance and comfort, initially they may be aimed at producing sensory comfort, but quickly they result in the creation of a defensive self or identity. This is the process that Gemma is going through in seeing herself as "someone with an eating problem."

People get into entrenched patterns of habitual behavior, which then become established. These behavioral patterns form a kind of cocoon around them, which cuts them off from the painful feelings, but also cuts them off from experiencing the world. They start to think of the patterns of behavior as "me" and to cling to the identity they offer. These processes are barely conscious. Because of the familiarity of the patterns that they enact, people assume that they represent permanent attributes. The patterns are repeated many times, and individuals do not know other possibilities; so they assume they are "how it is." This is what is referred to in Buddhism as ignorance or avidya. By ignoring much that is going on around them, people limit their behavior and interest to things that relate to their own self-view.

Out of a collection of repeating patterns and preferences each of us starts to grasp for something to hold onto that seems permanent, calling this "me" or the self. Because there is always some degree of pain in being alive, this process has been going on all your life. Even being born is dukkha. By the time you reach adulthood, the self has become multi-layered and powerful. The self has in some sense been effective, in that it has kept you distanced from the worst of your pain, but it also gets in the way of experiencing life or really encountering other people.

The self, according to Buddhist psychology, is the fortress you create to protect yourself from experiencing the pain of loss and impermanence. It is your greatest defense mechanism. It is also your prison. Keeping this fortress in place becomes a life project and consumes large amounts of your energy.

The creation of identity or "self" is the second way in which we try to escape from dukkha. Creating an identity can provide some pleasure and comfort, as did the first level of escape into sensory distractions. Both sensory gratification and self-formation, as the Buddha points out, are things you are likely to find attractive. For this reason they will generally, but not always, evoke those impulses that are broadly categorized in Buddhism as *greed attachments*.

Sometimes, however, just as sensory attachments can be unpleasant, self-formation can be negative. A person who is full of self-loathing or lacks self-esteem may be just as deeply entangled in self-attachments as a person who is full of pride. A negative self-image can be very powerful and limiting. Sometimes, too, self-formation can be based on hate attachments to others. You may create an identity upon the basis of being better than another person or more entitled than another social group. Ultimately, though, self-formation represents a distortion of perception or a deluded state. The self is a limiting factor in people's lives and one that cuts them off from others. They have created the self-prison.

Buddhist Psychology as a Psychology of Addiction to Self

Buddhist psychology offers a model for understanding mental process. It suggests that you form an identity or self as a response to the apparently overwhelming pain of some life events. In reaction to this pain, you discover ways of dulling your experience. You alter your perception so that you enter a state of delusion, or avidya. The state of avidya is created through habitual patterns of escape, which are in turn perceived as a self.

The self is both a protection and a prison, creating a *cordon sanitaire* between the individual and the world. The illusory safety which this self provides is held together by the ever-repeating patterns of habitual behaviors. The familiarity of these old patterns creates the illusion of permanence and reliability. Buddhist psychology denies the permanence of self, seeing it merely as the illusion generated by repetition.

All these aspects will be explored further in later chapters, but it should be clear from the discussion so far that what we are looking at in Buddhist psychology is a psychology of addiction. But addiction to what? For most of us, it is an addiction to self. The self you create is the source of security and comfort to which you turn when life gets difficult; and this habitual pattern of refuge is just as persistent and just as falsely based as any substance addiction.

The Metaphor of the Self-Prison in the Buddha's Story

We have already seen how the story of the first part of the Buddha's life can be viewed as a representation of his later teachings. The early part of Siddhartha's life mirrors the process of samudaya. The Buddha's birth involved great suffering. Siddhartha's mother died shortly after he was born, leaving him to be raised by an aunt. The young prince was immediately offered a life indulged with every sensory delight as compensatory distraction. He also learned that he was expected to be someone with a strong identity. He was, after all, a prince. Here there was much dukkha; here too were the potential routes of escape. Behind the enjoyment of the palace life, a deep grief lay unacknowledged. Like a dark specter in his charmed life, his mother's death provided a sad backdrop to his childhood. The situation in which he lived was an escape from reality, a false construction of pleasure and status, hiding painful experiences that were not to be addressed.

The palace had strong walls against the troubled world beyond. Like an image of the defensive self, it was built inward-looking and self-preoccupied. Within these walls, Siddhartha lived in ignorance of the suffering of ordinary people. We could say he was in a state of avidya. It took a further shocking encounter with dukkha beyond the palace walls to free him.

Just as the young Siddhartha did, you too can live a comfortable life for a time within the strongly fortified palace which your self-structure has become. You may feel as if you need to do so. Building this fortress, you cut yourself off not only from potential pain but also from the wider countryside around. The self-structure creates insulation not only against pain but also against many of the real delights of life. You can indulge your senses with distractions and enjoy your well-built defenses, but you do not really encounter life. To be in a state of avidya is to be anaesthetized against fully living.

The Buddha escaped by leaving the palace and facing the reality of suffering. He saw the four sights, symbolic of all the pain of impermanence. He set out, leaving the palace with all its self-deluding grandeur, on a search for the spiritual life. It was dukkha that released him. Similarly, if it was through encountering dukkha that you built your fortress, it is also dukkha that has the power to release you. For this reason also, dukkha can be viewed as noble.

Once in a while an opportunity arises to break through the palace defenses. Once in a while, as happened to Siddhartha, a person sees something that disturbs his or her equilibrium. Once in a while an encounter with the harder side of things creates a chink in your armor through which you can start to glimpse the world more clearly. Seizing such opportunities, you make spiritual progress. Helping others to seize them, you enable them to grow.

Dukkha as a Means to Encounter Life

If Buddhist psychology is a psychology of addiction, psychology of encounter. Encounter is the antidote addictive patterns that hold us trapped. By encountering the world beyond the walls of the self, you break through to freedom. The path to health is in encountering that which is not self. In other words, you need to encounter that which is other. It is when you break out of your patterns of habitual and clinging behaviors that encounter with the world becomes possible.

Often, the route to this encounter comes through a meeting with dukkha. If at these points of pain you can stand firm and face the real situation instead of retreating into your habit patterns, you may encounter the world in a fresh way. You may break out of the self-prison. This will not necessarily be comfortable, but it may be releasing. Meeting the world fully, you let go of the defense structures of the self.

For those schooled in western approaches to understanding the mind, a psychology based on something other than an assertion that self is a good thing may seem remarkable. Self-effacement is out of fashion. Self-interest is the order of the day. Shadows of childhood injunctions not to be selfish and stories of the self-sacrificing wife or mother—for women have often been accredited with selfless virtues—have left only images of starchy piety for anyone who does not seek self-assertion. Programs to raise self-esteem and improve self-image abound. Problems are frequently attributed to a person's having a "poor sense of self." When I present Buddhist psychology to students, I am often met with disbelief and even hostility, so strongly are people attached to their views of self—and yet the real liberation comes from stepping out of the self-structure into a new relationship with life.

So this book offers a different perspective from that offered by many psychologies. It explores the mechanisms by which people create and maintain the self-prison which restricts their lives. It looks at ways in which they can take opportunities to break free. Buddhist psychology is a non-self psychology.

The subject of self and non-self is complex, and many of the labels that we apply in this context are distorted by beliefs about what is good and useful. There are parts of your self-prison that you do not recognize as part of the fabrication and with which you do not actively identify. Likewise, there are things that you may attribute to self, such as acting courageously or being clear about your intentions, that are not necessarily part of a defensive structure. In the chapters that follow these things will become clearer, and some common ground will emerge between self and non-self psychologies. But differences will also remain. They are important, for the Buddha taught a revolutionary message that should not be lost as you try to re-fit the teachings to your previously held systems of thought.

The Three Poisons: Valences of Attachment

In the samudaya response we form attachments. The Buddha spoke a great deal about grasping and attachment. Patterns of grasping are said to be of three kinds. Traditionally they are known as the three poisons. There are three valences of attachment, most commonly known as greed, hate, and delusion (*lobha, dvesha,* and *moha*). You can think of them as three ways in which you can become hooked by things.

The process of becoming hooked involves the arising of energy in a person and its almost immediate attachment to an object. Experiencing dukkha, feelings arise which are painful and difficult. The energy of those feelings transmutes into craving or thirst for something that will provide an escape. This is the samudaya response. Buddhist therapists call this "something" which is craved an *object*. The term "object" is here being used in a technical way. More colloquially, you might say "I am attracted to something," "I want to be something." This object can be something real, but it may also be something more abstract, like an identity. Being hooked by something is often an experience of attraction or wanting. This kind of reaction is a lobha, or greed, response.

The opposite response is the dvesha or hate response. When you hate or reject something, there is also a hooking-in process, just as there is with the positive attachment, lobha. Once more, feelings are aroused and refuse to subside quickly. You have only to think of a time when a difficult phone call has left you lying sleepless the following night, thinking of responses you might have made, to recognize how powerfully a negative attachment can preoccupy the mind. The power of hate responses to dominate a mentality, not only of an individual but also of a group, becomes frighteningly clear when you look at feuds that have continued through generations.

The third response, moha, is generally translated as delusion or confusion. It may take the form of ambivalence, rationalization, or outright folly. Often it is a mixed response in which both lobha and dvesha reactions are present. This kind of reaction is perhaps the most difficult to deal with, as its confused alternations create a semblance of instability while remaining strongly attached to the object. As I waver in ambivalence, I am least able to let go of my attachment. We have all met people who are stuck in relationships that they seem to be able neither to settle in nor to give up. One day they are full of feelings of love for the other person; the next day they are full of negativity and the desire to leave. Such confused emotions can be difficult to fathom, but one thing is generally apparent. It often takes a long time for such situations to be resolved, and people caught in such ambivalent feelings can remain stuck for years.

All these three valences of attachment involve self elements. They are the bricks of the self-prison. One feels lobha, dvesha or moha responses because one has a personal investment in the object to which he or she is responding. The stronger that investment, the stronger the reaction is likely to be. Those things that support identity are likely to evoke the strongest responses. I am likely to be strongly attracted to those things I identify with and strongly reject those things I actively dis-identify with. In this way, the self-structures are further defined and reinforced.

THEORIES EXPLAINED IN THIS CHAPTER

- the three levels of escape in the teaching on samudaya;
- habit-energy and addiction;
- the self-prison;
- liberation through encounter; and
- the Three Poisons.

THEORIES BRIEFLY INTRODUCED TO BE ELABORATED LATER

- non-self psychology; and
- vijnana: the dualistic mentality.

· 3 ·

Mind Models and Senses

The self is a defense that we humans create against the uncertainties of existence. Faced with our day-to-day encounters with dukkha, the afflictions that we inevitably experience as part of being alive, we find ways to protect ourselves from the natural feelings that arise and threaten to overwhelm us. The ways in which we escape from these inevitable reactions are outlined in the teaching of the Four Noble Truths. Each of us creates our own patterns of escape, which fall into the three levels of sensory indulgence, self-creation and self-destruction.

Buddhist psychology shows how people are constantly recreating themselves out of the patterns of reaction into which they fall. It shows how these patterns are self-reinforcing and self-perpetuating. Although psychologists refer to the self as if it were an entity, in fact this use of language reifies a process that does not result in anything substantial at all. Rather, the self is a collection of experiences that constantly forms and re-forms. Like a flock of birds or ripples on a pond, it creates patterns and shapes that often repeat, giving an impression of substance, but it is ultimately non-substantial or empty. Buddhist psychology uses terms such as "self" for the sake of convenience and to avoid convoluted language, but we must be on our guard against allowing these to become substantial in our minds. In its pure form, Buddhism is radical in the extent to which it seeks to avoid reification.

The self defends people against the experiencing of pain, but it also limits their capacity to really experience and interact with the world. It becomes what I call the self-prison. From within this limiting construct, one sees the world from a narrow perspective and enacts the same escapist behaviors over and over again. When people act in new ways, they are surprised and even shocked by themselves. "That just wasn't me!" they might exclaim.

Buddhist teaching aims to help you break out of this false imprisonment so that you can live a more free and useful life. Over the years, Buddhist scholars have put much energy into studying the nature of mind and its propensity to create a self-prison. The understanding that they have reached has evolved during that time. The models that have been produced are detailed and demonstrate the depth of observation that has gone on in the process of creating them. Some relate to process, others to a search for understanding of the nature of mind itself. This chapter will explore some of the different models of the mind that have been developed.

The Nature of Mind

What is mind? This question seems fundamental to our whole exploration of who we are and who others are, yet answers remain elusive. Before continuing to read, sit for a while with the question. Can you find your mind? Can you know it is there? If so, how? If you see something that you think is mind, with what do you see it?

Sometimes you may catch yourself watching yourself. Is the mind capable of performing the functions of watching and thinking simultaneously? A thought arises. You spot it. Now you are thinking. Now you are watching your mind thinking. Now you are watching yourself watching yourself thinking. You can go back in an endless regression, seeking the watcher but always just missing. Keep searching.

An emotion arises: perhaps frustration at not being able to find the watcher, or maybe excitement at the discovery of something so tantalizing. How do you recognize this as an emotion?

What is frustration? Or excitement? Spend a few minutes asking yourself this. How do you know you are feeling an emotion? Probably you will find a bodily sensation. Maybe you will find images or words. Explore them. What does curiosity really feel like? After you have sat with these questions for a while, ask yourself: "Is any of these experiences *mind*?"

Imagine you have a dream. You are running down a street between tall buildings. You meet someone you know. Picture the scene of the dream. Spend time making it vivid. Get a clear image of the buildings. Look at the person. What are they doing? How are they dressed? When you have conjured the scene, ask yourself, "Where are these images? Are they connected with mind?"

Phenomenological Exploration

Phenomenology is a western philosophical school that has influenced our ways of seeing and researching the world over the past century. This school of thought has been introduced into many fields of research, particularly those concerned with human relations. Primarily focused on direct perceptual experience, it has attempted to get beyond the positivism that has limited so much work in these fields, exploring subjective experience rather than restricting itself to what is objective and measurable.

In psychology, phenomenology has attempted to let go of the models and preconceptions about the mind and mental process that have built up over the centuries and to achieve a fresh perception of the processes of mental function. It has wrestled with exploring experience directly, in ways similar to those which you have just been invited to try. It then attempts to use descriptive methods to represent authentically what is discovered.

Parallels exist between this quest for direct experiential knowledge and understanding and that of the Buddhist path. Edmund Husserl, father of phenomenology, defined his purpose as the attempt to get beyond the layers of personal assumption and interpretation and the *natural attitude*, which is the collective body of assumptions and norms that any group holds in common, to reach direct experience of "the things themselves." This quest has much in common with the Buddhist attempt to get beyond the conditioned mind (I'll return to the Buddhist understanding of "conditioning" later in this chapter) to a state of enlightenment. In trying to understand mind, one must return to this fresh perception and view the different models in the light of direct experience.

Clarity and Contamination

When you look at the world, you rarely see things exactly as they are. There is generally some distortion in any individual's view. You may see selectively, finding your attention drawn to some things and ignoring others, or you may see in a distorted way. Things get in the way of direct perception. You can think of your experiencing the world as analogous to looking through a sheet of glass that occasinally gets dirty. Let us explore this analogy.

Perhaps the glass is the windscreen of a car. You are going for a drive on a summer afternoon. The sun is shining and you see before you the open road. The windshield seems clear and transparent. You can see through it easily and are not really conscious that it is there. As you drive into the country, you leave the main roads and find yourself on a country lane. It deteriorates into a farm track. There is a lot of mud on the road where the tractors have driven, and some of this mud splashes onto the windshield. You find that your view is clouded by spots of dirt. At this point you may attempt to clear them with your windshield wipers—but it just seems to make the mess worse. The wiper blades smear the dirt around. You squirt water onto the windshield from the washer system to no avail. Eventually you do manage to get enough water onto the windshield to clear the mess. You drive on, enjoying the view.

The afternoon is getting on, and the sun is lower in the sky as you turn for home. Now the sun is ahead of you. Suddenly the whole windshield becomes opaque with traces of the mud. You had no idea it was still there. Again, you are struggling with the washers, trying to see where you are going.

The mind acts rather similarly to the windshield. Sometimes it seems clear and transparent, while at other times it is clouded with thoughts and distractions. Different circumstances evoke different mind states. When your mind feels clouded, you may try to clear it, but sometimes your frantic search for peace may actually make matters worse. You scrub away furiously, trying all the latest therapies or practices, but just end up more muddled than ever. At other times you may be able to bring enough insight into the situation to get a clearer perspective.

Even when you think you have dealt with the things that were clouding your mind, though, the traces of mud may still be around. Just as the evening sun can catch fragments of residual dirt on the windscreen, so too new situations may reawaken old troubles in your mind. You may think you have dealt with a life issue only to find it reappearing years later in new circumstances.

Conditioning

Another way of describing this contamination or distortion of the mind is to say that our mentality is conditioned. The concept of *conditioning* is one that is fundamental to an understanding of Buddhist psychology. The use of the term "conditioning" in Buddhism differs from that in western thought. Its meaning is both broader and simpler. All things arise in dependence upon causes and conditions. This includes your mental states. Your mind states come about in response to the conditions to which your mind is exposed, such as the environment you are in and the things you are doing. The things to which you give attention condition your mind. Changing the focus of your attention changes the mind state.

You can see this simply demonstrated if you look at what happens when you go for a walk in the country or when you revisit a place where you have had unhappy experiences. The first situation may leave you feeling calm; the second may leave you agitated. A different environment can have a marked effect upon your preoccupations. For this reason, Buddhist psychology particularly advocates working with conditions. We will return to this subject at length in Part Two of this book.

Attention can be focused on what we might think of as internal objects as well as external ones. In this way your mind can be conditioned by thinking about a situation in the future. You might, for example, create a lot of worry by thinking about an exam that is coming up. Similarly, you can think about a past incident and feel sadness, remorse, satisfaction, or fear.

In particular, your mind states are conditioned by what you do. The things you do have the strongest conditioning effect, so the processes of distraction and escape described in the teaching of samudaya, as they involve repetition of actions, are likely to have a strong conditioning effect on the mind. Patterns of escape become self-perpetuating. They also themselves give rise to dukkha, which then leads to further repetitions of the action. Thus habit-patterns have a strong conditioning effect, not only in creating the conditions for their own repetition, but also more broadly in creating general mental states.

A mind that is conditioned is a mind that carries the traces of earlier states and actions. The previous experience provides the conditions for the present mind state, just as driving through a muddy farm lane provides the conditions for a dirty wind-screen, and the sun and the direction of travel provide the conditions for the residual dirt to show up. Because the mind has a kind of stickiness, old patterns remain and certain ways of seeing the world or doing things predominate. This provides a first model of the mind.

The Sense-minds: The Six-Vijnana Model

When you encounter things, you do so through your senses. The Buddha taught a lot about the senses, and in the earliest models of the mind it was the senses that predominated. The senses were seen not as passive receptors but as active agents in mental processes that grasp experience. The Sanskrit term used to describe the senses was *vijnana*. Vijnana implies an active intent, a grasping mind. Each sense, then, was seen as having a mind of its own—as a "sense-mind."

As we saw in the last chapter, vijnana is a term that suggests splitting off. Sanskrit is linked to English through the Indo-

European family of languages, so we can recognize similarities between words. The suffix -jna is related to the word meaning "know." Vi- has two possible derivations, either "divided" (as in the prefix "bi-") or "seeing" (as in the word "vi-deo"). Either of these possibilities suggests that vijnana means consciousness that is split off. This may refer to the observer consciousness. When you experimented with watching your mind, you probably experienced something of this split—between an observer, director mind and an active one. Within this split awareness are the seeds of self. There is an implication of self in the word vijnana. It implies a feeling of "me." You watch the scene. There is a separation in this experience between you and the world. So the senses not only have their own minds; they are also split off from their objects. The sense—say, the eye—grasps after its object—say, a beautiful sunset. In doing so, it creates a separation from that experience. This is the separation between observer and observed. It creates the self-experience.

There are six senses in Buddhist psychology. These are the five senses of sight, hearing, touch, taste and smell, plus a sixth sense, called *mano-vijnana*. This sixth sense is the mind's eye, or the mind as a perceiving organ. Effectively, it is the imagination. You can understand why mano-vijnana is regarded as a sense if you think phenomenologically. In the experience of thinking about the dream described earlier, you probably "saw" the scene before you. You perceived it using mano-vijnana. This sixth sense operates experientially just as any of the other senses, perceiving objects that appear to it.

The Content-Free Mind

In order to understand how the mind can be conceived of as a sense organ, you must to put yourself in the position of a member of the society in which the Buddha lived. It was a society in which people had a very different notion of the world, and of their relationship to it, from that which prevails in the West today. It was a world populated by forces that modern society does not recognize. It was experienced as possible, for example, for someone to travel by miraculous transportation and to converse with supernatural beings. It was a time of prophetic signs and magical influences. In that society, such experiences as visions and dreams were respected parts of everyday life. They were received as gifts and visitations.

Anthropologists have reported that in some societies today the dream life of people is quite different from that which we experience in modern Western society. The belief that a messenger might visit a person during their sleep, bringing important news or wisdom, is quite common. In such societies, people may experience waking during the night to find a figure standing at the foot of the bed. This figure may be a stranger or may be known to the dreamer. If it delivers a message, this is treated with high regard by the recipient.

Although the Buddha taught against belief in magic and ritual, there are many accounts of him talking with *devas*, or gods, and making mysterious magical journeys. Such stories illustrate the social norms of his society. People of his day lived in a world of visions.

In such a world, many of the events and processes which are now thought of as located within the mind were experienced as occurring outside the person. Having explored your own experience as suggested above, you may well have discovered that this way of experiencing is actually not so hard to enter. When you set aside the modern conception of the mind and explore your experience directly, it is often closer to the early models than to modern conceptualizations.

Reflect on this. Your experience is shaped by your conceptualizations. Perception is easily influenced, and you often see what you expect to see.

Let's try another experiment.

Imagine an old friend—perhaps someone you knew in childhood. Think about meeting this person. What do they look like now? Where might you bump into them? How are they dressed? Shut your eyes for a few minutes and allow the image to form.

Now reflect on the process. As you thought about your friend, it is likely that scenes came to mind. Perhaps they were immediately clear, or perhaps they were only partly formed. Recall the process. If necessary, reread the last paragraph to remind yourself.

Now ask yourself: How did my mind select an image? Was it based on a rational choice, or did it appear out of the blue? Did your mind keep on task or did it run off at tangents? Probably there were points when uncalled-for images arrived.

When you settled on an image, where did you experience it? Was it inside your head or outside it? Where were you in relation to the image? Did you see yourself meeting your friend, or were you part of the scene? How big was the scene? Was the image of your friend larger or smaller than life-size?

Now ask yourself: Why did this person come to you? Did they have a message for you?

You may find some of your answers surprising. It is likely, for example, that a number of scenes flashed into your mind. More correctly, they probably flashed before your mind. Probably you experienced your friend as in front of you, not inside your head. Probably also, although you were attempting to direct your mind, the images were spontaneous and somewhat unruly.

In the Buddha's day, the mind was thought of as something akin to this raw experience of mental process. People now tend to think of the mind as having contents—memories, unconscious processes, thoughts and so on. People of the Buddha's time did not. The experiences that we think of as *in the mind* were then thought of as external. They came to a person in the way a vision might. Mental images were thought of as coming from outside the person and beyond that person's control.

So the mind was seen as a sense organ, perceiving a range of images, thoughts, and ideas. You may have found that your experience of imagining your friend was actually closer to this early model than to the more modern conceptualization. By setting aside conventional models of western psychology, it is not difficult to see the world through the eyes of this simpler mind. Experiment again with your imaginary friend and see if you can experience the shift of perception that comes from adopting this model.

This six-vijnana mind model represents the content-free mind. By this I mean that the mind is simply the focal point of the six senses and is completely without substance. Experience comes and goes as the senses attach to different things in the environment. This attachment follows patterns because each of the senses is conditioned by previous attachments. In other words, each sense tends to be attracted to things to which it has been attracted in the past and repulsed by things it has previously avoided. This creates an illusion of continuity, but is in fact a process of constant repetition or re-creation.

Implications of the Six-Vijnana Model

The problem modern people have with the early mind model is that it challenges our view of ourselves. How can a mind not

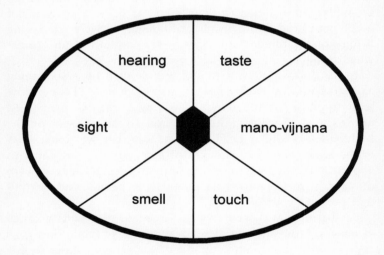

Figure 3.1 The six-vijnana mind map

In this model the six senses operate as outwardly focused, independent vijnanas. They clutch at experience, because each is conditioned. These senses are sight, hearing, taste, smell, touch, and mano-vijnana, the mind's eye (the order in which they are given is not significant). The mind itself is simply a point where these sense experiences meet. It does not have lasting content. The six-vijnana model is nearest to the way of thinking of the Buddha's own day. It suggests that all mental experience is a kind of "visitation."

have mental contents? If you have no mental contents, do you exist at all? The six-vijnana model of the mind does not leave room for the self. According to this model, everything that you perceive is a visitation or object. It is not you. The delusional nature of the self becomes more evident.

The Buddha taught many practices that involved observing a mental process without identifying with it. There are many sutras in which the Buddha teaches practices that consist of taking different physical or mental elements, and reflecting: "This is not me, I am not this thing, this is not myself." You can see an elaboration of this teaching in the Chachakka Sutta (MN 148), which attributes to the six senses what are described as their "six bases." They are:

- the sense organ (eye, ear, etc.);
- its objects (the thing that is seen, heard, etc.);
- its consciousness or function (sight, hearing, etc.);
- its contact (which is the bringing together of organ, object and consciousness, i.e. the point of seeing, hearing, etc.);
- its reaction (the response to contact); and
- its craving (in response to the reaction).

Dependent on the eye and forms, eye consciousness arises; the meeting of the three is contact; with contact as condition there is reaction; with reaction as condition there is craving. (MN 148.9)

This sutra describes the process whereby the sense organs and their processes condition reactivity and attachment. In other words, each sense conditions the same process, as is described in the Four Noble Truths. It attaches to an object and so develops craving. Each sense-mind builds up self-patterns through its contact with objects.

Modern psychology has tended to make us introspective. Buddhist psychology, on the other hand, tends to work in the opposite direction. Westerners are preoccupied with their mental processes and identify with them. We find it difficult to believe that our thoughts are not part of "me." Buddhist approaches, particularly those associated with the six-vijnana model, tend to be outward-focused. The focus is not "Who am I?" but "How do I see the world?"

Later Models of the Mind

The early Buddhist model of the mind describes the experience of perception. As people struggled to understand other aspects of their mental experience in the light of the six vijnanas, it began to be elaborated. In particular, people found it difficult to describe the processes that create continuity of experience or memory using this model. So theory continued to evolve as later Buddhist scholars and philosophers, notably those of the Yogacara school in the fourth century CE, struggled to reconcile the anomalies with observation of direct experience. Important figures in this process were Asanga and his half-brother Vasubandhu.

The problem these theorists faced was that of how continuity was achieved in the mind. It was perplexing and struck at the roots of Buddhist theories that there was no enduring self. Earlier mind models had simply treated the mind as one of six senses. Like the five physical senses, it could be caught by any passing object, be it a physical one such as a person or something to eat or a mental one such as an image or thought. Yogacara theorists struggled to understand how some aspects of mental activity could be carried from one moment to the next. How did memory operate? Was a person the same person as he or she had been the day before? Was there continuity from one day to the next?

In response to these questions, Vasubandhu and Asanga restructured the Buddhist understanding of the mind to include *alaya* or *alaya-vijnana*. Alaya is a word that means "store" (the word occurs in the name Himalayas, which means "store of snow"). Like the English word, alaya can be used as a verb or as a noun. It can refer to the accumulated things or the place where things are kept. Originally the meaning seems to have been intended to indicate a quality of mind—a kind of stickiness. As images and thoughts passed through the mind, this stick-

iness allowed the mind to carry a kind of after-image. Initially
the idea of the mind with alaya was still not of the mind as a
container. It was more a sense that, as the mind perceived or
experienced things, images became stuck to it. Later, however,
accumulation of experience began to be seen in a more concrete
way.

Storing Karmic Traces

The term alaya came to be used to mean a repository in the
mind. The alaya became the place where mental contents—like
karmic traces, or *bija*—were stored. Bija, meaning "seed," was
a term used to describe the imprint or action trace of a thing
a person had done. The theory of karma suggests that the bija
remains in the alaya until it ripens. This happens when particular circumstances or conditions arise. Such conditions mimic
those conditions in which the seed was first laid down. For
example, a person goes shopping. He is in a bad mood and is
rude to a shop assistant. This person may find himself being
rude again when he next goes shopping.

This illustration demonstrates well the two possible interpretations of alaya. The seed could be thought of as residing in the
person's mind, or it could be thought of as residing at the shopping center waiting for him to encounter it again. After all, there
is no evidence of its being in his mind in the interlude.

When conditions arise that are perceived to be similar to
those that were present the last time something happened, the
seed may ripen and the person repeat the same action he
committed the first time. In this case, he again acts rudely and,
as he does so, lays further karmic seeds of rudeness. At the time
when the seed ripens, however, there is always a choice point.
The action that created the karmic trace in the first place may
be repeated, laying down new seeds; or it may be avoided,
allowing that seed's effect to be spent.

According to this theory, once spent, a particular seed is
used up and the karma played out. Repeating the action, however,
sows new seeds, so that effectively a persistent pattern emerges.
If you buy a newspaper from a certain shop on the way to work
creates karmic seeds: you are more likely to buy a newspaper the

next day when you pass the same shop. You will feel an impulse as karmic seeds ripen. At this point you may enter the shop and buy the paper, or you may decide not to. Either way, karmic seeds will have ripened, and these seeds are now spent. If you enter the shop, however, new karmic seeds are created.

The process of exhausting karma, however, is not quite as straightforward as it might seem. Although individual seeds are used up, tendencies to continue repeating certain actions remain. The image of seeds is particularly relevant in understanding this, since just as a single flower produces many seeds, so too each action can be seen as sowing many karmic traces. The theory of karma suggests that many seeds are sown on any occasion, not just one. For this reason, repeating the action will expend some of the seeds completely but still leave others. Thus a particular seed may be exhausted but others remain, just like weed seeds in a garden. A dandelion sheds many seeds. When some germinate, they will either grow or die but will no longer remain as seeds. Other seeds will not germinate immediately and so will remain in the ground to grow in future. Each dandelion flower produces many more seeds than will germinate in a season; so, if unchecked, the garden will gradually become more and more overgrown with dandelions and will continue to grow more weeds for years after it has been weeded.

We draw a number of points from this analogy:

- Repeating actions multiplies the number of karmic traces you carry, since the previous seeds are never fully exhausted during the next repetition of the action. The quantity of karmic material gradually increases and a habit becomes more entrenched.
- If you resist an action, eventually the karma will be exhausted. There is no enduring element in the process.
- If a person who has had a long history of a particular problematic behavior, such as alcohol abuse, slips back into the old pattern, he or she will immediately sow many more seeds. This will make it harder to get free of the habit again. It is a bit like allowing a dandelion to go to seed in the vegetable garden. One year's weeds can mean seven years' seeds.

Individuals tend to follow old patterns of behavior in this way, but it is not inevitable. Where behavior patterns have been repeated many times, many bijas will be left in the alaya, meaning that a lot of restraint is needed to avoid old patterns being repeated and thereby to ensure that karmic traces are exhausted. The theory of bijas suggests that everyone constantly faces possibilities to resist following the old patterns. In addition, it suggests that, as you do this, you reduce the likelihood of repeating the pattern on another occasion. This theory underlines the importance placed by Buddhist teaching on not acting out negative states or behaviors.

The Illusion of Self

The concretization of the concept of the alaya introduced the danger (from a Buddhist perspective) of belief in the substantive self. As mental experience and response were seen to arise from the alaya, they were increasingly reified and identified with: "This is my memory, my feeling, my image, my idea." In fact thoughts, feelings, impulses, and imaginings that arise from the alaya are more accurately to be understood as transitory occurrences, dependent on particular triggers and conditions for their arising. They are the fruit of ripening bija and are not intrinsically self-entities. The idea of bija themselves is only a metaphor. These distinctions, however, can be blurred quickly by consciousness looking for identity.

Manas, the Mind Moderator

Having introduced the concept of the alaya, Asanga then considered how the six senses might be connected to this phenomenon. Some kind of mental activity clearly linked the senses to the mind store. Asanga proposed an eighth element in the structure of the mind. He called this element *manas* or *manana-vijnana*. As this latter name indicates, manas was considered to have some of the elements attributable to an organ of perception. It was a vijnana. So was the alaya. Both alaya and manas undertook self-conscious activity and were subject to the forces of grasping and rejecting.

Manas was conceived by Asanga as the regulator of the mind.

It had two aspects: transitory process, and what Asanga termed "defiled thinking . . . yoked to the four passions of belief in selfhood, self-pride, self-love, and primal ignorance" (p. 16 in Asanga's *Summary of the Great Vehicle*). Manas's four passions of defiled thinking can be translated as:

- atma drishti   self-view
- atma moha   self-delusion (i.e. blindness to whatever does not fit the self image)
- atma mana   self-pride
- atma sneha   self-love

As you can see, these "defiled aspects" are all ways in which self-investment can contaminate our thought processes. The aim of Buddhist practice was to eliminate these aspects of manas, leaving its more spontaneous aspect, which was that linked to transitory process. This aspect provided *wisdom, which saw all things as equal*. In other words, it did not discriminate in its regulating functions on the basis of self-motivated choices.

The introduction of these further aspects to the model of the mind created a quite different conceptualization of mental process. While the earlier model consisted of six sense vijnanas which were "visited" by experiences, the new eight-vijnana model suggested a mind with mental contents. Thoughts and emotions began to be thought of in a much more personalized way, and patterns of behavior to be perceived as "me acting." The introduction of the concepts of the alaya and manas provided a new way of thinking about how the delusion of self arose. Manas was the perceiver of self, and the alaya was the phenomenon which was mistaken for a self.

Manas should not be confused with mano-vijnana. The later Buddhist mind model includes the sixth sense, as well as manas. The functions of mano-vijnana, however, were now somewhat reduced, as the alaya came into the picture. In later models mano-vijnana, or the imagination, is secondary to the other senses. It is described as resting upon them, since it relies upon material already brought to awareness by the other senses for its existence. You cannot imagine something unless

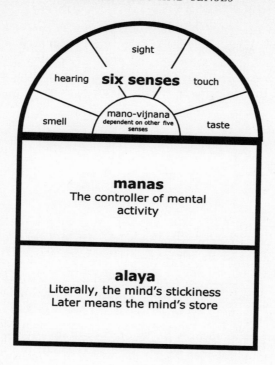

Figure 3.2

The eight-vijnana mind map

This later mind map developed as people struggled to understand continuity of experience.

you have already seen something like it. This shift reflects a move to a view of the mind more akin to the modern one. The mind became a phenomenon with continuity and contents.

Whether this is actually an improvement is an open question. Asanga and Vasubandhu, who introduced this terminology, do not appear to have intended it to develop in this way. They were themselves still close to the Buddha's original conception of a content-free mind.

Guarding the Sense Doors

Now return to the six senses. To understand how Buddhist psychology conceptualizes the senses, you can look at four terms that are often used to describe them. Each throws some light on the Buddhist conceptualization of their nature. They are:

- the sense doors;
- the six uncontrollables (shadayatana);
- vijnanas; and
- chittas.

Sense Doors

The senses are frequently referred to as "the sense doors." Through our senses we experience the world. Doors let things in. The Buddha frequently urged his followers to guard the sense doors. Texts often refer to the practice of *guarding the sense doors* as an essential precondition for the forms of mind-training that we call meditation or samadhi. It is still commonly used in Buddhist training.

You can experiment with the practice of guarding the sense doors for yourself. Try sitting for half an hour in a crowded place such as a coffee shop or railway station. Take a notebook in which you have marked out six columns, one for each of the senses. As you sit, focus on watching where your attention is going. In your notebook, put a check in the appropriate column as you notice yourself being caught by a sound (hearing), something you see (sight), a thought (mano-vijnana), and so on. When you have finished, look at your sheet and notice which sense predominates. Reflect too on how you responded to each stimulus. Do some senses predominate? Does one sense lead you into a process that involves other senses? For example, seeing a person may lead to a series of thoughts. Craving a coffee may follow smelling one being delivered to the next table.

The Six Uncontrollables

When you start to become aware of the different things that catch the attention of your different senses, you may recognize just how much your senses follow their own direction. I may want to concentrate on writing these words, but my senses may keep being drawn away. They might be caught by the rain on the window or the smell of dinner cooking. This wayward quality of the senses is captured in one of the other terms used to describe them: *shadayatana*. This word literally means "the six uncontrollables." When you practice guarding the sense doors, you will quickly discover that your senses have indeed got minds of their own. Far from being under your control, they are caught by sounds outside the room or by sensations in your body. The mind sense, mano-vijnana, as many people know from meditation, also behaves in an uncontrolled way, running off in various streams of thought and conjuring up images from nowhere.

Vijnanas

The senses, as we have already discussed, are *vijnanas*. They cut you off from the world in that very attempt to grasp it. They also are self-invested. Using your senses, you relate to the world in accordance with your self-interest. You grasp or reject experiences through your senses, according to whether they enhance or undermine your sense of identity and your personal preferences. You may also perceive things in distorted ways through your senses, as you attach your own interpretations to them. Most importantly, though, it is through the senses that you divide the world into self and non-self parts, identifying with that which you consider "me" and perceiving everything else as separate and different.

Chittas

Finally, the senses are called *chittas*. Chitta is a word that can be translated as "mind" or "heart." The word carries the implication of seeking or grasping. Chitta means the mind that goes out looking for an object. It longs for it. Each sense is a chitta, which implies that each sense "has a mind of its own." This is rather like the idea that the senses are "uncontrollables." No doubt you someimes find yourself looking at something without intending to—notice when you find your eye wanting to stare at someone who looks a bit odd, even though you may tell yourself this is rude or inappropriate. Notice how your ear pricks up at the sound of your name being mentioned across the room, even if you believe it is wrong to eavesdrop. In both of these examples, you can see how the sense has grasped its object, without your being in control of the process. This is why the Buddha told people to be vigilant in guarding their sense doors. The word chitta, however, not only describes the uncontrollable nature of the senses; it also suggests that there is intentionality involved when they act in this wayward manner. The senses not only run off in their own directions, they intend to do so.

The Three-part Nature of Senses

The senses are often described as each being made up of three parts: the faculty, the power, and the object. As there are six senses and each has three aspects, this produces a list of eighteen sense bases or *sense dhatus*—the elements of which the mind is really made up. You have already seen reference to this idea in the earlier quotation from the Chachakka Sutta (MN 148). The sutra lists six bases for each sense, giving thirty-six bases in all. The later elements in this list, however, are often not included. In this way the senses are generally referred to as having eighteen bases: the eye faculty is sight, the eye power is the impulse to see, and the eye object is the thing that is seen. The eye and its function are generally conditioned so that, rather than "just seeing" the world, the eye has an impulse that drives it to direct itself to particular objects. Through this impulse the process of attachment or aversion operates. The eye is attracted to particular objects because it sees them as "signs" or, in Sanskrit, *lakshanas*. It is attracted not to the object itself but to something that the object indicates. In particular, one's senses are attracted and attached to the things that one sees as signs or indicators of self. That's why the sound of one's name is so powerful.

So, the senses are understood to be a collection of functions that each operate with some degree of independence and insistence to draw one into states of attachment. The impulses that drive the senses are grounded in the previous actions of the senses that have conditioned them. For example, the ear is likely to be conditioned to recognizing and taking an interest in your own name. The eye is conditioned to be caught by people whom it finds sexually attractive. You become fascinated by things that give you pleasure and support your sense of identity. You find your senses are drawn to things that function in this way, even when your intention is that they should be focused on something different. A driver may be distracted by a provocatively dressed passer-by. A person sitting an exam may find her mind being caught by images of an embarrassing incident at the party she attended last night. A patient who is anxious about his own illness may not be able to resist overhearing the doctor's conversation with the patient in the next bed. Despite your best intentions, your senses are drawn by objects that support or threaten your sense of identity.

Your senses draw you into building identity through selective attachment to particular objects in the world. This goes on all the time and is a constant challenge to the spiritual practitioner. If you are to reduce processes of self-creation, you must remain vigilant, for mind is constantly trying to re-create the self.

THEORIES EXPLAINED IN THIS CHAPTER

- the six-vijnana model of the mind;
- the eight-vijnana model of the mind;
- the sense doors; and
- the eighteen sense dhatus.

· 4 ·

Rupa: Seeing and Not Seeing

Perception is a complex matter. You may think you see the world as it is, but in fact your vision is constantly being distorted by the pull of various mental influences. The senses are selective in the way they respond to the world, and this selectivity is based on past experiences. They pull your attention to those objects that already hold fascination for you. They are conditioned.

Conditioning creates a desire for contact that is like a magnetic attraction: the eye latches on to the eye object. The eye-power has been conditioned by objects that the eye has already seen. It seeks out more of the same.

Laura used to be a fashion journalist but has now become a nun. In her new identity, she has no reason to be interested in fashion, yet as she walks down the street she constantly finds her attention drawn to clothes in shop windows. This is because her eye faculty has often been drawn to clothes in the past. This habit of eye-grasping was closely connected to her previous identity formation and self-maintenance. Now that Laura has a new identity, the old habit will take a long time to reprogram and will never be completely extinguished, though it may eventually be transformed in a way that suits the new purpose of her life.

In the ordinary mind, contact gives rise to grasping, grasping to attachment, and attachment to identity. Identity itself becomes a new object to which mano-vijnana attaches. This second level of grasping reinforces the first level, since the eye is drawn to those things that function as signs of identity. Self-formation and habit-energy together create a cycle in which each element is constantly triggering the other.

When you experience your eye-faculty being caught in this way, it may seem as if the eye is indeed operating independently, outside the control of the will. The eye is seen as a mind in its own right or as being a chitta. At the same time, you can consider these events in terms of the pull that the object, in Laura's case clothes, has for the eye. Some objects fascinate and catch the attention. This fascination is a function of the power they have for you as lakshanas, or signs that you take to support your identity. So you cannot separate the attraction your eye feels from the pull the eye object exerts. The process of attraction to particular objects happens at all levels of your mentality. The mind attaches to objects depending on its predominant interests and preoccupations, and this can happen through any or all of the senses.

The Root of All Things

In the first sutra of the Majjhima Nikaya, called the Sutra on the Root of All Things (Mulapariyaya Sutta, MN 1) the Buddha gives a teaching that provides an explanation of the way in which people commonly distort perception. The title of the sutra indicates the centrality of this teaching. It focuses on how people create states of *avidya*. Commonly translated as "delusion" or "ignorance," avidya is the unenlightened state. It is the state of "not seeing," or avoidance. This sutra describes how people create self and seek reinforcement of that self through their surroundings. If you are to encounter the world directly, you must reduce this grasping after self-reinforcement and see things as they are, free from the distortion of mental conditioning.

In the sutra, the Buddha takes a series of elements and describes the ways in which people at different stages of the spiritual path relate to them. Of the common, untrained person he begins:

an ordinary person, who has no regard for noble ones and is unskilled and undisciplined in the dharma [Buddhist teaching] . . . becomes entranced by earth as earth. Having become entranced by earth as earth, he conceives [himself] as earth, he conceives [himself] in earth, he conceives [himself] apart from earth, he conceives earth to be [his], he delights in earth. Why is that? Because he has not fully understood it, I say. (MN 1.3)

Here the term "earth" means any solid object. The sutra continues, describing a similar process in relation to the other elements, thus covering all objects. In each case the Buddha describes how the common person conceives himself as being the element, as in the element, as apart from the element, as in possession of the element and delighting in the element. The Buddha then describes a similar process that the more advanced practitioners might go through. Here, however, he shows that the advanced practitioner has learned not to rebuild the self-construct on the basis of objects of his attention. Objects are directly known as they are, and not perceived as indicators of self.

People commonly impose distortion onto the object world. They take it as implying themselves and, in the process, create self-material in relation to it. We may loosely refer to this process as "investing" self in the object, although in fact the process is circular. You see in the object signs that lead you to construe a self, and from this you create a sense of self. The object is an indicator of that self. This object is called a *rupa*.

In the Sutra on the Root of All Things, the first experience described is *becoming entranced by earth as earth*. This describes the first contact that the person has with the element. At that point, the person becomes entranced. He does not simply see the element; instead he becomes hooked by it. Having become so entranced, the person immediately creates a series of distortions. The word translated as "conceives" (*mannati*), used in many of the phrases in this text, actually means distorted thinking.

The self-perspective infects the person's vision and leads to distorted vision. The four forms of conceiving represent four ways in which the person may mistake an object for an indicator of self or lakshana, contaminating his perception and creating a rupa. These can be read as follows:

- he identifies with it;
- he sees himself in it;
- he sees himself as different from it (in contrast to it);
- he sees himself as possessing it.

These are four ways in which a person ceases to encounter the object and starts to see the object as a rupa. The object no longer exists in its own right but starts to be a signpost for an aspect or extension of the person's self. At this point the person delights in the object. Craving has been aroused, and he has a sense of possession of the object. As the process unfolds, attachment grows. The four forms of *conception* all involve a degree of attachment or hooking on to the object. Three of the forms are lobha, grasping attachments, and one is aversive or dvesha. The lobha attachments are identification, dependence or mirroring, and possession; the dvesha response involves creating self through differentiation or conflict.

These attachments are concerned with identity formation and operate at a level western psychology would probably consider to be unconscious. The final statement, that the person *delights in* the object, denotes a sensory involvement, which grows from the identification. When you feel attracted to something, you may or may not be aware of how your attraction is based in your identification with it. The Buddha teaches that this process of seeking out objects that support one's sense of self continues because a person does not understand what is happening. Being ignorant of the process of attachment, the person is at the mercy of that process.

Selective and Collective Viewing

The view we have of the world is colored by our desire to see our self indicated or confirmed. This process works at a number of levels. First, we are selective in which objects we allow to catch our attention. We can think of the senses searching out particular sorts of objects. We can also think of objects exerting a pull on our attention. Generally, people tend to seek out things that reinforce their sense of identity.

Imagine a man and a woman going to look at a new house that they are thinking of buying. After they have seen a couple of houses they sit down to discuss what they have seen. One of them starts to talk about the houses:

"I liked the one with the blue wallpaper in the sitting room."

(Partner looks blank.)

"With those pretty flowery curtains . . ."

(Still no response.)

"Oh, you must remember, the one where they had built that alcove for the washing machine . . . the second house we looked at . . ."

"Oh yes—you mean the one where he had that great music system!"

Though this may be stereotypical, such conversations are not unusual. People see and remember the things that interest them, and this interest is focused on things they take to be pointing to themselves. Let us suppose that, following the stereotype, the first speaker was a woman, and that she generally chooses the decoration in the house, makes the curtains and does the washing. Notice that the man's memory begins to be jogged by the mention of building an alcove (well, after all, he is into DIY); but for him the defining factor is the music system. In their viewing, each has registered the features that support their interests and sense of identity. That is to say, they are fascinated by those things that they see as confirming their own role or identity. Each partner looks from his or her own invested perspective. Even if they agree on which house will suit them best as a couple, the criteria on which the decision is made may be quite different. More than this, they may actually have *seen* two quite different houses while walking round the same building. They have certainly been entranced by different features of it.

The wider experiences of some couples can offer an interesting perspective on this theory. The processes operating with one mind and one set of eyes can just as easily work with two. Couples, and indeed bigger groups, can develop a sense of shared identity. As with many of the processes of Buddhist psychology, the collective and the individual processes mirror one another. In the case of a couple, the self-prison can be created around two people rather than just one. As this happens, a couple start to think in terms like: "We are the sort of people who . . . " As time goes by, collective tastes and opinions build up, over-lying the individual identities that each partner brought into the relationship. This collective identity is less isolating, but it is still deluded. It can be even more powerful than the individual self, and it creates a greater sense of permanence and reliability. If we are an indivisible unit, we imagine that we cannot lose one another through death or separation.

The kind of shared perception that develops in such collec-tive situations is also less likely to be challenged in the course of interactions. Usually we tend to test reality against other people's perceptions. When there is a shared view, the re-sponses that are received from the other person simply confirm the self-invested view. The confirmatory words of the other person thus become lakshanas. As this phenomenon of shared selves occurs in bigger groups we start to understand how cultural expectations are built up. This is the *natural attitude* of phenomenology.

Rupas: Putting Our Stamp on Things

Attempts to provide reference to the self contaminate the view a person has of an object. Self-creation also occurs when we identify or name that object. In doing so we create a powerful rupa. This is something we do continuously, although we may not be aware that we are doing it. When we enter a room, we see chairs and tables and carpets and people, rather than a collection of colors and shapes. The process of labeling objects of perception is so automatic and universal that it is only when it fails that we become aware that we are doing it. When we come across something that we cannot name, we are disturbed.

Imagine being in a room alone and catching a glimpse of

something out of the corner of your eye that looks as if it is moving. What responses go through you mind? Maybe you try to explain it—could it be a reflection or something caught by a draft? Perhaps you try to dismiss it. Perhaps you become afraid that you are "seeing things." Whatever the response, there was probably a moment of unease. This was a bit of the world not under your control.

Naming is a form of possession. In the act of putting a word to an object, you put your mark on it. We can think about the process in several ways. First, in naming an object you are picking out that object from its surroundings. You see "a chair" as opposed to "a room" (which happens to have a chair in it) or "a cushion" (which happens to be on the chair). This is a kind of extension of the selective viewing that we have already seen operating. It is an effect of self-material creeping into your world-view.

Second, the name you choose to give an object in your mind has its own set of associations both for you and for others in our culture. There will be a difference of meaning and association if you label the object as "a chair," "Dad's chair" or "a Windsor." With each of these labels the object is invested with a subtly different personal and cultural meaning. More than this, though, in your labeling of the object you are in fact ceasing to see the object in itself at all. What you are seeing is your image of the object. This image is closely associated with your sense of identity. You are using the object to confirm your sense of identity, and the objects you have around you confirm the identity others will see in you. Thus a rupa is the personal manifestation of the object. It is the object as a phenomenon rather than the object itself.

Naming objects is a particular case of the general process of seeing self-indicators that occurs through perception. It is a powerful process. Some societies place great significance on names and even give secret names to people so that others cannot have power over them by naming them. As we name our world, we structure it. These structures reflect our mental structures. They are personal and unique. They are also a manifestation of our deludedness.

Exploring Your Own Rupa Process

You can explore your own process of attraction and naming.

Think of a room with which you are familiar, one you will be able to visit easily—perhaps another room in your house, but not the room you are currently in. Write a description of the room. It can simply be a list of the things you remember from the room, which you can do quite quickly. When you have finished, go into the room and take a look. Notice what you have remembered and what you have forgotten. Notice how you have described things and the words you have used for them. What does this tell you about what you see and what you don't see? Does your choice of words signify particular associations? If you were reading this description written by someone else, what would you learn about that person?

Now reflect on your experience of going into the room after having written the description. How did you see things having done the exercise and become more conscious of your process of naming? Did you see new things? Were you aware of how things that you remembered were in some cases indicators of self for you?

When you have tried this exercise, you may be left with a feeling that your description was accurate—just a list of what was there. If this is so, try inviting someone else to do the same exercise and compare your results. Alternatively, you could imagine being someone else—one of your parents, for example, or your own child. Go into the room and imagine how it is to see the room through their eyes. What do you notice as different? Like the couple described earlier, you may be surprised by the differences in your views of the same room.

Sometimes when my husband David and I have run courses in our center looking at these topics, I have invited the whole group of students to each write a description of the room in which we have just had coffee. I always find it interesting how different the descriptions are that people write, and what different things different people have noticed. Often things are pointed out which I have forgotten are there, even though the room is in the house where I live. It makes me realize how much I just don't see because I have stopped really looking.

One's vision is limited by what he or she expects to see, and each of us cuts out a great deal.

Rupas and Dharmas

An object that is labeled in the way we have been describing is called a *nama-rupa*. Literally, it means "named object." A nama-rupa is something I see as an indicator of something else that is important to my identity; in other words, it is something I am seeing in a distorted and ultimately self-interested way. The term nama-rupa, or rupa, can be used in contrast with the word *dharma*.

A dharma is "the thing itself." It is the object, perceived directly without personal investment. It is uncontaminated reality. The word dharma also has the meaning of "the thing that holds." It is the foundation. It is that which we can trust. Dharma is also used to mean the Buddhist teachings. These teachings are what we are left with when we have stripped away the layers of delusion. Seeing dharma could be described as enlightened seeing. It means seeing the irreducible reality. In the passage from the Sutra on the Root of All Things in the Majjhima Nikaya, quoted earlier, the first statement could be said to describe seeing dharma. It describes direct perception. The person perceives earth as earth. The other statements all refer to ways in which perception is distorted by the impulse to create and maintain identity. Rupas are created as the mind uses different means of deriving signs of self from the element earth.

The formal act of becoming a Buddhist involves taking the three refuges. When you do this you are saying that you place your faith in these three pillars of Buddhism: the Buddha as the source of your inspiration; Dharma, which is the Buddhist teachings: and the Sangha, which is the spiritual community. Taking refuge is an important act because it means giving up self.

When you take refuge in the Buddha you acknowledge that the teaching you are receiving has a source. You recognize that none of the teachings you receive in life comes from yourself. None of your thoughts is original. All that you learn comes from sources beyond yourself.

When you take refuge in the Sangha you acknowledge your interconnectedness with others and your reliance on others for support and spiritual nourishment. Here, once again, you give up your attachments to being a separate self and to your individualistic thinking.

When you take refuge in Dharma you recognize the Buddhist teachings. In particular, you recognize that these teachings are pointing out reality. The fact that the same word is used to mean the teachings and to mean reality indicates the practicality of the Buddhist message. The Buddha intended his teachings to be tested. He told his followers not to take his word for things but to try them out for themselves. You are encouraged to test the reliability of dharma, to encounter it. We will discuss later the importance of feeling your connection to the material world in achieving groundedness. When I recite the refuges, I like to bow to the ground and feel the solidity of the floor beneath me. Bowing is itself a good practice for letting go of self. When you bow fully you can rest on the earth and feel the solid contact. You can feel the earth as dharma. It holds you and supports you.

There are times when going for refuge feels like the only reliable thing left, when you start to recognize the illusion of permanence that you have built up around you. I recall one night recently when this realization became very much alive for me. This night followed a day in which my husband had left to visit a part of India where there had been some terrorist troubles. Although he was not likely to be in immediate danger, I had some concerns for his safety. During the day we had also talked a lot about future plans and possibilities for our joint work. I had come to realize, however, that I was building up a set of ideas in my mind about the next few months that was actually very unlikely to come into practice. As I went to bed that night, the various conversations of the day went through my mind. I began to feel unsettled. I remembered the parting at the airport. What if this had been the last view I would have of my husband? I recalled watching him go through the baggage checks, jovially chatting with the security people as they searched him. I imagined recalling the same image in future if I were never to see him alive again. Would I be able to remember that image for ever? How poignant that last sight of him would seem, as he light-heartedly turned for the official to scan his left side with his metal detecting machine.

As I lay in bed, the thoughts seemed to multiply—as can happen in the night—and I found myself getting increasingly anxious as the realization came over me that I could actually count on nothing in my life to be permanent. We can all talk about impermanence and accept it at one level, but as I allowed the awareness of its reality to unfold, I realized how often I had not fully allowed myself truly to know this. As most of us do most of the time, I had been living as if the important people and things in my life were permanent. At this point the world seemed to spin away. I felt caught in my fear and uncertainty.

This was when the reality of refuge hit me. Whatever happened, the inspiration could not be taken away. Nor could here-and-now reality. The dharma was all around me, beneath me. Whatever happened, there would be ground to stand on. I could take refuge in that encounter.

Knowing that the ground will always be there is an important realization. It can be a source of tremendous strength to those going into difficult situations. It can also be very helpful to those caught in anxiety states or other forms of mental confusion. Taking refuge in our encounter with the material world helps you to get beyond the cycles of self-preoccupation and delusion.

Rupas as Spiritually Invested Objects

A rupa is an object that has the power to draw your awareness. It commands the attention of one or more of the senses. The rupa is a phenomenon, something that appears to you. The word "rupa" is also used to describe sacred objects that hold spiritual power for you. All of these meanings indicate that the rupa is not the object itself, but rather the power associated with the object. The rupa is distinct from the object itself, which is the dharma. In this way, you could say that the object itself holds the rupa's power. The dharma holds the rupa.

So far, the rupas that have been described have been invested with what I term self-indication. The object in question takes on significance because it represents something significant in your psychological world. You cling to these objects because they shore up your sense of self. Your identification has created an energetic link between the object and you.

The word "rupa" is not always directly linked to self-indication, however. For example, the word is used to describe the sacred images that stand on the shrine. A figure of the Buddha is called a Buddha rupa. In this case, the power of the rupa derives from an investment that is not personal in the same way as it is in the self-indicating rupas that we have been looking at so far. Here the rupa points to the possibility of freedom from self. It is a positive lakshana.

A Buddha statue on a shrine provides a strong spiritual focus for the practitioner and is treated with great reverence and devotion. This response to the rupa is not, however, intrinsic to the object itself. To the person who has no associations with the religion, the figure is simply a statue and may be appraised on its artistic merits or disregarded. Of itself, the object has no special status. The power of the religious rupa comes from the symbolic function it performs. It is created out of the collective process of the religious community. As such, it is relational; yet the investment is not the personal investment of one person's experience. The object points towards something that is beyond self, and its function is to create a focus for the practitioner's relationship with the other and to offer a shared focus for religious practice.

The religious rupa is significant to the whole religious community, often carrying associations and investment from many generations of practitioners. At the same time, for it to have significance for any practitioner, that person needs to create a personal link to the object. This may occur through a gradual building of associations, or it may be created through deliberate use of certain practices. In this sense the object becomes a repository for the person's faith. It becomes the holder of religious experience and understanding. We can say that the rupa becomes a repository for Dharma.

There is a circular relationship between the rupa and the dharma. The practitioner has religious experiences through teachings and practice associated with the religious artifact. Through these, powerful associations are built up between the experience and the object. Thus, the object becomes a rupa, giving direction to the practitioner's spiritual experience. It can then be a source of inspiration for further practice. In this way, the practice can be built up and the rupa can be an aid to its maintenance.

This kind of rupa, however, does not ultimately point to self. The religious experience is, or should be, an experience of connecting with the other. Of course, for the average spiritual practitioner, there is frequently an intermediate stage in which the Buddha rupa does function as a lakshana, offering the person an identity as a Buddhist. The challenge of practice is to get beyond this "spiritual materialism" (Trungpa 1973). What the Buddha indicates is not the self, but the vitality of what is other—or, in technical terms, *other-power*.

The experience is in one sense individual but in many ways collective. It is passed on from one person to another through shared practice and teachings. In this way, the rupa can be seen as a channel for transmitting the religious experience, a link in the chain of practitioners.

In our French retreat center, our meditation hall is an old barn. When we first arrived at the house, the barn was a ruin, its roof caved in and several trees growing in the debris of shattered roof tiles, old straw and rotting timbers. Over several years we worked to clear the site and then asked a local builder to put a new roof on the building. The hall is still open to the elements. The big arched doorway lets in the sun and rain and, at full moon, wonderful shafts of silver light that fall directly onto the main shrine. The floor is still bare earth, pounded hard by years of use and now covered with loose rugs.

We have practiced in the barn now for five or six years. Most of the retreats have been held in summer, but sometimes we have sat there in winter, wrapped in blankets, the occasional flake of snow blowing in to settle on our woolen hats.

The space feels very different now from that original ruin.

When I sit down for the first time each summer retreat, I feel a strong sense of coming back to my spiritual base. It is like coming home. The experience is one of mind and body. I see the old walls, the rough stone shrines, the Buddha rupas, the view across the yard through the doorway, and something settles in me. I feel very in touch with the Dharma.

I think that most people will identify with such an experience. We all have special places that seem to hold a powerful link to the spiritual dimension. At the same time such links are, in part, ones we have created for ourselves. The associations that give a place the power to hold our spiritual experience are built up over time. The repeated experience of Buddhist practice in our meditation hall creates the conditions for mind and body to respond by becoming quiet and meditative when I next enter it. Added to this, though, the meditation hall contains many elements that already had spiritual significance. The old stones remind me of the generations of farmers and animals who have occupied this land, and the cycles of life by which they lived. The earth floor brings me into contact with the solid ground that supports us all. The Buddha figures and other religious artifacts have grown in significance over the years I have been practicing Buddhism. There are many layers of meaning. Through a combination of deliberate and accidental processes these have been brought together to create the practice environment. This environment is redolent with associations, most of which speak to many of the people who use it.

Shared associations are part of common culture and part of being human. The deepest levels of associations are universal. As Carl Jung's concept of archetypes suggests, it seems that certain images have a significance that is built into the human psyche at a fundamental and universal level. For these reasons, although rupas are created out of your relationship with them, you may still experience the power of a rupa image on first encounter.

Some objects that are described as rupa seem to have no self-element. Buddha images, sacred pictures, and items of religious clothing can all take us beyond self-preoccupation into a stronger connection with the other. They act as antidotes to self.

Other-invested Rupas

Some objects are self-indicating in another way, representing people who have been significant in one's life. These may take on particularly strong significance for us. Family heirlooms, for example, can have a particular potency.

I always wear three rings. One is my wedding ring, and the other two belonged to my grandmother. They were her wedding ring and her engagement ring. My grandmother was a woman of considerable energy and strength of character. She loved people and conversation and was an ardent campaigner for many causes. One of her regrets was that she had been too young to chain herself to the railings with the suffragettes. She was also a wonderful grandmother, always ready to read a story or share a joke as we cooked together in her big kitchen. Wearing her rings, I carry with me a reminder of her, even though she died some years ago. Wearing rings is often a symbolic way of being in touch with a relationship. Wedding rings, engagement rings, even funeral rings are worn in many cultures. They represent the relationships that are significant for us. When I look at my grandmother's rings, they provide a reminder of her and of the relationship that we had.

The symbolism contained in a rupa connected with a loved one has a number of elements. There is the element of self-indication. This is *my* grandmother, it implies. The ring is associated with my past, my memories and my associations. It is also, however, her ring. It had special meaning for her. It represented her engagement to my grandfather just after the First World War. It was of that time when life was precious and full of hope. I remember her showing me a cushion she had made at that time. She had stuffed it with the cut-up remains of my grandfather's army uniform. Inside it she had buried a tin with all his army buttons in it and a note expressing her hope that there should be no more wars like the one they had just gone through.

As I look at her rings, old-fashioned and rather solid, I think of that relationship. Perhaps it sometimes felt a little old-fashioned and rather solid to her too, being a schoolteacher's wife in a village in the 1920s. Looking at the rings, I can feel close to her and imagine her life, even though there is much I do not know about it. I can imagine her with me, picture her house; imagine being with her in the kitchen baking yeast buns. Developing my sense of her life, I can start to break through the rigidity of my own.

In this way objects can help you to explore your self-world—but they can also take you beyond it. They can be a physical way of keeping in mind the other person and the influence for good that they can have in your life. Buddhists, like followers of other faiths, may carry some object that acts as a reminder of spiritual commitment. Doing so helps us to stay in touch with our training and to keep the Buddha in mind.

Using Rupas to Develop Better Mental States

Other-related objects can be used in other positive ways to help free yourself from entrenched habit-patterns and compulsive behaviors. They can also support people who are in distress. Thus you should not think that rupa-investment is necessarily to be done away with. In Chapter 1, I described how the music and dance of Kurdish people brought comfort and a sense of belonging in the midst of terrible tragedy. Dances and traditional clothes are rupas that hold an experience of home in a foreign and often unfriendly country. For people who are cut off from that home and family, as a refugee may be, such objects are poignant but at the same time precious reminders. They may help the process of grieving and facing what has been lost.

Objects can be used to evoke positive states of mind. When we deliberately create an object that can be a rupa in this way, we call it an anchor. It anchors positive feelings and can be used to re-evoke them. Methods for creating such anchors will be discussed in later chapters. We have seen how this happens in religious practice, but a similar process can be used in more mundane circumstances. People naturally use objects in this way. Many people carry items that have personal significance or sentimental value in order to give them confidence or encourage them. It may be a photo in the wallet, or a piece of jewelery, or some small gift that a child slipped into a suitcase. In situations of stress the likelihood of doing this increases. Soldiers go into battle with love-letters or memorabilia from home in their pockets.

Object-Related Work

Mental states arise in association with objects. An important area of Buddhist psychology theory rests upon this fact. It is called *object relation theory*. (It is important to note that this is a completely different set of theory from the Western theory of object relations. There is no "s" on the end of the word "relation" in the Buddhist theory.) Object relation theory states that the mind is conditioned by its object. Here an object may be a physical object, but it may also be an idea, an image, a scene, a sensation. It is whatever you give your attention to; or, you might say, whatever is the object of your attention. This means that your mental state will change according to where you place your attention.

If I think about the exam I am taking next week I will be in a different mental state from that which I will be in if I think about going out for the evening. Making the object more vivid increases its power to influence the mental state. If, instead of thinking about the exam, I imagine the exam room . . . where I will sit, the layout of the tables, the monitor sitting at her desk, the pen I will be writing with . . . as the details become clearer, it is likely that my feeling response will intensify.

Because mental states are so dependent on the object of attention, the choice of an object to which you give attention is important. To some extent, this gives you a choice about the mental states you experience. Looking at your own habitual patterns of attention provides one way in which you can improve your mental state. It may seem simplistic to tell someone who is deeply unhappy to "think of something nice," but it is generally the case that someone who suffers from depression habitually brings their attention to negative objects.

Recognizing and changing this pattern may not be the whole answer, but it may help. As a person changes the pattern of their attention, so, gradually, increasingly positive thoughts may start to predominate. This has implications for those who are depressed. It may not always be helpful to talk endlessly about their problems. This is particularly the case where such talk seems to have a compulsive aspect, or where it seems to be building an overly negative world-view. It may be more helpful to turn the conversation to subjects with more positive associations, or to engage in a practical activity.

Self as Rupa

The mind and the rupa are like mirrors for one another. Within the perception of the object can be seen a reflection of the mentality, and within the mentality can be seen the reflection of the rupa. Since there is some choice in what a person gives their attention to, however, there are opportunities to influence the process of conditioning. The process can be positive or negative in its effect on one's mental state.

The concept of rupa is, in one sense, an explanation of the way in which people use the object world to create and maintain a self. At the same time, it demonstrates that the self they each create is not independent. It is bound up with their experience of that which is other. Some objects are significant because they represent something that is not self, that is meaningful to you. At the same time, that meaningfulness contributes to your sense of identity. Some objects of this kind, such as religious objects, represent collective or universal values. Even these carry the possibility of creating self-material (albeit positive) unless you are vigilant. If you simply use your spiritual practice to *be* a Buddhist or a Christian or whatever, there is a level of identity formation involved. At the same time, such rupas have importance in helping to reach out to the world beyond self. Many objects that become rupa, however, are more directly concerned with self-indication, and there is always the danger that, as you give too much of your attention to them, the self becomes more deeply reinforced.

There is one further step in this process. The self is itself a powerful object. When you think of self, that self, even though imaginary, is perceived by mano-vijnana, the mind's eye. It becomes rupa. This is the self-image. The self as rupa will itself exert a conditioning effect upon the psyche. As a person becomes preoccupied with his self-image, whether positive or negative, that image conditions his mental structures, making them more rigid. For this reason, psychological work that focuses on the self as an object of attention may be counter-productive, increasing the power of the self-prison and the person's entrapment in it. Moving towards a more healthy mental state involves deepening engagement with the real other, as opposed to a world of rupas, so that we cease to see things as self-indicators.

THEORIES EXPLAINED IN THIS CHAPTER

- lakshanas;
- rupa formation;
- self- and other-invested rupas;
- four forms of conceptualization of self;
- object relation theory; and
- rupas and dharmas.

· 5 ·

Skandhas: A Process of Avoidance

Mental states arise in accordance with what the mind gives its attention to. Technically, we refer to this as the mind being conditioned by its object. In the last chapter we looked at how, during this process, the object comes to be experienced as an indicator or sign (lakshana) of self. It becomes rupa. We also saw that this process is cyclic. Objects have the power to condition the mind; and we perceive objects according to the conditioning the mind has already undergone. We have also seen how this process supports the impression of an enduring self, and how this then creates a second-level cycle, as the self becomes a powerful rupa in its own right.

In this chapter, a further dimension of the process whereby perceptions condition the mind will be explored. We will look at another central Buddhist teaching, that of the *five aggregates of grasping*, or *skandhas*. The Buddha gave teachings on the five skandhas many times. His injunction to his disciples again and again was to let go of the five skandhas. We can interpret this as an injunction to let go of the processes by which we create a self-structure.

So what are the skandhas? In Sanskrit they are rupa, vedana, samjna, samskara, and vijnana. They are commonly translated as form, feelings, perception, mental formations, and consciousness—but these translations are not necessarily entirely accurate and may not be the most useful translations in assisting our understanding of this teaching. The skandhas are often presented as the five elements that make up the person, listed simply as a rather random collection of components. This is not, however, the most helpful way to view them. In the interpretation that I will present here, these elements are seen as stages in a process whereby the self is re-created and maintained.

Dependent Origination: The Process Nature of Buddhist Teachings

All the themes we have examined, and will be examining, in this book are variations upon a single theme. That theme is what the Buddha gained deep insight into, and it was the substantive content of his enlightenment. It is called dependent origination, the most fundamental teaching in Buddhist psychology.

In brief, the theory of dependent origination states that all mental events arise upon a basis of conditions. This does not mean that conditions *determine* events. It simply means that for any given event to occur, certain conditions must be in place.

The Buddha generally taught in terms of process. The teaching of dependent origination is a process teaching. All things depend upon causes and conditions. One thing rests upon another. One thing happening leads to a probability of something else happening. Changing the causes, we change the possibilities. This teaching is fundamental to Buddhist understanding and, in its general form, underpins all other Buddhist teachings.

The Four Noble Truths can be interpreted as a teaching about process. Dukkha leads to samudaya, which leads to nirodha, which leads to marga. Affliction leads to the arising of feelings, which need to be contained; this process puts one on the spiritual path. This teaching emphasizes the choice between distraction and spiritual progress, between the path of escapism and that of the engaged life. These are respectively the paths of self-creation and of non-self.

The Mahahatthipadopama Sutta, number 28 in the Majjhima Nikaya, uses the image of the elephant's footprint to demonstrate that, just as all other animals' footprints can be fitted within the outline of the elephant's footprint, so too all the Buddhist teachings can be fitted within the teaching of the Four Noble Truths. The teaching is given by Shariputra, one of the Buddha's leading disciples. In particular, Shariputra places the teaching of the skandhas within this framework.

> *Now this has been said by the Blessed One: "One who sees dependent origination sees the Dharma; one who sees the Dharma sees dependent origination." And these five aggregates affected by clinging are dependently arisen. The desire, clinging, personal attachment and holding [chanda, alaya, anunaya and ajjhosana] based on these five aggregates [skandhas] affected by clinging is dukkha samudaya. The removal of desire and lust, the abandonment of desire and lust for these five aggregates affected by clinging, is the containment [nirodha] of dukkha.* (Majjhima Nikaya 28.28)

In this passage, we can see a number of important points.

First, the theory of dependent origination is given central importance. It is linked to teachings on attachment and self-investment. In the earlier part of this sutra, Shariputra demonstrates that it is not the actual experiencing of things which causes problems, but the attribution of self-indication to them. This investment creates attachment, which arises out of the contact between the senses and their objects. In seeing something, the eye creates a possession of it. Shariputra explains that all these elements are, however, dependently originated, and so insubstantial. Your eye attaches to things only because it has been conditioned to do so.

Shariputra then says that the process of attachment represented by the skandhas is a source of suffering and that *chanda* (will, impulse, sensual desire), *alaya* (possessiveness or clinginess), *anunaya* (attachment to people) and *ajjhosana* (holding or attachment to things) arise in dependence upon the skandha process. He says that what is required is that you contain the desire and craving in this process. In other words, you must become less personally invested. (It is interesting in view of the discussion in Chapter 3 to notice that the word alaya is used here simply to mean possessiveness.)

The Skandhas

The teaching of the skandhas is an analysis of the processes of self-creation in terms of a five-stage cycle.

Rupa

The first skandha is *rupa*. Rupa is traditionally translated as form, and as such is often taken to mean the person's body; but the word "rupa" actually refers to things that have a power over you on account of the fact that you see them as indicating something that is important to you. The most important thing to you is your self-image. When the Buddha advises giving up rupa, he means that you should stop seeing everything as indicating your self.

The American psychologist and theorist Carl Rogers developed the concept of the *frame of reference*. The frame of reference is a person's individualized perception, and it is shaped by that person's previous experience. It is the way that particular person sees the world. Rogers saw it as essential that a counselor was able to enter the client's frame of reference through empathic listening and response. This injunction suggests that Rogers believed it was possible for the practitioner to leave his own frame of reference and take on that of someone else. He did, however, seem to see this as particularly beneficial to the counselor and did not advocate that clients should be encouraged to give up their own frames of reference.

A Buddhist view suggests a different approach. While a level of empathy is necessary to understand the other person's perspective, and to establish a caring relationship, simply responding from within the other person's frame of reference will reinforce the illusion that what is perceived as real is in fact real. It will contribute to the maintenance of the illusion of a substantive self. It is only by encountering others and experiencing difference that people start to loosen their grip on the deluded views they are carrying. You need to get beyond your investment in

things being a particular way. The Buddha was quite unequiv-
ocal on this matter. He instructed people to give up the skandhas,
thus letting go of personal investment in their world-views.

Rupa is perceived through the senses, and guarding the sense
doors is one means of increasing your awareness of your biases
and distorted view. The Buddha gave a vivid description of the
dangers of leaving sense doors unguarded. In the sutra of the
Greater Discourse on the Cowherd (Mahagopalaka Sutta, MN
33) he likens the senses to open wounds, which need to be
dressed lest they allow unwholesome states to enter.

> On seeing rupa with the eye, a bhikshu does not grasp at its
> signs and features. If he left the eye faculty unguarded, evil
> unwholesome states of covetousness and grief might invade
> him, [so] he practices restraint, he guards the eye faculty, he
> undertakes the restraint of the eye faculty. (Majjhima Nikaya
> 33.20)

In continuing, the sutra shows how each of the other sense
faculties also needs to be guarded.

Vedana

The second of the skandhas is *vedana*. Vedana is often translated as "feelings," but this is really too broad a term. A better
translation is "reaction," but even this is still wider than the
Buddha's original meaning. Vedana has only three possible
forms—attraction, aversion and confusion. These three possibilities are the same as the three possibilities offered in the
teaching of the Three Poisons or negative root reactions
(discussed in Chapter 2).

Vedana is an instant response. It arises from sensory contact.
It is an immediate, visceral reaction. We can think of it as rather
like the response of an amoeba coming up against an object.
Imagine the amoeba going about its world encountering objects.
When it bumps into something, it reacts either positively or
negatively. If something is food, it engulfs it. If something is
unpleasant or dangerous, it shrinks back. Humans are not so
different. You see something, and unless you are on your guard

you have already reacted. You experience something (rupa) through your senses. This experience evokes an immediate response, which seems to catch you almost unawares. You either want the object or you push it away. You see something, and in a moment you have reacted by grasping or recoiling—or you feel confused and disconcerted.

"Veda-na" literally means "knowingness." The ancient Indian texts are called Vedas, and this means "the knowledge." Vedana is the feeling of recognition: "I know what this means." People judge things according to what they imagine them to be indicating about themselves. A feeling arises (samudaya) that is powerful and visceral. Anything that a person takes to be threatening to self makes him go hot. The Buddha describes this as a fever. The same is true of things that flatter one's pride.

Vedana follows rupa. Technically it involves the attachment of the senses to the object. The Sutra on Right View (Sammaditthi Sutta: MN 9), which, like the Mahatthipadopama Sutta, is a teaching given by Shariputra, elaborates on the experience of vedana. It describes how vedana arises out of the experience of the six senses:

> There are these six classes of vedana: vedana born of eye-contact, vedana born of ear-contact, vedana born of nose-contact, vedana born of tongue-contact, vedana born of body contact, vedana born of mind-contact. With the arising of contact there is the arising of vedana. With the restraint of contact there is the restraint of feeling. The way leading to the restraint of vedana is just this Noble Eightfold Path. (MN 9.42)

This particular exposition is interesting in terms of a general understanding of the way the different Buddhist teachings fit together, because it shows how vedana arises out of sense contacts. This seems to confirm that the process interpretation of the skandhas is correct. It also offers a bridge between this teaching and that of the Twelve Links of Dependent Origination (discussed in detail in Chapter 10 below). The term "contact" (*sparsha*) occurs in the latter teaching, where it is presented as providing conditions for vedana. Further evidence that all the main teachings of Buddhism can be taken to describe the same phenomena is found in the reference here to nirodha (translated as restraint), which connects this passage to the teaching of the Four Noble Truths.

Transforming vedana   If you want to do something about your habit-patterns and get out of compulsive ways of reacting, transforming vedana can be crucial. Because vedana is so immediate, it can be very difficult to catch yourself before you have reacted. Yet it is often that immediate reaction that is so damaging. If I meet someone with a disfiguring disability and, despite my intention to be friendly, react with revulsion, I may cause a lot of hurt. If someone tells me of their involvement with atrocities in a war situation, and I spontaneously react with feelings of disapproval, these will show on my face and make it difficult for the person to trust me.

Showing a feeling reaction is not always harmful—indeed, if you are really going to encounter others, you need to be able to respond spontaneously—but the reactivity described by the term vedana is ultimately based on self-interest and may be quite inappropriate to the real situation. It is particularly difficult to handle because it is generally non-verbal and precedes intentional response. For the same reason, however, it gives others a strong message about your intentions toward them. People trust what they see and, although they may not be aware of doing so, form impressions of others' reliability through watching their reactions.

In situations where feelings are high, overcoming vedana responses can be especially important. A friend of mine works as a mediator. He has gone into many conflict situations around the world, listening to the pain of people on both sides. When he is with people he hears many terrible stories. He hears of killings and mutilations, families ripped apart, and hatred going back generations. He visits people on both sides of a conflict and often brings them together face to face, hoping to build reconciliation through enabling encounter. In these delicate discussions, there are many times when he is moved by the accounts of suffering that he hears. There are many other occasions when he is angered or repulsed. In both situations, it is important that he is not hooked into reacting inappropriately. If confidence is to be maintained and healing to occur, he must be able to stay neutral but compassionate. Achieving this involves a deep caring for the other and a letting go of personal agendas and interests. Inasmuch as his vedana reaction is diminished, he will be able to be present and witness without judging.

Vedana responses occur at the body level. They are often called "gut reactions." You can learn to notice them by increasing your detailed awareness of moment-by-moment process. Sharon asked for my help in dealing with angry outbursts she was having at work. She had lost her temper several times in meetings and was frightened she might lose her job as a result. I encouraged her to replay the situation in her mind, starting as she entered the meeting where the last outburst had occurred, and to notice the way her body responded as she did so. She pictured her office; the pile of papers on her desk that she would take to the meeting; her thoughts before she entered the room. We went through the scenario moment by moment. She imagined the meeting starting, and her feeling of rising anxiety. Then she noticed that when she thought of a particular person speaking, she had a strong bodily reaction. She had previously been unaware of this. In the past, she had lost her temper with this person. Having noticed this response, we were able to replay the scene imaginatively a number of times. First, this process enabled Sharon to see that she had particular expectations and assumptions about this person. She was attributing qualities to them that might or might not actually be present. In this, she was creating a rupa. Second, Sharon was able to notice how her reaction began with physical sensations long before she actually lost her temper. By observing such details, she was able to interrupt the reactive process and recover her composure. This way she avoided the outbursts that were threatening her job.

By observing vedana you can see how you are self-referencing things that may really have little to do with yourself. You can also see that vedana itself is just a knee-jerk reaction. The Buddha taught followers to notice vedana and respond by thinking "this vedana is not mine, it is not me, it is not myself." The observation of the process, similarly, allows you to separate from it and so dis-identify with it. This in turn allows you to take a wider perspective so that you do not get caught in details. This observation is part of the awareness that you bring to training. Shariputra suggests that the way to escape from powerful vedana reactions is to follow the path of training.

Samjna

The third element in the skandha process is *samjna*. The word "samjna" is made up of two parts: "sam" means "with," and "jna" means "knowing." It is the same root as in "vijnana," with the same prefix as in the word "samudaya." The word "samjna" means the knowledge that comes with something. In other words, the samjna response occurs at the point when associations come up after you experience something. Following on from the immediate vedana reaction, associations and imagery come into your mind. Samjna is when you really become hooked into a process. The initial visceral reaction leads to patterns of response that are strong enough to make you lose awareness of the process. You become drawn into a whole set of associations and images and start to act in ways that follow old patterns.

If vedana is an immediate, limited, gut reaction, samjna is a slower, more diverse response. Samjna is, in fact, the creation of a kind of trance state. You experience something that arouses a reaction, and on the basis of this you slip into a pattern of responses based on past conditioning. You are on automatic pilot. This may or may not be appropriate to the real situation you are in. You are carried along by your associations and the expectations that go with them. You are already embarked on a habitual pattern of behavior.

Sally goes to an adult education class. The group leader, a tall woman, seems pretty confident. Sally has never met her before but immediately feels dislike. During the coffee break the class leader walks past Sally to talk to another woman in the group. Sally feels very upset and snubbed. Later in the session, when the participants are asked to share their ideas, Sally is unable to think of anything to say.

When she thinks about it afterward, Sally realizes that her response to the situation was probably not reasonable. She has no evidence that the class leader snubbed her and no basis for her feeling of dislike. She realizes that she feels quite put down and, perhaps as a result of this, unconfident. Yet these feelings, again, are not justified by the real situation. Sally tries to make sense of her experience.

Sally realizes that a pattern of reaction has been going on that owes more to old habits than to the present situation. An image comes to her of a teacher she had when she was eight years old. This woman was very strict with the class, and Sally found her frightening. She coped with her fear by becoming quiet in class. The teacher had been tall, with blond cropped hair, rather like the present class leader.

Sally now recognizes that she has become hooked into an old pattern of responses. When she first saw the woman, she felt an immediate pulling back into herself. She felt dislike, even though, on reflection, she knows there was no reason for it. Nevertheless, she wanted the woman's attention, which left her open to feeling rejected during the coffee break. This immediate negative reaction took place at the level of vedana. It was a gut feeling. After that she felt carried along by the situation. Her inability to respond seemed linked to feelings of longing for attention.

Sally's response in the coffee break felt awkward and inappropriate. She was not aware of why she was acting as she was. It was only later that she was able to recall the schoolroom and the teacher. Although the memories had not been in Sally's mind, the habit-responses were, in a sense, programmed in. They led Sally to act in ways that she had at a much earlier time.

Sally had in fact entered a mild trance state. She was seeing things and responding to them as if she were in a different reality. This is nothing out of the ordinary; we all spend much of our lives mildly entranced. According to Buddhism, this is the condition that ordinary people are in most of the time. Samjna is entrancement. In it we see not the real world but a self-indicating one. Our actions are not fully under our conscious control and our vision is distorted. We are in the grip of delusion.

Samskara

Sally did not contribute to the class discussion as she might otherwise have done. Her confidence dropped and she retreated into silence. She became preoccupied with the situation and found herself unable to sleep that night. As she brooded over the evening, her mind ran over and over what had happened, trying to make sense of why she had responded so strongly. These thoughts proliferated, creating great anxiety about how she would approach the next class. Such rumination is the fourth stage of the skandha process, called *samskara*. "Samskara" is often translated as "mental formations." Etymologically, the word "samskara" is made up of a combination of the words meaning "with" and "do." The second part of the word has a similar origin to the word "karma," which means "action." So samskaras are what arise with doing. They are action traces, the mental structures that result from the traces of what we have done. They are patterns of habit-energy, or behavioral tracks, that then elaborate themselves. The root meaning of the word samskara, then, has two implications. First, it implies leaving a track or trail. Second, it implies the elaboration of these traces.

The image of a samskara as a track is a useful one. Some tracks are deeply worn ruts. If you are driving along a road with deep ruts in it, it is hard to keep the car wheels from falling into them. Even if you want to drive on the ground to the side of the rut to avoid getting stuck in the mud at the bottom of it, the wheels seem to keep falling into the hollow. Some samskaras are so deeply worn that we find ourselves repeating the behavior again and again.

Other tracks are old and nearly grown over. These tracks may come near to being abandoned, but they are never completely lost. When I was younger I trained as an archaeologist. It was fascinating to look at photographs taken from the air at different times of year. On them we would see many marks and lines, often crossing modern field boundaries at strange angles. These crop marks, as they were called, appeared in many different conditions. Some showed up when the field was parched and dry in summer, others in the differential growth of crops. These were the impressions of old trackways and buildings, often dating back to Roman or prehistoric times. I remember seeing pictures of one Roman fort, completely outlined by a thin scatter of snow, which had settled in the shallow impressions on the ground, normally invisible to the eye. Few people realize just how much history lies beneath the countryside and how many remains of past generations we share our space with.

Just as an old pathway becomes apparent when a field is parched in summer, so too old patterns of habit-energy emerge at times of stress. The Buddha told his disciples many times to let go of the samskaras, but to do this you first need to let go of the hold that particular ones have over you. The theory of samskaras suggests that once a track has been laid, it will always be there, creating the possibility of repetition. So, in order to let go of samskaras, you need to find new responses so that you increase your repertoire of behavioral patterns. In addition, there are suggestions in the Buddhist teachings that you can work to create positive samskaras or *kushalas*. If you cannot give up the skandhas completely, you should aim to create and repeat patterns of positive behavior.

The term samskara also carries an implication of proliferation. Once a pattern of behavior has been repeated, the creation of the samskara includes a process in which the material in the action trace is multiplied. This is because a person repeatedly rehearses the action in her mind. Sally goes home and spends hours running over the scenario with the class leader in her mind. As she does so, she imaginatively repeats the actions of the day many times. She recalls what she did, trying to find ways out of the difficult feelings. One may run over the day's material through intentional thought, or—through what in the West would be termed unconscious preoccupation—in dreams. This process is described as *fuming by night* in the Ant Hill Sutra (there is an analysis of this sutra in Chapter 7). Thus actions that carry a strong emotional charge have a stronger effect in creating samskaras; for when you feel very emotional about something you have done, you become more preoccupied by it and rehearse it more often in your mind.

Samskaras are closely associated with the concept of karma. Karmic bijas, or seeds, stick to our alaya, and ripen when appropriate circumstances arise, providing the likelihood that an action pattern will be repeated. Sally's experience of meeting the class leader provided the circumstances in which seeds laid down during her previous experiences ripened. These created a propensity for her to act in the same way, which she did, laying the seeds for the next time she was faced with a similar situation. The karmic model offers a similar explanation to that offered by the theory of samskaras. The latter theory suggests that Sally followed old behavioral tracks, so increasing their depth. Both the theory of karma and the theory of samskaras suggest that if she could have recognized what was happening and managed to speak up in the group, she would have created the future possibility for different action.

Samskaras are created through action, but this does not mean that thoughts are not also subject to habit-energy. Thought has an action dimension. Thinking of, or imagining, doing something is not as powerful in creating samskaras as actually doing it is, but thought does have a conditioning effect. Our minds and bodies are not separate entities, and as we think we often imagine acting. This has a bodily aspect, as muscles respond to imaginary scenarios. If you imagine running away, your leg muscles may tighten; if you imagine shouting, your jaw tenses; and so on. Thus the emotional impact of an imagined situation leaves its impact in your samskaras.

Buddhist psychology is action-focused. What you do creates the conditions for future actions. It could have been the action of speaking up which would have made the difference for Sally. Had she done so, new samskaras would have been created, or new seeds sown. It is not necessary for Sally to feel comfortable about her actions (in this case, speaking up); it would be the fact that she acted differently that would create the new samskaras. Actions condition the mind. These theories suggest a more behavioral approach. In the words of Susan Jeffers' well-known book, you must "feel the fear and do it anyway" (Jeffers 1987).

If you are trying to change your behavior, you need to look at the way that you act now. This can also be true if you are trying to help others. People do not learn to be more peaceful by endlessly expressing angry feelings. They do not learn to be happy by talking continually about their troubles. They do not learn to be healthy by dwelling only on their sickness and disabilities. Although there is a time to express feelings, there is also a cost. Think about the behavioral tracks you are creating through such actions.

Similarly, think about the way that positive behavioral patterns are created through dialogue. In talking with others, you can learn to listen better and develop compassion. If a person does not simply talk about his drinking problem, but practices the words he will use to say "no" when asked to take the next drink, he will be more likely to be able to refuse the drink he does not want.

Vijnana

The final skandha is *vijnana*, commonly translated simply as "consciousness;" it is really the mentality associated with self-investment. This is the outcome of the skandha process. The skandhas are the stages in a process whereby the self-prison is created and maintained. At each stage, perception is infiltrated by personal agendas that create distortion. Delusion predominates. Vijnana is the ordinary mind that separates the world into "me" and "everything else." It is the mind that seeks confirmation of the self's existence. It is the mind that places you at the center of your life story and construes everything else as indicators of yourself.

In this way, the skandha process is circular. Having a view that is dominated by self-indicators, a person goes through life seeking to bring everything encountered into the same self-reinforcing structure, thereby refining and consolidating the self-image.

Buddhist psychology presents models suggesting that what you perceive conditions how you react. How you react conditions the kind of mental structures you carry. The mental structures you carry then condition how you approach life. How you approach life conditions what you perceive. This pattern is a loop that reinforces itself constantly. Each of us continually seeks affirmation that weave that person who we have assumed ourselves to be. Situations that disturb this process are avoided or reinterpreted, and the self appears to become more substantial. What you need to bear in mind, however, is that this process is in origin a defensive one. Its effects are to limit potential, to cut off possibilities for new action, and to tie up energy in the maintenance of the self-structure.

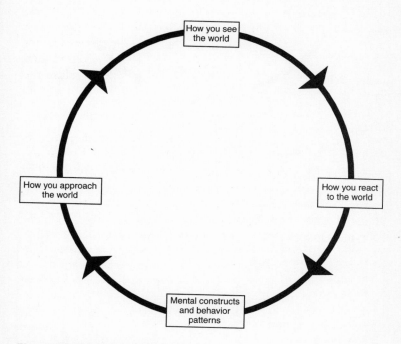

Figure 5.1 The basic skandha process
This process is built on the way that we relate to the world. At its simplest this can be reduced to a four-phase model.

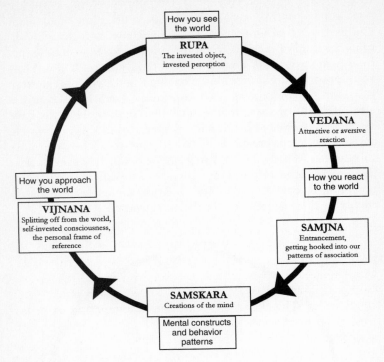

Figure 5.2 The skandha process, represented as a cycle.

This model elaborates the aspect of the process relating to reaction to the world.

THEORIES EXPLAINED IN THIS CHAPTER

- the skandha cycle;
- rupa;
- vedana;
- samjna;
- samskara; and
- vijnana.

· 6 ·

Beyond the Skandhas

The teaching of the skandhas provides a model of the circular process whereby the self-prison is created and maintained. It is a five-stage model describing the process of creating and activating habit-energy. The skandha process operates on large and small scales. The skandhas create the accumulation of behaviors, thought patterns and assumptions that narrow our lives and stop us really encountering the world, and the Buddha taught his followers to abandon them. To do so, however, it is necessary to step out of the rut of conditioned thought and action, which is not easy. Acting in familiar ways can feel comfortable and natural just because they are familiar, but it is really a form of delusion, a backing off from the world. To encounter the world, one must let go of this delusion. This takes courage and faith.

Escaping the Self-View

How are we to know what is really right and what is part of the delusion? If I trust my deepest intuition, am I in contact with primordial wisdom or am I simply unearthing long-established samskaras? Buddhism is not a matter of just going with the flow. It is about changing course.

This problem of knowing which intuitions to trust is

multiplied when we look at society as a whole. Here just the same processes of conditioning and identity creation operate as in the individual. Shared norms create a collective view, known as the *natural attitude*, which is rarely questioned. Only by moving outside the common consensus do we begin to recognize that there are other possible views, and that our individual or shared view has been narrow or distorted.

In this respect, the Buddhist practitioner is fortunate. Buddhism offers a different perspective from that of the cultural norms prevailing in the West, and this difference frequently throws into question preconceptions and assumptions about how things are or how they should be done. My own experience of becoming more deeply involved with the Buddhist path has been that my eyes have been opened to how many everyday assumptions I had been making. I was previously unaware of how often I did things in particular ways simply because everyone around me did. I had assumed that what I saw was accurate, and that it was how the world was. Now I saw there were alternative ways to look at things.

Among these assumptions was the belief that having a strong sense of identity was a good thing. As I began to understand and work with Buddhist models of the mind, I realized that such views actually reflected just one set of opinions, and that in many ways they were flawed. I began to realize that much of what I thought of as offering people freedom was actually extremely limiting. I saw that often, when we think we are making a free choice, we are in fact simply following old habit-patterns. Even these patterns are not always, or even mainly, our own, but are often learned from others. I saw that people do not direct their own lives, although they may think they do. I saw that much that went under the name of empowerment and encouraging personal expression in community groups was the reiteration of old patterns of ideas, learned from community workers. At the same time, I was confirmed in seeing the value of community and communal practice. My faith in the idea that psychological growth meant creating a strong self was gradually eroded.

In some respects, I became more relativistic in my view of things. Many things could be done this way or that way. There was not always a right approach. Non-attachment to views is a basic principle in Buddhism, and we need to be vigilant that we do not hold on to even Buddhist views rigidly.

Buddhism is not, however, afraid to say that some things are wrong—eating meat, for example, which involves killing. This is not just a matter of preference. It is harmful. Buddhists will speak out about such things. The Buddha refuted ideas he thought of as pernicious on many occasions, and was willing to condemn certain behaviors as wrong. Choosing how to live and what to do is, in many instances, very important. You cannot avoid acting, so how are you to know what action is right? How do you decide on matters of right and wrong and guard against the dangers of simply assuming something is right because it fits with your self-view? Buddhism puts emphasis on right view. Right view is a step on the Eightfold Path. Right view involves keeping Dharma in mind. Right view also means view that is not clouded by self.

Dharma does not come from within. It is that which you encounter in the world when you stop seeing everything as indications of self. This wisdom has been passed down in the Buddhist teachings by generations of people who have also struggled to achieve a cleaner relationship with life. It has been passed down from person to person. It is a collective vision. But, since dharma is reality, the things themselves, it is also the truth that you can test out for yourself and that you must find through encountering the world. Ultimately, you cannot take anyone's word for it, least of all your own. The only way to find it is to look.

Buddhist psychology presents a psychology of encounter. The challenge is to get out of your self-preoccupation and encounter the world, in whatever form it presents itself at any given moment. It is a psychology in which the important principle is to know deeply that which is other.

Getting Beyond the Self-Model

One of the difficulties with creating models is that they start to look substantial. When we start to think of karmic traces and samskaric structures, we begin to think of something akin to the western model of a subconscious. It is not long before we return to an illusion of a substantial self under a different name, grown out of the model itself.

Models are just diagrams. They are maps to help you make sense of complex patterns of things. The map is not the territory. You should not take them as too literal a representation of the actuality, though you may find them very useful. The map you use may depend on your interests and your existing knowledge. A tourist will use a guidebook that marks museums and other places of interest. A geologist uses a map with the different rock types marked on it. The map will also shape what you see. If you use an orienteering map, your attention will be drawn to rocks and trees. If you use a railway map, you will be more aware of the main lines and bus connections. None of these maps tells the whole story. We use them, but we should not imagine that they show everything that is at the location they represent.

Because we live in an age where the idea of the mind as a repository predominates, it is tempting to think of the teaching of the skandhas as better related to the later Buddhist mind models. In fact, the Buddha himself probably thought in terms of the perspective offered by the six-vijnana mind model. It is useful to bear this in mind when you are tempted to create something substantial out of the theory. Thinking of the mind in terms of the six-vijnana model can be liberating, but getting an experiential sense of it challenges our usual manner of perception.

Special Objectivity: Seeing Ourselves as Other

The kind of observational practice offered by meditation is very similar to the process of observation that in western methodology would be associated with phenomenological approaches. The practitioner deliberately lets go of assumptions and explores his direct experience.

Phenomenological enquiry is descriptive rather than a process of evaluative conceptualization. In phenomenological method, the researcher or practitioner herself is included as a subject of observation. It is recognized that the process of observing creates particular circumstances and influences the environment of that which is observed. The observer and the object being observed together create an inseparable system. For this reason, a phenomenological researcher will use reflexive questioning as part of her method. What am I experiencing? How am I reacting?

When this kind of approach is adopted, mental formations, just as much as apparently external phenomena, become the objects of exploration. As this happens, they cease to be viewed as personal possessions. The self-investment in them diminishes and they become merely interesting objects to be studied. Processes of reaction and attachment become phenomena that appear and disappear. They become transient rather than enduring entities. They are no longer experienced as personally owned.

The Buddha taught many practices which involve deliberately challenging identification and moving toward a more objective view of mental process. As a person observes the arising and departing of thoughts in meditation, he feels less personally involved with them. He develops objectivity both about mental process and about the world around him. This is not the kind of distanced attitude that is often associated with the word "objectivity," but rather an attitude of respectful appreciation toward whatever presents itself to the mind. Objects of attention are treated equally and with a respectful attitude, whether they are thoughts, things, people or emotions. This way of approaching experience we may call *special objectivity*. Special objectivity involves shifting the boundary between the categories of subjective and objective phenomena, so that we reclassify many apparently subjective things as non-self. A spontaneously arising feeling, for example, is something that happens to me, but not something I create. It is other, not self. Special objectivity involves letting go of self-attachments and perceiving things with as much clarity as possible. It is about trying to get to the position of seeing dharmas instead of rupas. Buddhist practice aims to help us to perceive everything in this way, free from personal investment.

Some meditation practices involve observing mental process in this way. As the mind becomes relatively quiet, mental processes become easier to observe. We can watch a thought or a reaction and be aware of its arrival and departure. We can notice that we have little control over this process and that these thoughts are indeed not part of our selves. At these points, it is easier to see how the six-vijnana mind model describes mental experience.

At other times, when your mind is cluttered with thoughts, maintaining the objectivity required in order to see phenomena as passing elements becomes harder. It then becomes easier to return to seeing the mind process as a substantial self. At such points, the model of the mind as a container with contents can seem more appealing. The eight-vijnana model seems to correspond more closely with the subjective experience of the busy mind. You become more caught in the processes of self-formation. It is harder to hold on to the simpler six-vijnana model. The mind's quality of alaya-ness becomes stronger, and patterns of habit-energy more enduring.

Approaching the World

The Buddha taught for forty years. His message was that, in attempting to escape the pain of suffering, one creates delusion. This delusion is the delusion of self. It cuts the individual off from direct experience. Spiritual practice provides a means of breaking through the compulsive patterns that make up the self to a direct encounter with the world.

This understanding is rooted in material reality rather than in metaphysics. Buddhism is a spiritual path that reveres what is real. Life is the miracle. The earth is the miracle. Person reaching out to person is the miracle. Once you step beyond individualism, you cease to worry about personal survival or ambition. Metaphysics becomes unnecessary. The Buddha's message has a big vision for the world.

Omnipresent Factors

In the Abhidharma, an early collection of writings on the theories that underlie the Buddha's teachings in the sutras, there occurs a teaching on the common or omnipresent factors, elements that make up the unenlightened state. There is considerable parallel between this and the teaching of the skandhas. It provides a list of stages in the process of the ordinary, conditioned mind. There are a number of versions of the teaching, but all of these roughly fit the same pattern. The Sanskrit list of omnipresent factors has five elements. We have already introduced three of them. These are sparsha (contact), vedana (reaction) and samjna (association or fascination). The two remaining factors relate to how we approach the world. They describe ways in which self-material prevents us from approaching the world in a clean way. These last two factors are *chetana* and *manaskara*. These latter elements can be considered as subdivisions of vijnana. Unlike the list of skandhas, however, the list of common factors has a corresponding list of rare factors. The rare factors are elements into which common factors can be transformed through spiritual training. Because we have these two lists, we can discover more about the meanings of the elements in both lists by making comparison between the common elements and their transformations (see Figures 6.1 and 6.2).

Sparsha

Sparsha is generally translated as "contact," but the term also implies that it is contact with a self-indicator. Sparsha can be transmuted into *smriti*. Smriti is generally translated as "mindfulness." Mindfulness is often taken to mean awareness but can also describe the practice of keeping the Buddha in mind. In this context, what is being described is an experience of perception without grasping. When linked to the senses, smriti involves holding an object in reverent attention. This contrasts with the grasping attention of sparsha. The common factor involves self-investment. The rare factor does not.

Vedana

Vedana, which was discussed in the last chapter, can be transformed into *samadhi*. Vedana is the mentality that grasps or rejects experience. It is the point in the process when you react to experiences, categorizing them according to your personal mentality. Samadhi is a word that is often used to describe deep meditative states. It refers to a state of mind that is open and responsive, but not unsettled. It describes a poised mind, bright and clear, but without reactivity. The mind of samadhi is one that has let go of self-attachments.

Samjna

Samjna, also discussed in the last chapter, is associated with the rare factor, *prajna*, into which it transforms. Samjna is the factor that describes how we fall into old patterns. It is the point at which perception is dulled and one becomes entranced. Prajna, on the other hand, is transcending wisdom. This wisdom comes when the self is no longer clouding perception. It is what one knows is right when he or she lets go of egocentric interests.

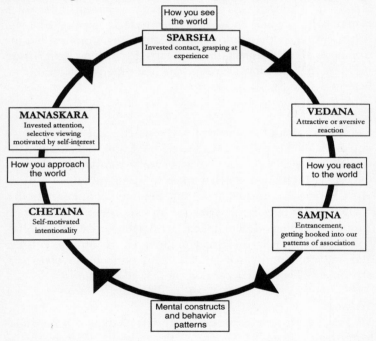

Figure 6.1

The five omnipresent factors, related to the skandha process

The teaching of the omnipresent factors can be represented as a cycle. This representation elaborates the aspect of the cycle involving our approach to the world. The list of omnipresent factors includes vedana and samjna, two of the skandha elements.

Chetana

Chetana is described as the most powerful of the omnipresent factors. It is the driving force in the process of self-creation. The word "chetana" derives from "chitta-na" or perceiving mind-ness. Literally, it means "the mind that goes out looking;" in other words, it is the part of the mentality that seeks out

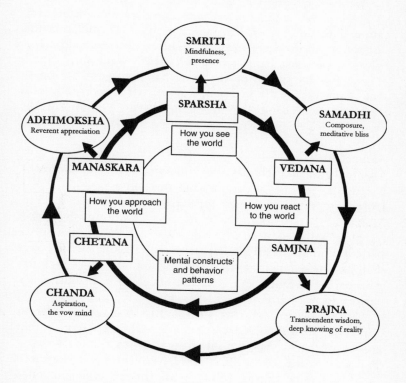

Figure 6.2 *The transformation of the five omnipresent factors*

The omnipresent factors are transformed into rare factors through spiritual practice. Thus each common factor has an enlightened equivalent. The rare factors can also be seen to create a cycle of enlightened perception. Each common factor contains the seeds of its rare counterpart. Indeed, it is the same factor, contaminated by self-material. By loosening the grip of the self-perspective, one moves toward a more enlightened world experience.

objects in order to attach to them. Chetana is volition or intentionality. It is the part that approaches life with the intention of getting what it wants.

The English word "intention" does not entirely represent the grasping quality of chetana. It does not necessarily convey its self-invested nature. It is, in fact, the self-invested nature of all the common factors that makes them problematic.

Chetana can be transformed into *chanda*, which means aspiration: intention transforms into aspiration. Formulating this distinction, the grasping quality of chetana becomes clear. It is driven by personal acquisitiveness. It says "I want this," "I will achieve this." Chanda, on the other hand, suggests aspiration that is not personally invested, aspiration that comes from a connection with something outside ourselves. Aspiration is the expression of one's faith in something other.

Manaskara

The final element in the list of omnipresent factors is *manaskara*. Manaskara means "attention," but this too means more than mere attention; it means attention that is self-seeking. Manaskara is attention that is focused toward an object that has personal interest to a person. We each choose where we place our interest. This kind of attention is seeking out an object that has rupa qualities. It is looking for the thing that has personal significance, so that it can attach to it. In this, it is a narrow form of attention.

Manaskara transforms into adhimoksha, or reverent appreciation. Adhimoksha is a gentler kind of attention that appreciates the world without trying to grasp it. It is respectful and broader in its view. It is not driven, since it is not motivated by habit-patterns. More importantly, it is not impelled by the kind of insecurities and fears that drive the conditioned processes. Manaskara clutches at the world because it is driven by all the pain and anxiety that underlies the whole process of conditioning and self-creation. Adhimoksha means liberation.

The omnipresent factors form a process model that is very similar to that of the skandhas. Sparsha (contact) leads to vedana (reaction). This brings us to the entranced state of samjna. From this state arises the grasping intention of chetana. This directs our attention (manaskara) toward renewed sparsha (contact) with the object world and so on. All the omnipresent factors point toward self, whereas all the rare ones point to liberation.

Expanding the Model of the Skandha Cycle

The theory of the skandhas and that of the omnipresent factors are parallel. The list of omnipresent factors allows us to expand the original skandha model to create a fuller picture of the cycle. By adding chetana and manaskara to the other elements, you can see how the process of approaching the world creates the conditions for objects to be perceived in an invested way.

chetana (intention) leads to manaskara (attention);
manaskara leads to rupa (invested object);
rupa leads to sparsha (sense contact);
sparsha leads to vedana (reaction);
vedana leads to samjna (entrancement);
samjna leads to samskara (habit-patterns);
samskara leads to vijnana (self-interested mentality);
vijnana leads to chetana (intention) . . .
. . . and so on.

The different stages of the process can also be related to the different aspects of mental function. This is probably most easily demonstrated using the eight-vijnana model, because some parts of the cycle are carried out through sensory functions, while others relate to accumulated habit-energy. In fact we see a progression in which mental process creates a cycle. It starts from sense contact, then transfers energy to the alaya through the mediation of manas, and so creates the propensity for seeking out new sense contact. We can represent this diagrammatically (see Figure 6.3).

The senses, or sense doors, are the interface with the world. It is through the senses that experience is mediated. Through the senses you perceive rupa. This is because the senses are

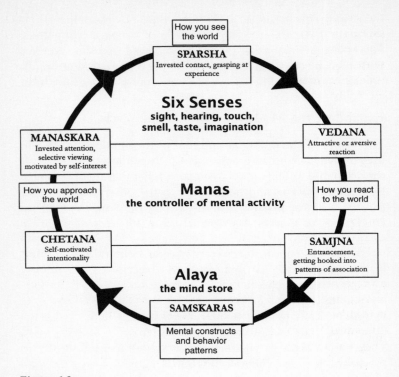

Figure 6.3

The extended skandha process model and eight-vijnana mind map

The extended skandha model can be applied to the mind map. Here sparsha and samskara form opposite poles, which can be described as "internal" and "external." Vedana, samjna, chetana and manaskara sit at the interfaces between the areas of the mind map, mediating the boundaries between the senses, manas and alaya.

conditioned and therefore looking for self-invested objects. If your senses are not conditioned, you see dharmas. The action of the sense attaching to its object, the rupa, creates contact, or sparsha.

When you make contact with something that is rupa for you, your self-patterns are activated. As manas attempts to moderate the experience (as described in Chapter 3), its self-invested aspects are provoked. These accompany the vedana reaction. The vedana reaction can be seen to bridge the area between sense contact and the regulatory processes of the mind. The vedana response is basically a felt response, arising through the mentality's discriminatory process.

Samjna, on the other hand, rests in the space between manas and alaya. It is the process that moves you into an entranced state. It moves you from the conscious control of manas into the automatic process of old habit tracks, the samskaras, which are located in the alaya. Vedana arouses manas, whereas samjna puts it to sleep again.

Chetana rests at the point when these habit-energies propel you into intentioned action, taking place at the interface between alaya and manas, while manaskara occupies the space between manas and the senses. Manas provides its directive aspect, while the senses provide the attention. Manas is thus stirred into brief awareness at two points in the cycle: by vedana before samjna sets in, and by chetana before manaskara takes over. The term manas-kara means that manas has been hijacked by chetana into karma-forming activity. These two interludes are very brief. They represent the points at which awareness of the process is possible; the points at which, in principle, the cycle can be most easily interrupted and transformed.

In this way, the cycle is completed. The six points in the process occur at the two poles of "inner" and "outer" experience, and at the four transitional points between the areas of the senses, manas and the alaya.

Breaking into the Cycle

This model of the skandha process provides a practical system for understanding the process of conditioning. It also provides a useful aid for those who want to work with mental process, since it demonstrates that there are potentially a number of points at which it is possible to make changes.

Unless it is disturbed, the cycle is self-perpetuating; it creates a logic of its own. The mind is conditioned by what it sees, and what it sees is conditioned by its samskaras. Rupa conditions samskara, and samskara conditions rupa. To break free of this cycle, you must not only recognize that it happens, but also do something to change it. The remainder of this chapter deals with specific approaches that a person might use in making such changes.

Working with Rupa

The mind is conditioned by the objects to which it gives attention. Attachment to self-indicating objects is linked to powerful emotions. We have also already seen how an object can be used to carry positive associations, providing comfort and even inspiration. We have seen how being selective about the objects we surround ourselves with can either help to create calmer states or help us to work through difficult feelings. In this section, we will look at other ways in which experience of objects as rupa can be worked with.

Decreasing Rupa Investment

One way to divert rupas from their self-indicating function is to explore the reality of objects you perceive. You can seek a shift from rupa perception to dharma perception. The level of investment a person places in an object varies, so you can work to reduce the amount of delusion in your world-view, in various ways. You may use grounding exercises, which will be described further in Chapter 9, to focus attention on physical contact, for example with the floor. Focusing on practical tasks also brings you into contact with the physical world. The Japanese Morita therapy (Reynolds 1980) puts a lot of emphasis on practical tasks as a way of combating anxiety. In our center in France there is much physical work to be done. Occasionally we have visitors who arrive in some state of crisis. It is striking how often simply digging the garden for a few days can bring about healing that months of conventional therapy might not.

Exploring Rupa

Sometimes it is helpful to explore what the self-investment is that is creating a powerful rupa. In the last chapter, you met Sally. In order to let go of the pattern of entrancement, Sally needed to understand why the course leader had been such a powerful rupa for her. Her therapist suggested that Sally begin by imaginatively recalling the image of the woman. This image was powerful for her.

At that point the therapist helped Sally to explore her associations so that she came to understand how the woman represented the teacher she had feared as a child. That first phase of work involved intensifying the rupa so that the samjna reaction became stronger and the origins of the process clearer. Sally's therapist asked her to imagine the teacher standing in front of her in the room. She asked her to describe the woman in detail. How was she dressed? How tall was she, relative to Sally as a child? What expression did she have on her face? As Sally started to see the teacher towering over her, her face filled with emotion. Sally knew then why she had felt so upset in the adult education class.

Having reached some understanding, a second phase of work began. Sally's therapist encouraged her to hold the image of the teacher in mind. Her intention in doing this was to help Sally to perceive the teacher more realistically. In this way the rupa's power would be reduced. Sally focused on trying to see the teacher through her eyes as an adult. She was encouraged to speculate about the woman's real thoughts, to imagine what her home life had been like, and to think about how it might have been for her to teach at that school and what friends she had among the other staff. She thought about what kind of childhood the teacher might have had herself and how this might have affected her teaching. All this, of course, was speculative. Sally knew very little about the woman. In one sense, the story she told came out of her own experience. Nevertheless, the purpose was to break the hold that a particular image of the teacher had on her and to help her to start to see that the teacher had no doubt been an ordinary woman with ordinary human failings and concerns.

Having done this, Sally was encouraged to think about the tutor on the adult education course in a similar way. She was encouraged to recognize that this woman was not the teacher whom she feared as a child, but an ordinary person whose job was to run the class. She increased her sense of the woman's real qualities by exploring what the reality of this woman's life might be. She could even try imaginatively being this woman. As she did so, the patterns of reaction generated by the past experiences became less powerful. She realized that both teachers had their reasons for being as they were, which were unrelated to her.

Rupa in Ritual

Another potential way of working with rupa investment involves the use of objects as ritual items. This type of work can be very potent. If I wished to create a ritual in memory of my grandmother, I might use her rings in it. This would bring a strong sense of her presence. Ritual is a creative medium with a language of traditional elements that can be combined to generate personal meaning in a dramatic way. As a Buddhist community we are frequently asked to create and participate in rituals. These can be very moving occasions in which shared action creates the possibility for transformation, letting go, and healing.

Working with Vedana

Because it involves a bodily response, vedana can often be easier to spot in someone else than in ourselves. We can help one another to become aware of reactive responses of this kind. This will, in turn, help us with developing our awareness. We saw an example of this in the last chapter, in the account of Sharon's work. People can develop skill in noticing these responses. Sally might also work with vedana and learn to pay attention to that immediate sense of rejection she felt when she met the class leader. By reliving the scene imaginatively, she could learn to recognize and be alerted to the process on future occasions.

The advantage of learning to catch the vedana response is that it occurs before the samjna entrancement, so it can be identified consciously. This kind of observation can be useful in many settings. It can, for example, be an important part of a Buddhist sangha's training practice to spend time reflecting on our own experience of reactivity and giving each other feedback on the reactive behavior we have noticed, provided this is done in a sensitive and respectful way. This helps people develop the skills needed in more sensitive helping situations.

Working with Samjna

Samjna is the point of entrancement, when your mind is hooked by a compelling object. Samjna builds on rupa. Work with rupa and samjna can therefore often go hand in hand. Because the mind is conditioned by the object of its attention, when focusing attention on the rupa you can easily slip into a samjna response. You saw this happening when Sally encountered the class leader. Samjna responses also arise through imagery or role play. In our own work, my husband and I use psychodrama, a technique developed by the western psychologist Jacob Moreno. Psychodrama relies on creating samjna states. In psychodrama, setting the scene and putting auxiliary characters into role are an important part of most pieces of work. These processes are concerned with increasing the power of the objects as rupas so that the person working on the psychodrama becomes more entranced by them. In such a state, it becomes possible to work in a variety of ways to change old patterns of behavior or to test out old beliefs.

Working with Samskaras

Samskaras are mental formations related to habit-energy. These patterns are dynamic action traces. They tend to recur in different situations when conditions are similar. The focus in Buddhist psychology is on the current patterns of behavior, so it is often useful to explore how samskaras manifest themselves in the present. This can be done in many ways. First, you can work to understand the origin of patterns, thus developing more alertness to patterns that may arise in particular situations. This gives you more awareness and choice when the samskaras are activated again.

Other work may involve looking at patterns that are currently being played out in relation to significant people in your life—a partner, a therapist, a teacher, a friend. The enactments may well have their roots in old patterns, often going back to childhood and relationships with parents or other significant others.

The Buddhist understanding of karma emphasizes the possibility of change at the point where an old pattern is triggered. It is important that at this point the person doesn't simply go through the same pattern of behavior but finds a new course of action. For this reason Buddhist approaches place a lot of emphasis on encouraging people to do things differently, rather than placing the primary emphasis on understanding or expressing feelings. Furthermore, importance is placed on current action rather than understanding past experiences per se. Although understanding the past can be important in unravelling the detail of a samskara, it is a means to an end and is not seen as the primary route to change.

Working with Chetana

Chetana is self-centered intentionality. It is intention that is concerned with building identity, and in this is an obstacle to aspiration, which seeks a higher purpose. Chetana is said to be the organizing factor for all the other factors. We humans are driven by our intentions.

Developing aspiration is an important Buddhist practice and plays a key role in the process of change. There will be more on this in later chapters.

Living purposefully leads to mental health. For those people who lack a sense of purpose, life becomes meaningless and self-preoccupied. Many people who are in the midst of affliction have lost any sense of purpose or vision in life. It may be hard to hold on to aspirations when one is displaced, homeless, a refugee, or suffering long-term mental illness. Yet finding aspiration can be the beginning of change. Over the past few years we have been keeping contact with a group of people in Sarajevo. These people, living in the aftermath of the recent Balkans conflicts, bore many privations. In the early years when we visited, material conditions were particularly difficult. They had experienced terrible hardships during the siege of Sarajevo and had witnessed awful sights. We imagined this group might want material aid or psychological support and counselling. In fact they asked if we could run a Buddhist retreat. Their hunger was not for psychological comfort, but for spiritual support. They wanted to rediscover their vision.

Religious faith can be the most important thing left for people in extreme circumstances. In many situations of imprisonment and abuse, it is those with faith who survive best. Contrary to the view put forward by Abraham Maslow (Maslow 1954), the hierarchy of human needs often seems to start with the spiritual rather than the material. The spiritual level provides the foundation for everything else.

Points of crisis can be points of transformation. It is often at such a point that a person discovers a higher purpose in life. When this happens, change really takes place. Buddhism is not alone in emphasizing the need to discover purpose. Programs such as the twelve-step program, used for working with addictions, make similar emphasis on the need to give up self-effort and surrender to a higher authority. It seems that it is the spiritual dimension that gives these programs such a high success rate.

Working with Manaskara

Manaskara describes the way we clutch at things in which we have an interest. Change may involve becoming more aware of what objects our attention is drawn to and which circumstances we seek out. People are often unaware of the ways in which they create situations that will provide the conditions for old patterns to be repeated.

Manaskara transforms into adhimoksha, which implies appreciation or reverence. In order to make this transformation you must develop your capacity to appreciate situations as they arrive rather than wishing they were different. One way that adhimoksha can be cultivated is through life review retreats. In our center in England we run Nei Quan retreats. These events, which are similar to Japanese Naikan methods, use introspective Quan meditation. This enables participants to explore early childhood relationships, working with set questions to discover new perspectives on these early influences. The method particularly encourages participants to develop an appreciative attitude toward those who cared for them. It frequently brings them to a realization that they have received far more from the universe than they can ever repay and that their whole existence is a gift. Such realizations create an overwhelming sense of appreciation and gratitude. This type of work initiates a cathartic transformation in which the self-view is decreased and a new, more open appreciation emerges.

Developing appreciation is really a matter of how you think about things. Lack of appreciation is often a lack of imagination or awareness. If I look out of my window, I see blue sky with small white clouds. How beautiful! How much would it cost to buy so much glorious blueness? And then, it is all full of fresh air for me to breathe. If my breath were metered, how large a bill might I run up through a year? The sun shines in, and solar panels gratefully soak up the heat. Light and warmth, and even hot water, all for free. Rooks fly by into the tall lime tree beside the house. If I had to feed and care for these creatures along with our rabbit and cat, what would that cost? And there are trees, every shape and color you can imagine, decorating the landscape as far as the eye can see. Just imagine going to your garden center and ordering all those. Of course, the trees help replenish the air. Attractive eco-friendly machines that just go on working, day after day. I could go on. How often do you catalogue all the gifts you receive in life? How often do you calculate your debts? Reflect on the situation into which we are all born on this planet and you will begin to think in different ways. Let go of your sense of entitlement, which can lead to resentment. Start to feel gratitude and wonder.

THEORIES EXPLAINED IN THIS CHAPTER

- special objectivity;
- rare and omnipresent factors;
- the expanded skandha cycle model;
- the expanded skandha cycle related to the eight-vijnana mind map; and
- cultivating gratitude.

· 7 ·

The Ant Hill

There is a fascinating sutra in the Majjhima Nikaya called the
Ant Hill Sutra (Vammika Sutta, MN 23). This text is particularly relevant for those of us interested in psychology because
it describes the interpretation of a dream. This dream came to
one of the Buddha's followers, the bhikshu Kassapa. In the
sutra, the dream is interpreted by the Buddha. It reveals a
complex and very illuminating model of the layers of resistance
that must be overcome in order to release our spiritual energy.
This chapter focuses on the sutra.

The Sutra

Kassapa's dream is brought to him by a deva, or deity. In the
dream, Kassapa sees himself standing beside an ant hill. This ant
hill "fumes by night and flames by day." A brahmin appears and
tells Kassapa to delve into the ant hill with a knife, which he
does. Brahmins were of the priestly classes, so in the dream the
brahmin represents a wise man. When Kassapa digs into the ant
hill he finds a whole series of objects. The first object he finds is
a bar. This the brahmin tells him to throw away. Kassapa is then
told once more to delve into the ant hill. This time he finds a
toad and again is told to throw it away. This process is repeated
a number of times. Kassapa goes on to find, in turn, a fork, a

sieve, a tortoise, an axe and block, a piece of meat, and finally a Naga serpent. Each time he is told to throw out the item, and each time he follows this instruction until he reaches the Naga serpent. This he is told to leave unharmed. "Honor the Naga serpent. Do not harm the Naga serpent," says the brahmin.

Delving into the Ant Hill

When Kassapa takes the dream to the Buddha for explanation, the Buddha offers a detailed analysis, interpreting each of the items in the dream in turn. The Buddha tells Kassapa that the ant hill represents his body. It is an impermanent structure, made of rice and porridge, and subject to constant processes of decay. It broods by night, pondering on the day before, and by day it acts on the basis of those thoughts. The knife represents wisdom—a symbol that is often used in Buddhist iconography. Manjushi, the figure who represents wisdom, carries a sword to cut through to the truth, for example. Wisdom cuts through delusion. The process of digging into the ant hill seems to represent cutting into the body. In Buddhist thinking, the body and mental process are perceived as two sides of a coin. This means that delving into the ant hill represents cutting through the layers of the mentality, revealing the person's patterns of behavior and disrupting the layers of habitual processes. This is described as arousing energy. Habits lock up energy. When we disrupt our habits, energy is released.

This image of digging into the ant hill is somewhat reminiscent of introspective enquiry. In doing this, we stir up energy, which often, but not always, takes the form of feelings. Working in psychological ways, one can learn to recognize when energy is being stirred. You can feel the energy in your own body, or see the look of engagement in another person's face when the discussion is meaningful and relevant. This is distinguishable from the dullness that arises when familiar material is being discussed. When a person is simply regurgitating an old story, they may not be emotionally engaged, and the conversation will become flat, an indication that the person is simply revisiting old speech patterns rather than working to make changes. They are simply re-creating old habit tracks.

Emotional expression is not, however, the aim of this type of enquiry. The tool of discovery is sharp, but wisdom does not simply rely upon cathartic expression. It requires clear understanding and mental rigor. Energy and intellect come together. Affect and insight are partners.

Objects in the Ant Hill

The items that are found in the ant hill are each interpreted by the Buddha. First the bar is discovered. The bar means ignorance, or shutting out. There is an allusion here to the bar that was located across the road at the entrance to towns or villages in the Buddha's day to prevent unwelcome arrivals from entering. The bar is a closed gate.

Next comes the toad, representing despair due to anger.

Following the toad comes the fork. The fork represents indecision. (As in English, this could mean a fork as either an implement or a forked path; either image clearly has associations of a split between two possibilities.)

Next comes the sieve. The sieve represents a set of items called the "five hindrances." These are sensual pleasure, sloth and torpor, ill-will, restless worry, and doubt.

Next comes the tortoise, representing the skandhas.

Next come the axe and block. The axe and block represent the five cords of sensual desire, which are basically the attachments of the eye, ear, nose, tongue, and body.

Next comes the piece of meat, representing lust.

Finally, the Naga serpent represents the spiritual energy which emerges when a person has eradicated all the other items that are hindrances to his practice.

Understanding the Sutra

The symbolism of the dream is complex. We will look further at the elements listed above and at their psychological significance. We will also look at the structure of the whole dream. This overall structure offers an understanding of the way in which different levels of resistance are created and describes the process of uncovering them. It describes the stages a person goes through when trying to eradicate the different blocks to personal or spiritual growth that they have built up over the years. We will find that the patterns in these processes offer interesting parallels to other theory in both Buddhist and Western traditions. Thus, the images provide a model for the different levels of conditioning that people create and for understanding how these fit into an overall pattern.

The sequence of items represents a gradual process of shedding layers of avoidance. The first items discovered represent the highest levels of denial and are highly socialized, while the later items represent more basic patterns of escape into more bodily distractions.

The Bar

The first block that is encountered is the bar, representing complete denial. It symbolizes a refusal to look. Just as the barrier across the town gate was intended to keep all comers out, so too this first barrier represents complete resistance. A person who resists looking at his or her patterns of behavior in this way avoids any kind of self-examination. If compelled to explore his behavior or attitudes for some reason, the person is likely to be very resistant to the process. Someone who is stuck at this level is likely to find it very difficult to look at his part in difficulties that may be arising for him. The person is likely either to pretend that everything is all right, even when it patently is not, or to blame others rather than look at his own role in things.

Although for some people the denial represented by the bar seems total, creating a barrier to any personal work, for most there are points at which you hit some similar block when you start to do introspective work. Such blocks may not operate across your whole mentality; you may run into them in discrete areas of the psyche. You may decide that you need to tackle some aspect of your thoughts or your behaviors, yet may hit complete resistance in certain areas of your exploration. You may experience the bar falling across your thoughts—sometimes quite palpably, as you forget what you were going to say mid-sentence. Facing the bar is not easy, as there is no ground on which to stand. There is no room to maneuver and no point of entry.

The Toad

The toad represents despair due to anger. This is an interesting image, as it has two emotions bound up in it. The precipitating emotion is anger. It is a resentful anger. By contemplating the image of the toad, you may begin to understand the kind of anger being represented. Lying camouflaged in the dank grass near to a pond, it is mostly still but can nevertheless spring up if startled. Gnarled and ugly, it likes dark places. This brooding anger prevents a person from looking at their own role in a situation or problem and leads them to blame others. It creates a defensive barrier to communication, which neither allows others in nor allows the person to be really honest about his own position. Toads exude poison. Repressed anger can be poisonous. This is the anger represented by the toad. At the same time, the image of the toad carries upon its back despair. It presents the martyrish stance. It says "What's the point?"—blaming others and at the same time destroying itself.

The attitude of the toad is destructive. Potent emotions such as despair and anger create psychological deadlock. It is a stance that might be labeled passive–aggressive. As anger turns to despair, it falls back upon the person who experiences it, bringing depression and self-destructive feelings. This is the most entrenched level of samudaya attachment. It is a level in which there is little scope for psychological intervention. Someone caught up in this kind of anger may spend much time expressing resentment and despair, but may never recognize that they have become enmeshed in problematic behavioral patterns. Energy is caught up in a fruitless cycle of blaming self and others. But the self-blame and accompanying self-effacement often sound hollow, for they are not based on real insight. Although the person may say things like "It's all my fault" and "I am a terrible person," there is no real remorse, and the statements are a distraction from real responses.

Most of us can recognize when the toad gets loose in us. We can recognize that painful state of feeling alienated and alienating. Despite that pain, however, it is not useful to respond to someone caught in this pattern with bland reassurance. The toad represents a highly defensive state, and the only way to get onto a deeper level of communication is to get beyond it. When you try to help others who are stuck in this pattern, you may try inviting the person to take more responsibility. "Is it really your fault?" you might ask, inviting the person to look deeper and find a more authentic position. "What *did* you do?" you might ask, inviting them to look at their own actions in a concrete way instead of blaming the actions of others.

The Fork

The fork represents indecision. Committing to a course of action is the first step to making progress. If someone does not commit, they will not make progress. This is the case whether the person is intending practical action, spiritual training, or personal enquiry: the process will flounder if time is spent in avoidance and procrastination.

People fail to commit in many ways. They may "go through the motions" of seeking change. They may waste time talking about things that, although possibly interesting, do not get to the heart of the matter. They may fritter time away on unimportant details to avoid looking more deeply at their behavior. They may repeat a story they have told many times before. They may skate around the subject rather than addressing it. At other times, someone may avoid facing their own patterns of thought and behavior by looking to many different people for support. They may enter into a number of relationships with different therapists, teachers or helping professionals, either simultaneously or by flitting from one to another. By this means they may avoid getting depth in any one relationship and avoid the personal issues they need to face.

This defense level can also describe the situation where a person seems stuck in a life dilemma that never seems to resolve. Stuckness in life can be mirrored by stuckness in helping relationships. For instance, Tony seeks help because he does not know whether he wants to leave his partner or not. He tells the therapist who is working with him all the things that are wrong with the relationship and all the advantages there would be in leaving. The next week he comes back and goes over the same list. The following week he comes back and says he thinks things are getting better. The next week he is sure the relationship has to end. Each week he rehearses a list of good reasons for leaving or staying. Often he is emotional, and sometimes he seems desperate, but nothing actually changes. He never actually leaves. Nor does he fully commit to staying.

A situation like this can go on for years. In some ways the therapist is supporting it. Venting his irritations, Tony is able to keep just below the level of discomfort that would force him to do something. He stays within an uncomfortable but endurable margin. Why does it persist? There is perhaps a clue if you look at the overall analysis offered by the second Noble Truth. The pattern of delaying a decision in this way is basically a destructive pattern. Its purpose is distraction. It is escape into a kind of misery—but it is also a way of avoiding another kind of pain. Holding oneself in a life dilemma of this magnitude creates a powerful distraction from the existential fears of death and impermanence. Ironically, too, it mirrors impermanence in a small way, with its uncertainties and its constant experimentation with coming and going in the relationship. It is almost as if Tony is trying to reassure himself that the end is not the end. This process starts to look a bit like an inoculation. In creating uncertainty ourselves we seem to bring impermanence under our control. Sadly, however, this is illusory, and the pain that drives the cycle simply creates more misery for all involved.

So the kind of indecision described here differs from the kind of productive struggle that is part of a spiritual search. Rather than moving toward breakthrough, this kind of indecision is a delaying tactic. It prevents people from having to commit themselves to a course of action and thus risking being wrong and losing face. It creates a smokescreen that stops them from having to look at their real situation, and an illusion that they are working on the situation, but no real movement. Ultimately it is an attempt to deny one's own mortality.

The Sieve

The sieve represents a collection of items—the five hindrances. As the image of the sieve suggests, these are elements that exert a drag on our process. A sieve placed in running water slows down the stream. It does not stop the water flow, but it collects any object that is in the water. The sieve accumulates debris, which hinders the flow of the water.

The five hindrances are things that impede your progress. These are sensual pleasure, sloth and torpor, ill-will, worry and doubt. These elements create drag on your spiritual path and on your willingness to tackle your habit-energies. You are pulled up by your sensual desires: pleasant sights, smells and other attractions are constantly distracting you. Your senses are easily captivated and constantly hook on to objects unless you guard your sense doors. Attachments accumulate. People also accumulate baggage in the form of resentments, through ill-will, cluttering their minds with irritations. They become lazy and slow, stagnating in their practice.

The last two hindrances, worry (or restless guilt) and doubt, are both qualities that can sometimes be helpful to the spiritual path. In each case, however, you should recognize that, when these qualities are listed among the hindrances, it is that aspect of the quality that accumulates negativity and slows progress that is being referred to. It is not the aspect that might stimulate a person into positive transformation. Worry or guilt in this context means the kind of restless guilt that creates a circling mind, ruminating through endless repetitions of self-criticism and regret so that it achieves nothing. It is the kind of feeling that someone experiences who is constantly feeling needlessly guilty. It involves compulsive worrying and wishing things had been different.

Similarly, doubt here is not the avoidance through doubt that the fork represents but rather a deeper level of self-questioning and preoccupation with negativity. It is unproductive. It is the kind of doubt that might be popularly called angst. This level of resistance is associated with a mind that is accumulating unhelpful debris. The hindrances create attachments—compulsive behaviors associated with clinging. Circular thought processes predominate and stop the person from seeing life issues with clarity. Mental activity and even physical objects accumulate. The person becomes identified with these and becomes self-preoccupied.

At this level the Three Poisons (see Chapter 2), lobha, dvesha and moha, operate to create attachments that hinder spiritual growth. Lobha (greed) attachments operate in the clinging to sensual pleasure and often in giving way to sloth and torpor. Dvesha (hate) attachments predominate in attachment to ill-will and often in doubt. Moha (confusion) attachments predominate in someone caught in restless worry and guilt. Overall, though, all the hindrances have all three qualities, as they all involve a degree of clinging.

The Tortoise

The image of the tortoise represents the skandhas. (See Chapters 5 and 6). This delightful image seems particularly fitting for the process that is so much associated with creating the self. A tortoise has a hard armored shell into which it can retreat. What a wonderful image for the skandha process and the self-prison! The tortoise is also, of course, associated with slowness. The skandhas slow us down. Burdened by them, we become slow, lumbering creatures carrying our heavy loads of self-protection. We do not easily change direction in life but plod on round our habitual patterns of behavior.

Kevin has spent many years going to personal growth groups. He enjoys the warm contact that he feels encountering other group members. When he first started to go to groups, he felt quite shut off and out of touch with his emotions, but now he feels much more alive. Kevin sees himself as open and well adjusted, able to speak authentically about his experience and to make a stand about what he believes to be right. He leads assertiveness sessions for men and feels he has learned a lot about how to project his own ideas through this kind of training. Kevin is basically happy with life and sees himself as having reached a good level of personal awareness. He does not feel he has any real problem.

This is probably true in the terms that Kevin has defined for himself; yet in a way, Kevin has reached a ceiling. He has put a lot of energy into self-development and has let go of a lot of his earlier difficulties and hang-ups as a result. But, although Kevin sees himself as a risk-taker, he is actually keeping himself within a rather limited orbit. There is still considerable rigidity in his stance, which leaves him wedded to particular opinions about ways of interacting and lifestyle. This is seen by others who know him, but is not obvious to Kevin himself because his self-image is grounded in an identity as a self-aware, liberated man.

To go farther, Kevin would need to start to venture into new areas of his psyche and let go of some of the hard-won sense of identity. This search would involve facing some of the more instinctive drives and realizing the extent of sensory indulgence in his life. The skandhas create a shell around us, which protects us from threatening encounters with pain and impermanence, but they can also protect us from knowing our own darker aspects. We do not see the layers of conditioning that lie beneath the level of identity.

The Axe and Block

The image of the axe and block represents sense attachments or sensual pleasures. In this two-part image of axe and block we can discern the sense moving toward its object. It is a powerful symbol. The axe is heavy and cuts on to the block with impact. The sense attaches to its object with great force. The eye locks on to a sexually attractive person, inviting you to approach them. The sense of smell draws you to food, inviting you to indulge in gluttonous eating. The ears prick up as you hear someone gossiping across the room. You must be led by your senses into further layers of distraction and escapism. Too easily, drives are activated by the sensory world, and one is pulled toward craving and an unending search for satisfaction.

The commentary on this sutra suggests that the axe and block come from the slaughterhouse, alluding to the cutting up of a carcass, and, by extension, to the cutting up of the person by their attachment to sense cravings. People are at the mercy of their senses and can create havoc for themselves in pursuing them.

Earlier we looked at the practice of guarding the sense doors. Guarding your senses prevents you from being swept into sense attachments and thus prevents your falling into the creation of skandhas.

The Piece of Meat

The final image in the dream is of the piece of meat. This, the Buddha says, represents lust. It represents the raw energy that drives the sense attachments. Cravings for sensual pleasure lead us into sexual and other desires.

The image of meat is commonly used in association with raw sexual impulses. This association goes right through human societies and can be found in modern colloquial speech. References to some discotheques or clubs as "cattle markets" or "meat markets" implies that these are places where sexual partners may be easily found. There is an implication that women attending them will be open to thinly disguised, or even overt, sexual advances. Conversely, men may be referred to as "beefy" or "a hunk" by groups of women voicing sexually predatory and sometimes retaliatory sentiments. Such common phrases reflect the aspect of sexuality that is concerned with appetite and satisfaction. They are voracious, paralleling the other appetites for food and pleasure. In these expressions you can sense the primitive links between hunger and sexual drives. These drives in their unharnessed form make no allowance for the object of their desire. They see the other solely in terms of the agenda of the person making the advances, without appreciating that the other person involved has a personality, feelings, and responses.

Lust is a drive, purely directed toward satiating sexual appetite. It takes no consideration of the person who is the object of its attention. It recognizes only the body of the other, not the personality. The other becomes the focus of fantasies, and maybe of debauched indulgence. There is no relationship, only gratification. At this extreme, the energies of lust are indeed powerful.

Buddhist training has often put great emphasis on subduing the senses and the lustful emotions. The use of the image of the piece of meat is reminiscent of some of the meditations on the loathsomeness of the body which monks were encouraged to practice. Images of dismembered and decomposing corpses were intended to counter lustful feelings, to evoke disgust and to illustrate the impermanence of such attractions as a woman's body. The fact that such great emphasis was placed on these practices—even if they were sometimes misogynistic—points to the importance with which the subject was viewed. Great dangers were perceived in giving rein to this level of escape.

A Dangerous Place

The deeper levels of the ant hill model take us into the area of the more primitive, instinctive drives. These are the areas of human activity that are often hidden. People frequently find it difficult to face these aspects of themselves. These are the raw passions.

There is more energy in the deeper defense levels than in the higher ones. If they get out of hand, these passions have the power to drive a person into dark and dangerous states; so mastering and containing them becomes an important part of spiritual training and is important to our living fully. The deeper layers of psychic energy, generally locked away by the processes of socialization, are closer to the heart of the spiritual path, represented by the Naga serpent.

At this level, the potential is greater—both for spiritual progress and for disaster. There is a sense in which the spiritual path becomes more treacherous, the further you venture down it. Practitioners are at greatest risk of falling over the edge into disgrace or indulgence as they reach the most intensive levels of practice. This is why a strong ethical container for spiritual practice is so important. It becomes the crucible in which passions can be transformed and keeps both the practitioner and those around them from the dangers of falling prey to temptations.

Understanding that raw passion and spiritual depth are closely linked, you can see how transformation and great spiritual progress can sometimes be easier for the seemingly most unlikely people. There are many stories, both in the Buddhist texts and in those of other traditions, of mass murderers, prostitutes, sinners, and gluttons, who suddenly found religion in a deep and passionate way. Such people have often lived life on the edge and never acquired the levels of socialization and self-structures that prevent most people taking risks. They have little to lose and may be willing to throw themselves heart and soul into a new path because their hearts are not tied up with attachments. They have not buried the primitive spiritual energy so deeply.

The Ant Hill Sutra as a Representation of the Levels of Samudaya

As the account in the sutra describes the sequence of items discovered in the ant hill, it becomes apparent that there is a process of peeling away layers of defense, culminating in the discovery of the Naga serpent at the base of the mound. This serpent represents the person's spiritual energy. We have seen how the images that are presented represent diminishing degrees of defensiveness. The description starts with the highly defensive layers of the bar, toad, and fork, and progresses to the more primitive levels of the axe and block and the piece of meat. These representations also show how spiritual potential is more closely linked to the lower levels of the conditioned mind. There is less defensiveness in these lower levels than in the higher levels. The higher levels, though they appear more socially acceptable, are also more rigidly defensive just because they are highly socialized.

Now look at the way that this model can be related to other aspects of Buddhist psychology theory presented in this book. In particular, parallels exist between the material presented in this sutra and the teaching on samudaya, with its elucidation of the three levels of escape. The teaching on samudaya suggests that the first level of escape or avoidance which people adopt in response to dukkha is that of sensory indulgence. Comparing this with the layers of defensive structure suggested by the Ant Hill Sutra, one can speculate that this level corresponds to the last two layers of defense, the axe and block and the piece of meat. In other words, the

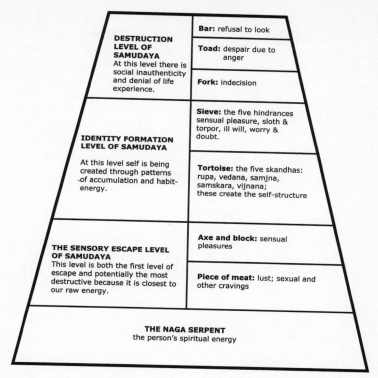

Figure 7.1   The Ant Hill Sutra

This sutra describes a dream analysis. The images in the dream provide an important analysis of the levels of avoidance in which a person may engage.

deepest layer of defense is at the level of sensory escape.

The second level of escape in the samudaya teaching is that of identity formation, or the creation of the self. The middle levels in this model of defense structures are the tortoise, representing the skandhas, and the sieve, representing the five hindrances. Both these images describe the defenses and habit-energies that feed the process of self re-creation. The skandhas are the stages of the process by which self is fabricated from the accumulation of self-indicators, and the five hindrances are the processes of attachment and accumulation that feed this process.

The third level of escape described in the teaching on samudaya is the stage of non-being. This level is the most desperate level. In the Ant Hill Sutra, the highest layers of defense are represented by the fork, which represents procrastination and uncertainty; the toad, which represents despair arising from anger; and the bar, which represents refusal to look at anything. All of these images represent an avoidance of any kind of encounter with the life situation and a deadening of response. These defenses are at the level of socialization in which the person gives up spiritual energy and becomes locked into life-denying behavior. Spirit is submerged.

A Comparison with Freud

The model suggested by the Ant Hill Sutra offers an interesting theoretical parallel with the Western ideas propounded by Sigmund Freud. The images that occur in the dream suggest a stripping away of levels of socialization, taking us from the complex dilemmas of intellect and relationship to the more basic drives of sexuality and greed. In these patterns, we can see similarities to Freud's model with its categories of superego, ego, and id.

Sexual and sensory cravings form the earliest and therefore most deeply entrenched defense levels in the Freudian model. When you think of the small child's encounters with the world, the first experiences are of sensual cravings. The baby seeks comfort in being fed or held. Thus the first patterns of escape are likely to be those of sensory indulgence. Only later does the child start to create identity. These ideas mirror the western understanding of child development. The two approaches differ, however, in the conclusions drawn from them. Freud's view was that id instincts required socialization, and that the development of the ego represented the process whereby this was achieved. A Buddhist model suggests that ego formation is a defense and that direct transformation of such energies provides the route to real spiritual progress.

The Buddhist model sees the passions and drives as something to be contained or harnessed—but harnessed to the process

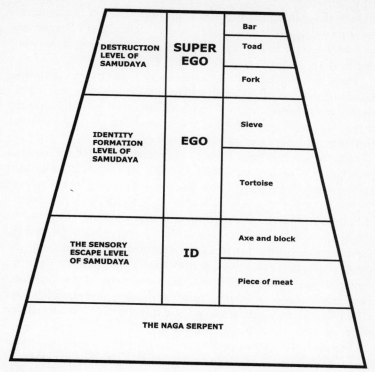

Figure 7.2

The Ant Hill Sutra related to Freudian concepts of id, ego and super-ego.

of enlightenment, not to social conformity. They provide the energy for spiritual practice. You see this particularly in tantric approaches, but you can also see it presented theoretically in writings such as the Ant Hill Sutra. Freud saw libidinal energy as a driving force in life, also acknowledging the place of this energy in human development. Buddhism draws on this raw energy to fire the spiritual journey. It suggests the direct transformation of this energy into the spiritual path. The process may have similarities to what Freud alluded to as sublimation, although his theories on that aspect of the psyche were never fully developed. You could say that the Buddhist model presents a theory in which it is the id and not the ego that is developed into the higher adult state. In this light, David Brazier has hypothesized that Buddhism may lead us to seek a super-id rather than a super-ego (Brazier 1999).

There are similarities and differences between Freudian and Buddhist psychological models. How do we explain the differences? If Buddhists eschew the path of socialization, what do they advocate? Are Buddhists trying to do something different through their practice?

One explanation may lie in the different nature of the settings in which Freud and other Western psychologists operate and the settings in which most Buddhist training takes place. Working with the deeper levels of the defense structure, those that lie beyond the self, requires a strong container. Without it, the path can be perilous. According to the Buddhist model, containment comes not from the creation of ego but from the path of practice and ethics. It also comes for many from living and practicing in community with others and from working with a teacher or spiritual guide who can provide advice and containment through their own experience of having made progress with these matters.

The aim of Buddhist practice is the transcending of self rather than its creation. To nurture and release the energies represented by the Naga serpent means harnessing forces in our lives that can create great trouble for us. Buddhist practice requires a strong basis in precepts and an ethical framework. At this level, Buddhist training generally takes place in situations such as spiritual communities, where containment is provided by the ordered lifestyle, observance of precepts, and commitment to the spiritual teacher. In such a setting, the lifestyle is often structured, with ascribed roles and a disciplined sequence of practice and other activities. This structuring provides an external framework for the practitioner, diminishing the need for personal internalized socialization of the kind suggested by the upper levels of the Ant Hill model.

For those living in a disciplined community, because the social ordering that usually takes place through repressive processes is achieved through external frameworks and roles, and because there is a commitment to awareness rather than avoidance, there is the potential to live with less psychological repression. This produces an environment in which a greater level of personal transformation can occur. Commitment to a spiritual training situation of this kind is generally much stronger than the commitment a patient or client might have to a psychotherapist. It often involves open-ended lifetime commitment as well as shared living arrangements. This is important, because the giving up of personal defensive or repressive structures involves working with higher levels of spiritual energy, which can create vulnerability and the potential for a person to "go off the rails" if their practice is not contained. Working with greater levels of spiritual energy is both potentially enlightening and potentially more hazardous.

For these reasons, it may not be a bad thing that most psychotherapy takes place around the level of the skandha process—even though Western models would not use this terminology—working with self-structures, loosening the hold of self, and creating positive rather than negative patterns in the conditioned mind. But we should not forget that in this model there are further levels of defense beyond the self, which may be emerging in our work and which ultimately have the greater power to bring transformation.

A Paradox

Although the deeper levels of the psyche are associated with the levels of sensory escape suggested in the samudaya model, this does not always mean that when you encounter sensory distractions you are dealing with deep material. Nor does it mean that you are working at a level where self-structures do not operate. This would clearly be a nonsense in the light of most people's experiences. Most sensory distraction is not at the level of deep trauma and instead suggests a less serious attempt to avoid difficult feelings in the present. Switching on the television or opening a beer is often simply the reaction to a hard day at work.

Although the Ant Hill model suggests that the deepest levels of defense consist of these raw impulses, there are clearly samudaya responses arising all the time. This is a paradox in the model. The levels of samudaya are constantly recurring, and sensory distraction is always the first line of escape. So, because you are constantly encountering new forms of dukkha, you are also constantly generating new patterns of avoidance. The deepest layers of the psyche are sensory. Delving into them, you reach back into the earliest layers of your conditioning, and thus the most entrenched response patterns, much like the archaeologist who finds the earliest material in the deepest levels of the dig. As new difficulties arise, however, your first line of escape is also likely to take the form of sensory distractions. So both the deepest and most superficial levels of escape may be concerned with sensory impulses.

Similarly, you certainly cannot dismiss self-destructive impulses as superficial on the grounds that they relate to the later levels of the psyche. They have, in fact, been created when the levels of identity formation have failed to provide enough distraction. So, besides representing the greatest level of repression, they also represent the greatest levels of desperation. These are the layers in which the person's responses to the world are deadened and flat. A person who is highly defended has fewest resources to deal with an unusual crisis if it occurs.

The Naga Serpent

At the bottom of the ant hill we discover the Naga serpent. The image of the serpent is commonly used to represent energy and healing. The Naga represents the spiritual energy of the person, cleansed of the last remnants of attachment, wholesome and healing. You can trust and nurture this serpent. The many levels of resistance, which block encounter with the world, imprison energy. Releasing that energy, you heal society.

The Buddha uses the image of the snake to represent the Dharma on other occasions, as we will discuss in Chapter 15. In the Simile of the Snake Sutra (Alagaddupama Sutta, MN 22), the Buddha talks of how one needs to take great care in catching a snake. Taking a forked stick, one catches the animal behind the head. The venom, which is a powerful healing medicine, can then be safely extracted. If the snake is caught carelessly, it will turn and bite. So too, the methods and teachings of the Ant Hill Sutra need to be properly understood and applied within a strong container of ethical behavior.

THEORIES INTRODUCED IN THIS CHAPTER

- the Ant Hill Sutra as an exposition of the layers of avoidance;
- the Ant Hill Sutra as an exposition of the samudaya process; and
- comparisons with Freudian theory.

· 8 ·

Beyond Self

Buddhist psychology offers models of the processes and structures of the mind. It shows how flight from the existential inevitability of loss, pain, and death leads to delusion, which is a subtle and pervasive refusal to face reality. Instead, we attempt to find and hold on to something that is concrete and substantial. This common mentality is one of grasping, which leads to attachment and creates an accumulation of habit-energies, preferences, and behavior patterns that support the illusion of an enduring self that can escape impermanence. Buddhist psychology sees this self as a defensive structure that lacks foundation yet dominates the ordinary mind.

The Three Signs of Being

A teaching that describes the unfounded nature of self is the teaching on the Three Signs of Being. This provides a succinct three-line summary of the teaching of non-self. It is formulated as follows:

> *sarva samskara anitya*
> *sarva samskara dukkha*
> *sarva dharma anatma*

This translates as:

all samskaras are impermanent,
all samskaras are affliction,
all dharmas are non-self.

In this translation I have left the words "samskara" and "dharma" in Sanskrit to emphasize an important distinction. Sometimes these statements are translated using the words "compounded things" for "samskara" and "things" for "dharma," but this translation does not give sufficient weight to the important distinction that is being made. As a result, the teaching has often been misunderstood to mean that all things are impermanent, affliction, and non-self. Making a clear distinction between the first two statements and the last, by using the words "samskara" and "dharma" in Sanskrit, the intended contrast becomes clear. The first two statements refer to samskaras and the last to dharmas. Leaving the words untranslated, as technical terms, makes this distinction apparent.

By failing to attribute specific enough meaning to the Sanskrit word, the use in traditional interpretations of the teaching of the term "compounded things" as a rendering of "samskara" has contributed to an understanding of Buddhism that may be overly negative. The Buddha's message is not life-denying. It is life-embracing.

The teaching of the Three Signs of Being does not say that everything is suffering and everything is impermanent. It says that it is our habit-patterns or self-structures that are impermanent and troublesome. It also says that the real things are non-self. The self is a delusion formed out of the samskaras. There is a real world beyond the self that can be reached if we stop proliferating self-structures or samskaras.

Comparing East with West

The Buddhist understanding that the self is unreliable, constructed, and basically defensive produces an approach to psychology that is founded in a very different paradigm from most western approaches. We can call this the paradigm of non-self.

The non-self paradigm has implications that deviate substantively from much popular western thought. To adopt a Buddhist perspective, and not fall back into a basically Western model of thinking, you need to understand and face these differences. On the other hand, you should be wary of abandoning everything Western psychology has to offer that is framed in terms of self. Not everything described as self-enhancing in Western models is at odds with Buddhist thinking. To suggest that this was so would be to lose a wealth of good practice.

Because the self has acquired a good image in the West, many ideas and practices that are useful and positive are theoretically defined here as being concerned with building the self or supporting identity formation. Something that is described in this way does not, however, necessarily function as a means of creating the self-formations that are described in the Buddhist models we have been exploring. Many qualities, such as courage, character strength, determination, confidence, and enquiring energy, which in a Western context might be associated with having a strong sense of self, are encouraged in Buddhist training. Here, though, they are not seen as building self-esteem, but as providing the capacity to do without it.

The teaching of non-self does not point the way to the martyrish self-sacrificing position. In the Buddhist paradigm, such behavior builds a negative identity and negative world-view. In this way it is just as much the product of habit-energy and attachment as the path of selfish indulgence. The Buddhist approach is neither to build nor to abase the self. It is to recognize the reality of our existential position in relationship with the world. It recognizes one's dependency upon conditions, and especially upon the physical environment. Who you are depends upon the context in which you live. Humans are dependently originated, and conditioned by events and circumstances. With events and circumstances, people change. The teaching of non-self is not a denial of the existence of the person as a complex entity, functioning in a complex world. Non-self theory places people in dynamic encounter with one another and with the environment they inhabit. It acknowledges the ever-unfolding social process and the ways in which people provide conditions for one another.

The Buddha did not see the theory of non-self as an abstract theory of the non-existence of the person. Rather, he offered a practical understanding of the ways in which people build false views of the world by imposing their own agendas on it. This becomes evident in the Samyutta Nikaya, where the Buddha has the following conversation with Vacchagotta:

> *Vacchagotta: Now, Master Gotama, is there a self?*
> *The Buddha remains silent.*
> *Vacchagotta: Well then, Master Gotama, is there not a self?*
> *Again the Buddha remains silent.*
> *Vacchagotta goes away.*
> *Ananda: How is it, Lord, that you gave Vacchagotta no answer?*
> *The Buddha: If I had told him there is a self, he would have taken it that I side with the eternalists. If I had told him that there is no self, he would have taken it that I side with the annihilationists. The reality is simply that all samskaras are impermanent, but whatever I had said to Vacchagotta, it would simply have increased his confusion.*

The teaching of non-self feels uncomfortable for many Western people at first. Western society is firmly attached to ideals of individuality and personal freedom. Ideas on non-self seem to threaten the basis on which these ideals are founded and to cut the ground from under us. In fact, however, they offer liberation of a much more profound kind.

A Conflicted World: Modern Attitudes about Self

The modern attitude about self is actually very recent. It has grown in the popular culture only since the middle of the twentieth century, though its roots go back a couple of hundred years. During this time, society has moved toward a more individualistic value system. We have seen the growth of assertiveness training and personal growth courses. Family structures have become more fragmented. There have been greater emphases on career opportunities for all and everyone's right to self-fulfillment. These developments are not necessarily bad in themselves, but they are often accompanied by an emphasis on self-interest rather than collective values.

Many factors, including the increasing role of multinational corporations in political decision-making, the increasing influence of the mass media, and a secularization of Western society, have pushed much of the world toward a philosophy of increased individual consumption and consumerism. Image formation has become big business. Designer labels, the glorification of celebrity and the high profile given to "lifestyle" features provide "selves" we can aspire to. Such self-making is an exercise in illusion. Our clothes, our houses, our cars, our leisure activities, even our children are all designed to enhance the personality we would like to be (though paradoxically they often create an image that is replicated by many: a phenomenon satirized in the film *The Life of Brian*, where people stand in regimental rows, chanting in unison "We are all individuals"). We have become a society quick to stand upon our rights and to insist on the services that we feel that we deserve. Being "taken for a ride" is a shameful experience. We are taught to be suspicious of people, whether strangers in the park or storm window salesmen. We are encouraged to fortify ourselves in every way against others. "Look after number one" is the message.

The echoes of previous times, however, have not long died out. Many of us grew up in the shadow of other value systems, which, even if they had been largely abandoned, still crept into our attitudes and created the conditions for inappropriate feelings of guilt and anxiety to arise. Women were expected to be caregivers and to stay at home, creating a smooth-running environment for husband, children, and often elderly relatives as well. Combining the old demands of homemaking with the new ones of career and glamour has created pressures for many women as well as men. These conflicting requirements have led many of us to feel caught between guilt at what we are not achieving and anger that we feel expected to manage so much.

In addition, many people have seen great hypocrisy in a society that advocated self-sacrifice for some while perpetuating many social inequalities and injustices. Those people who were most vocal in advocating high standards of morality and other virtues

140

for others were often seen to be condoning and hiding their own immoral or exploitative behavior. Not surprisingly, people rejected the values they saw associated with such double standards. We are not yet far enough removed from Victorian values of self-sacrifice and duty to be objective about the issue of self.

Contrition

Being haunted by feelings of guilt is a common problem in modern times. Feelings of negative self-preoccupation hang around, filling one with regret and self-reproach. You cannot let them go. You lie awake at night wishing you had done things differently. You feel overcome with embarrassment when you meet people who have witnessed your mistakes. You avoid seeing people whom you have wronged. You tell others how bad you are and what awful things you have done, or else you remain silent and hope others will not notice the consequences of your actions.

Such preoccupation with personal guilt is part of the process of self-creation. Uncomfortable as it is, it is basically a defensive pattern of behavior. Often it defends the self. When you are preoccupied with guilt, it is often because you feel your identity is under attack. It may be that you feel you have let yourself down by your behavior. It may be that "getting it wrong" was not part of your self-image. It may be you thought you were "better than that." Guilt and pride are often two sides of a coin. If pride comes before a fall, feelings of guilt may follow it.

Guilty feelings are often feelings that can neither be put down nor followed through. The person feels trapped in compulsive ruminations, often reliving incidents or rehearsing explanations to imaginary others. A process carries on in which rough edges of unwise actions are sandpapered with a proliferation of mental maneuvers, in an attempt to make them fit into the person's self-image. Alternatively, the incident is added to the evidence that supports a negative self-image, often carrying with it a sense of "I told you so." In either case, this sort of guilty feeling involves holding on to the experience of having "got it wrong," rather than letting it go. The guilt can even be free-floating. It can be a loose sense of having gotten something wrong, with no clear focus about what. Such diffuse guilt can arise from a general, but often rather peripheral, sense that there are discrepancies between reality and the self-image.

In contrast to this sort of self-orientated guilt, other feelings of regret may be grounded in a real desire to move on. The latter sort of feeling is often referred to as "remorse" to distinguish it from the chronic guilt that does not necessarily lead to change. When regret takes the form of remorse, a person looks toward action. Preoccupation with maintaining and restoring the self-image drops away, and the person becomes willing to look at their part in events. An important aspect of this can involve expressing contrition.

Expressing contrition can bring release. You cannot move on into new areas of your life until you have let go of the past, and it is often those parts of the past you feel you got wrong that cause the greatest hindrance to you. Clung onto, they create chronic guilt. Let go in an expression of contrition, and they create the possibility for growth and change. If you do not allow yourself to feel contrition, you become caught in restless guilt, one of the five hindrances referred to in Chapter 7.

Acts of contrition provide a route to freedom. Some Buddhist ceremonies begin with formal acts of contrition. These ceremonies emphasize the role of contrition in creating a new start. They are the antecedent to acts of commitment.

While a person ruminates on things he has done that he regrets or feels to have been wrong, he feels guilt. Unwise actions haunt us. In the Buddhist world-view, there is no external source of judgement. This is not a religion with an omnipotent God figure who sits over us. Actions are understood in terms of their complex grounding in conditions, rather than as examples of good or evil. Nevertheless, you suffer from the things that you have done wrong because the karma of those actions stays with you. The seeds that an action sows in the world and in your mentality grow and proliferate, unless you are able to break the cycle of self re-creation. We are all prisoners of our past actions. We are prisoners of the samskaras that we have created through those actions. These samskaras impact on our mentality at all levels.

An act of contrition acknowledges mistakes and ill-judged

actions and lets them go. In the formal ceremony of contrition, Buddhists start by bowing. This is a physical expression of the willingness to let go of self. After all, it is self-creation that has led us to remain attached to our mistakes. We then make formal confession of our wrong-doing and resolve to begin anew. What is important is that the act of contrition involves really letting go. The difference between the state of nagging guilt and true contrition is that in the first instance we really still wish to be vindicated, whereas contrition involves acknowledgement that we have done wrong and moving on.

Guilt is a self-invested state, based on feeling "Why did I do that?" The element of self is prominent. When you feel you have let yourself down through your actions, your regret is as much for the loss of face as for the consequences of the action itself. This kind of regret contains strong elements of pride. You regret having let yourself down. The act of contrition, by contrast, is quieter and more final. The person feeling contrition feels regret for the consequences of the action, acknowledges his or her part in it, and is willing to change.

Honestly acknowledging your responsibility for events takes you beyond self in a deep way. In recognizing how you make mistakes again and again, you come to abandon self in deeper ways. As you express contrition, you also recognize the futility of relying on your own capacity to always get it right, and you see that you are dependent on circumstances and powers greater than yourself. In terms of Buddhist theory, you stop relying on *self-power* and start to rely more on *other-power*. Contrition therefore involves an acceptance of the fact that you are intrinsically foolish and vulnerable in many ways.

You let go of guilt from the past by expressing feelings of contrition. It is important to realize this, not only for yourself but also in your responses to others, who may be struggling with their own feelings of guilt. It is often tempting to comfort and reassure someone who is expressing feelings of guilt. You feel embarrassed by their honesty and want to help them to feel better, so you might respond by saying things like "Oh, I'm sure it wasn't that bad," or "I'm sure you didn't mean it that way." These diminish the person's sense of the gravity of the action over which he or she feels guilt, but they may not help the person to resolve and move on from the feelings of guilt. In such situations it may be much more helpful to allow the person to express feelings of contrition openly and to talk about the regret he or she feels. Recognizing guilt in a clean way that does not pander to pride is the better way to express contrition.

If you have hurt others, there may be an opportunity to make amends in some way. It might be through verbal apology or through an act of kindness. Often, though, this is not appropriate or possible. Big gestures to those you have wronged can carry connotations of self-importance and may be the last thing that person wants. Sometimes, though, a simple apology can heal years of hurt.

Where direct reparation is not appropriate, an act of kindness to others, who represent that person symbolically, could be considered. Acts of contrition of this kind are sometimes undertaken even in circumstances where, to the worldly eye, no wrong has been committed. The Chinese Zen master Xu-Yun, for example, undertook an arduous three-year pilgrimage to atone, among other things, for his mother's death in childbirth while bearing him. This pilgrimage was both an expression of his remorse and an act of gratitude to her (Xu-Yun, 1988). It was also an important landmark in Xu-Yun's spiritual life.

There are obvious practical constraints, of course, in making reparation to those who have been hurt. At the extreme, it may be inappropriate for someone who has committed a serious crime to have any contact with the victim of that crime. Similarly, there may be reasons why it is not wise to allow someone to make recompense to a group who have been the subject of previous hurt. For example, in the case of a person who has committed child abuse, it would probably not be appropriate to seek further involvement with children. Generally, though, the principle of making amends can be valuable. Acts of contrition can draw a line under the wrong action. Holding onto the feelings of guilt can be an act of self-reinforcement.

The Fallacy of Creating a Self to Let Go of Self

Unease at the possible implications of the teaching of non-self has led to various attempts to reformulate the Buddhist teachings. One approach that has become popular is the idea that you have to create a self before you can let it go. This is a neat theory that allows the whole of the western therapy paradigm to be tacked onto a Buddhist model. It incorporates good Buddhist sentiments like compassionate listening and creating healing space, while proposing that people need to develop a sense of identity before they can start to do the real work of transcending self. Such a model satisfies some voices in the Western Buddhist community who find the notion of giving up self distasteful, but it misses the real point of the teaching of non-self.

Far from being a killjoy teaching, leading to endless hard work and suffering, the teaching of non-self is one of liberation. Self is a defensive prison of habit-energy that you construct around yourself, and the teaching of non-self invites you to step beyond this prison into vibrant relationship with life. The self-prison from which the teaching invites you to escape is just as likely to be a negative self-image as a positive one. There is just as much need to give up being the downtrodden partner in the relationship as the arrogant one. The Buddhist paradigm does not lock you into self, but offers encounter with that which is other. It is a joyous meeting with the universe in all its radiance and diversity. This does not require you to become mentally chaotic. Far from it. It simply encourages you to drop rigidities and live more directly.

The Buddhist concept of non-self rests on an understanding that the self-structure is built in response to affliction. It is the result of an attempt to feel safe by establishing a sense of permanence. We encounter difficulties and we retreat into various patterns of avoidance and rigidity. Initially this involves sensory distraction. Later it takes the form of self-creation. These processes are not generally conscious; they are delusion or avidya. The processes of self-creation have kept us distanced from the worst of our pain, but they also prevent us experiencing life or really encountering other people. They are like a broadly acting anaesthetic.

Negative Self-Creation

Getting caught in self can take different forms. When you think of someone having an excess of self or ego, you probably imagine someone who is very self-promoting and overconfident. You do not think of someone struggling to keep a house clean and feed the family proper meals. Yet, although the latter behavior can be grounded in real love and connection with others, it can often be founded in maintaining a self-position. The person's identity can be strongly tied up in the role of caregiver, whether this is as someone who is capable and efficient, someone who is oppressed, or someone who is not worth bothering with. The negative self-image is just as limiting to the person concerned, and probably their family, as the overconfident self-position.

In Buddhist psychology, the self has different modes, positive and negative, and it is just as possible to have an excess of negative self as of positive self. Negative self is not what is being described by the term non-self. You can be trapped by destructive behavioral patterns just as powerfully as by grandiose ones, and you can hold on to a negative view of yourself just as strongly as a positive one, if not more so. Many people are so caught in a sense of their own worthlessness that they are completely unable to see even the most modest achievements in their lives.

I have worked with many people whose difficulty had, itself, become an identity. They would say "I am an alcoholic" or "I am a bulimic." Such positions can be difficult to relinquish, especially where the problem has so dominated the whole of adult life that no other identity has been found. A person who lives a life of drudgery may be a saint, but it is also possible that they are caught in the hold of a negative self. The idea that "I am only good enough for this" can be just as powerful a self-statement as any positive assertion. For this person, all the indicators in their life seem to be confirming the assumed identity. They are surrounded by lakshanas that say "You are an alcoholic" or "You are a bulimic." Since the illusion of self is created through such signs, the person is kept in the negative identity. Reading signs, however, usually involves a lot of delusion.

Letting go of negative self-image can be frightening. It brings the possibility that a person might start to achieve things and therefore might be expected to continue to achieve them. Letting go of the negative identity also means "not knowing who I am." This is a frightening step. It can also be a freeing one. This is not always the case, however. Without support, a sudden loss of identity can lead to the creation of even stronger defensive responses. In supporting others, you need to hear not only the pain of the situation in which they have imprisoned themselves but also the pain that caused them to retreat into a strong identity in the first place. It can take a lot of time and caring.

The Issue of Self-esteem

Western practitioners with whom I have discussed these issues raise the point that many of the people they work with, commonly women, are burdened by a lack of self-esteem. Such people spend all their lives working for others and have no personal space or time to develop their own interests and abilities. How can such people have an excess of self? I can feel a great sympathy for this view, because I too have worked with many women who lacked confidence and had very low opinions of themselves. Often they were so handicapped by feelings of incapability and self-loathing that their lives had become extremely limited and felt meaningless.

There are several points that need to be made here. First, a negative self is just as much self as a positive self is. Self-loathing and pride are two sides of a coin. The real problem for a person with low self-esteem is that she is also trapped in self-structure. Her mind is often preoccupied with exaggeratedly negative thoughts about herself, and she may constantly criticize herself for things she does. Her view of others is also heavily colored with similar negative self-preoccupation: she sees others as more successful than herself, more capable than herself, and generally better than herself. She may even withdraw socially because she imagines everyone is looking at her and laughing at her behind her back, or speaking to her only out of pity. Instead of seeing things as they are, she sees only signs that confirm her view of herself.

Second you need to let go of those value judgements that you make around the issue of self. The modern self-culture is, in part, a reaction against the Victorian self-sacrifice culture; but neither culture was free from the delusion of self. Although "doing things for myself" is now seen by many as a good thing, there is still a note of defensiveness in the assertion that "I need to love myself more." Indeed, it may even become a pressure. A person may feel guilty for not fulfilling it—"I *ought* to love myself more." The injunction to love oneself may seem to imply a challenge to the listener, but it is also something about which people often secretly feel uncomfortable. The fear of being judged by a society that advocates independence and self-cherishing can lead to a great deal of internal conflict. You do not need to get caught in the kind of self-argument that statements about "having to love myself more" imply. If you love life, you will be happy and live well. This is a much simpler approach.

Third, the position of asserting that "I have to love myself" often masks a despair of receiving the love of others. Despair of the other can drive us into depression and ultimately into the self-destructive patterns associated with the third-level escape patterns of samudaya. The despair underlying this self-love position, albeit well hidden, often rests on a belief that "no one else can be trusted to love me properly." Learning to trust deeply brings us back into contact with the other and breaks this isolation.

Believing you have to love yourself creates a life of independence. A person who believes he should love himself probably also believes that only he is responsible for his feelings. He may well also decide to live alone, preferring freedom to a committed relationship. Such a situation of self-reliance creates an environment in which self-concept is not challenged and in this may provide a semblance of stability and contentment. This has its comforts, but it creates a lonely situation that denies the person's connection with, and dependence upon, others and with the world. While it is a common Western ideal, it yields no ultimate satisfaction.

Unidentified Self-Material

The term "self-material" includes both those things that a person believes to be part of his or her self and those things that they perceive as lakshanas or indicators of self. Items of the latter kind may not be recognized as related to self, and may well be mistaken for objective reality. In this way, a person can live with a highly distorted world-view, but assume it to be simply a view of things as they are.

Some years ago I worked with a group of women who had come together because, among other things, they felt that they lacked a sense of identity. They talked a great deal about feeling empty and not knowing who they were. What emerged was that, although the women talked very little about their experiences of themselves, they described in great detail the way that they saw their home and work environments, and other places and objects of significance.

Rather than seeing things with clarity, they described almost everything they talked about in terms of their personal involvement. When they talked about the room they were meeting in, their descriptions were entirely based on criteria associated with personal preference and identity: "I like this cushion because it's my sort of color," or "I like that chair because I find it comfortable," or "I like the colors in the room because they are like the ones I have chosen in my house."

It felt as if there were a kind of appropriation taking place. The women each seemed to be imaginatively moving into the meeting room and redesigning it to reflect their tastes. Those tastes strongly reflected the sense of identity that the women felt that they lacked. Their statements about personal preference and examples of personal identification made up most of the interaction.

There was no fixed theme suggested for the group, so the women talked about the things uppermost in their minds. In practice, most of the topics of discussion during the group were of subjects that offered possibilities for high levels of identification: my clothes, my family, my house, my garden, my job. The women still felt that they lacked identity, and did not recognize that their process in the group was associated with building a strong sense of self. At the same time, they were actually demonstrating a very limited world-view, based on processes connected with maintaining self-structures. In Western terminology, these processes might be termed identification and projection. In Buddhist psychology, they could be described as maintaining the self-world through the skandha process. This process, as Buddhist psychology would suggest, was founded on craving or thirst. They felt a sense of lack.

The women were right in thinking that they lacked solid identity. Their mistakes, from a Buddhist point of view, were that they saw this as a problem and that their preoccupation with lakshanas led them to cut themselves off from real interaction with others. The women did not seem to see the other people around them, or even physical things in the room, very clearly at all. Although they appeared to be talking about things that might be construed as "other," they were not seeing these things as separate objects in their own right. Their experience was not one of encounter. They were prisoners of their limited view.

The self-material that is invested in the object world is more difficult for a person to recognize and work with than that which is part of the perceived self. It is taken to be an accurate perception of the world. The person living in such a world can feel powerless and isolated without understanding that the isolation comes from the limitations of their own perception.

We have all experienced how we can wake up in the morning feeling down and then go on to experience the day as a series of things that go wrong. The mail is all bills, the bus is crowded, the weather is too cold, the people we work with are irritable and don't seem to have time to stop and listen to us, the work is boring, and so on. It always seems as if these are objective facts. The woman in the bus line *did* push in front of me. The coffee in the canteen *was* stale and cold. I *did* have to pick up that extra work because someone else was off sick. Of course, on a good day, these things would probably pass unnoticed.

The world you see is substantially a function of your mentality. Our viewing is selective and colored. Some things you distort by misinterpretation, some by imagination, and some by selectivity of view. Through all these processes, distortion takes place. It is a function of the thirst for lakshanas and is also the creator of new self-material.

Collective Selves

Self-patterns operate at a personal level, but they also operate at the levels of the group and of society. Skandha processes operate in groups, organizations and even whole nations. Groups have particular experiences that lead them to react in particular ways. These build certain habitual behavioral patterns that become the norms for the group. These group norms create expectations that then affect how the group collectively approaches the world. This approach forms the group experience and shapes the group's collective perceptions. These processes create a group identity and a group story about the world.

Recognizing the power and universality of these processes, you can appreciate the power of the self-process. You can also appreciate that, just as you cannot actually pin something down and call it a group identity, so too you cannot isolate any such thing as a self. Both are concepts. They do not have substance. In short, they are illusory. Nonetheless, both can be highly coercive and consequently limiting.

Both individual and group identities are persistent and hard to recognize because they are created through a cycle of stages. Everyone involved reinforces them. You become aware of the norms and assumptions of your culture only when you are faced with someone of a different culture. In this regard, it is useful to compare your experience with that of people with different social, geographical, or historical backgrounds. Meeting those who are different from yourself loosens your attachment to particular views and widens your perspectives. This is not always easy, though. Even when you meet someone with different views, you are apt to dismiss that person's perspective as mistaken or archaic or to reinterpret it in the light of your own cultural norms. This process is, of course, supported by your colleagues and friends, who live within the same social milieu as you do.

The group and social identities in which you live co-exist with your personal identities. You identify with your culture, creating identity in relation to it; and your culture, in turn, is created through collective identification. Bringing about change in culture requires adjustments of identity.

This means we are all under constant coercive pressure from society, as well as from our own need for psychological defenses, to create and maintain certain identities. Those who adopt behaviors and roles that challenge the social norms are commonly experienced as threatening to the sense of collective identity and are therefore often punished through ridicule, persecution, or isolation. These processes become more powerful when a group feels threatened. Yet it is through such exceptional people that society has the opportunity to expand its own limits and shake off restrictive patterns of vision and action.

Within smaller groups and relationships, too, the coercive power of collective identity creates pressure for the status quo to continue. Some groups form around the assumption that everyone is the same. Others require members to take differentiated roles. In both situations, however, the group norms and assumptions will be operating.

Many identities and behavioral patterns require someone else to play a complementary part. We call these complementary parts *counterpart* roles. One role supports the other. One person's identity is reinforced by association with a person whose identity pattern complements it. Within such a relationship, there is a pressure for both people to keep playing the game lest either let the other down and reveal the impermanence of their shared sense of identity. This kind of mutual support often exists in partnerships, but it can also exist in larger groups. Counterpart roles are highly persistent and an important prop to the skandha process. Once you have become established as part of such a pairing, you are likely to seek others who can fall into the complementary role to your own in order to support our sense of identity; and you invite those you become involved with into these roles.

Keeping the self-structure in place is a defensive position, but it is also a position that costs you highly in energy. Countries often spend huge proportions of their resources on supporting their armies against the possibility of invasion or threat. You too may employ a large proportion of your life-energy in trying to be somebody and then in protecting that identity. Breaking out of this cycle and getting beyond the self-prison offers the possibility of releasing this energy. You have the potential to live in a way that is more creative, engaged, productive, and happy.

THEORIES INTRODUCED IN THIS CHAPTER

- the Three Signs of Being;
- non-self;
- negative selves;
- contrition;
- unidentified selves;
- collective selves; and
- counterpart roles.

Part 2
Creating Conditions

· 9 ·

Grounding

In the countryside of Cheshire, as you walk or drive down little hedge-lined roads, you come across a huge white bowl resting on a lattice of iron girders and pointing up towards the heavens. Years ago, when I lived in the northwest of England, I would pass it regularly—an impressive structure, glimpsed through the gaps in the trees that shield it from the road. The angle at which it pointed varied from time to time, but it always reached toward some part of the sky. This is Jodrell Bank, the largest radio telescope in the UK, and once the largest in the world. Its huge structure is the receptor of faint messages from distant corners of the universe. Its sheer size enables it to pick up the smallest of signals from stars and galaxies millions of light years away. The parabolic shape of the large bowl focuses these messages so that they can be collected and deciphered.

If you are to live fully, you need to develop your capacity to be alive to the world, to move out of self-concern into an other-centered universe. This means listening, developing sensitivity, and broadening your perspective. The image of the radio telescope illustrates what is involved in opening up to the world in this way.

First, to be open to experience, you must establish groundedness. Literally and metaphorically, you can increase your awareness of the solid earth. The telescope cannot function without being well anchored on its base. It is not the sort of grasping contact of sparsha, which grabs at experience to possess it. Rather, it is the reverent contact of smriti, or "mindful presence," that respectfully meets experience.

Second, just as the telescope is able to turn its attention to particular points in the skies, so you must also learn to direct your attention in a focused way. Whether listening to the flow of another's story and catching tiny details or watching an insect visiting each flower of the honeysuckle in turn, you need to be able to concentrate well.

Third, you need to be empty of self-preoccupations—empty like the huge bowl of the telescope—so that you do not contaminate what you experience. To focus on the person or object of your attention, set aside your own agenda as far as you can. Of course, self-material has a way of creeping into our experience all the time, so this requires great vigilance.

Finally, you can develop understanding, so that you can see the bigger picture that emerges as you listen and look. Just as the telescope collects many small signals from different corners of the universe and builds them into a picture, so too can you bring together perceptions, appreciate what is there, and see what needs to be done.

This chapter will focus particularly on how to achieve the solid, non-grasping aliveness to the world that liberates you. We will look at ways in which you can create clear mental space, empty of contaminating self-material.

As members of an engaged Buddhist order, we at the Amida Trust have learned that there are many parallels between living fully, working in helping situations, and more traditional forms of Buddhist practice. For example, giving quality attention to another person requires the same concentration, groundedness, and focus that we apply in meditation. Quality attention cuts through lakshana, making us more available to others. When we are in contact in this way, we feel fully alive.

The ability to listen to others is important to all of us, in our relationships and friendships as well as in more formal caring situations. Too often when we listen, especially if we are close to the person concerned, we find that personal agendas are triggered very quickly. We tend not to hear what that other person is saying but only what we think it indicates about ourselves. The closer we are, the more we either reinforce our shared prejudices through the interaction, or else find ourselves drawn into conflict as aspects of our self-structure feel threatened by what is being said. Reducing our reactivity can be a first step in breaking out of these unhelpful responses. Developing groundedness helps to do this.

Buddhist practice requires a combination of solidity and flexibility. To give good attention to another person, you need to cultivate both these attributes. If you can give your attention to each new topic or piece of information as it arises, without being overly attached to your own theory about what might be going on for the person you are listening to, you will listen better. It is not easy. It is in the nature of your minds to keep pulling the process back to self-creation. All the time you are listening, the skandha process keeps erupting as you split what you hear into areas of interest and non-interest, approval and disapproval. You react and you filter.

The radio telescope is well anchored on its base and because of this it is able to turn in any direction, changing its focus to reach whichever part of the universe it is directed to observe. So too, if you are well grounded in the physical world, you will be better able to maintain your focus, less likely to be swept away by others' feelings if they become distressed, or to be distracted by intruding self-orientated reactions.

Solidity and Grounding

Jodrell Bank telescope sits on a massive iron frame. It must be solidly based on this structure so that it will not be affected by vibrations from its own movements or events happening nearby, for the signals which it receives become distorted by even the smallest accidental movement. At the same time it must be able to move so that it is not rigidly directed to one area of the sky, but can sweep the whole expanse of stars.

To be fully present, we can use techniques that deliberately cultivate stillness and solidity. They can help us to develop calmness and the ability to be present in situations where it might otherwise be difficult to avoid being reactive. Developing skills of this kind provides a basis for interactive or helping work you may be involved in. They can be particularly valuable when you are with those who are distressed or anxious. These techniques are called *grounding* practices.

Grounding involves developing your awareness of the solidity of the body and its contact with the material world; literally with the ground on which you are standing or sitting. There are a number of ways of approaching grounding, some of which will be described here. First, however, let us look at the benefits grounding brings.

The Benefits of Grounding

Grounding as a Source of Calmness
If you are grounded, you will less easily get caught in heightened emotions. You will be less likely to react hastily and more able to step back from situations to reflect on them before responding—and so less likely to respond unwisely. Also, you will not get swept up into the feelings of others as easily. Although it is good to be able to empathize with others' experiences, you are not much help if you simply end up getting overemotional yourself and identifying with their feelings in unhelpful ways. You may want to help others who are distressed; you will be able to do so only if you can maintain a level of stability. For the person whose lifestyle exposes them to a lot of traumatic situations, groundedness is particularly important. In the long term such a person will be more likely to avoid burn-out if they can maintain a level of calmness while working.

Grounding as a Source of Support to Others as well as Ourselves
If you are able to stay grounded, you will offer a calm presence to others. This may in turn help them to become calmer. Emotional states are very easily passed from one person to another. Anxiety can quickly spread through a group when a

difficult situation arises. Each person's reaction increases the tension for others, until a high pitch of emotion is reached. In such circumstances, the presence of someone who is not caught up in the turmoil can help reduce the tension.

The process by which emotion passes from one person to another through felt body experience is called *contagion*. Contagion generally operates at a level beyond conscious awareness, but it can be very powerful. If you know how to become grounded, you can deliberately bring calm into emotionally fraught situations.

There are times when the best support you can offer others is to deliberately increase your own groundedness. When with someone who is very agitated, particularly if the agitation seems to have a strong compulsive component to it, developing stillness may be the most helpful approach to adopt.

Grounding and Faith

Grounding methods increase your experiential awareness of the material world. You become aware of the reliability of things that are beyond self. These methods encourage you to take refuge in reality or dharma. As you become more aware of the ground beneath you, the air you are breathing, and the physical objects that surround you, you become more aware of the miraculous complexity of our world. More than this, though, you learn experientially its reliability.

We never question the presence of solid ground beneath us. We rarely appreciate it, either. By increasing your awareness, you subtly develop your sense of appreciation and wonder for the ordinary things that are so extraordinary. You experience increasing trust in the existential world. You grow in faith.

Grounding ourselves, we go for refuge. As I described in Chapter 4, there are times when the experience of touching earth is an important reminder that dharma is always there. Before we give a talk in our Buddhist center, we always make five prostrations. We touch the earth and remind ourselves that we are not alone or even independent. Whatever we say is simply a gathering of ideas passed down through us from those we have listened to in the past. We remind ourselves that we have to trust that words will come in a way that will be useful to those who listen. We may have spent time preparing what we will say, but even this does not guarantee that we will deliver what we have to say well. If we are self-preoccupied or become too concerned with the performance, words disappear and we fumble for concepts. Like a sportsperson, one needs to learn not to try to control the performance in that self-conscious way. When we start to speak, we have to let go and put ourselves in the hands of the universe. We have to have faith.

Sitting on the ground to talk, or maybe standing, it helps to pause and feel the solid floor and know one is not alone.

Increasing Your Awareness of Body Experience

Grounding techniques bring greater awareness of body experience. In Buddhist psychology, mind and body are not separate. Awareness of the body helps one to recognize the processes described in the teachings we have been exploring. Vedana occurs firstly in the body. Samskaras are action traces, so are the shadows of body activity. As you think about things and imagine them, your body generally responds, albeit in small, subtle ways. Just as a dog moves its paws while it is dreaming, so too, at a micro-level, your muscles tense and twitch in response to action impulses and shrink away or relax in response to stimuli. As you become more aware of these responses, you can learn to recognize when old patterns of response have been triggered. You notice the familiar sensation of embarrassment, anger, horror, defensiveness, or attraction. Thus you have the opportunity to avoid the pattern, to divert yourself away from the old tracks if you wish.

Awareness of body responses can be particularly helpful in learning to handle interactions more skillfully. Body states are subtly communicated. On an instinctive level you are programmed to recognize the body language of others and to respond physically yourself. If you experience hostility in another, your body tenses. If you experience friendly feelings, we relax. If you experience sexual interest, you become aroused. Often two people's body states mirror one another. You may not be consciously aware of this process and may wonder why your mood has suddenly changed as you are sitting with someone. As you become more aware of your body experience, against the background of a generally more grounded state, you may recognize unvoiced emotions of others, expressed through the body, and so better understand the complexity of their situations.

Grounding Techniques

Physical Contact

Grounding techniques rely upon increasing your awareness of physical contact with the material world, and particularly those parts of it that support the body, such as the ground or floor or the seat we are sitting on. This awareness is developed at a physical level rather than an intellectual one. Start by sitting or standing in a well-balanced posture. If you are standing, plant both feet firmly on the floor, weight equally distributed between them. If you are sitting, sit well back on the chair. Place both feet on the floor, with your weight evenly balanced across the seat of the chair.

Having found a stable, comfortable position, concentrate on the feeling of contact between the body and the ground or chair. This can take the form of an investigation. It is often best to shut the eyes in order to focus awareness in the sense of the body. Feel the distribution of weight over the area of contact. Ask: "What is the nature of this contact? Where do I feel myself to be touching the floor most solidly? Where is my contact lighter? Can I discern the texture of the carpet or cushion on which I am sitting? Is my body still, or do I feel small movements as I sit?"

Investigating in this way, you come to appreciate the reliability of the contact you are making with the ground. You start to trust that it is supporting you in a physical way as well as an intellectual one, allowing your body to rely more strongly on that support. You start to feel more solid.

Use of the Breath

To aid the process of grounding, you can use the breath. Imagine your breath flowing down into the lower parts of your body. Slowing your breathing deliberately, imagine it flowing down through your lower belly and on through your feet into the ground. You can imagine all the energy in your body moving downward, giving you a solid connection with the floor. Keep your attention on slowing your breathing and imagine a downward movement of air through your body, perhaps visualizing this process as a dark blue stream of light. Visualization techniques actually act as a distraction from detailed involvement with the breath at the body center. The breath is closely linked to emotional states, and focusing on the breath at the center of the body can increase emotionality. This is not generally useful to the grounding process, as it may bring a person to a state of heightened arousal or increased anxiety. For this reason, it is best to use the breath as the basis for visualization. If you are focusing on the physical experience of the breath, do so either at the nostrils or very deep in the belly. At least to begin with, avoid focusing on the main body cavity area, which may be the center of emotional energy. As you become more experienced, you can experiment with shifting focus to the breath in other areas of the torso.

Use of Imagery

In west London there is a Japanese temple that I visit from time to time. This temple is an ordinary suburban house, but in its back garden there is a surprise. The temple has a Zen garden, built with great care by Japanese experts using traditional methods and materials. The garden is bounded in a traditional way, with a wall rendered with sand-colored cement in subtle, waved patterns, and capped by neat terra-cotta tiles. Inside, the garden is enclosed by rows of dark pebbles from eastern Europe and Italian marble edging stones. The main expanse of the garden contains a number of embedded rocks, each circled by moss and resting in a sea of raked gravel. The rocks have been collected from all over the British Isles: craggy granite from Aberdeenshire, slates and shales from the Lake District, monolithic basalt slabs from Ireland. The rocks are buried deeply.

Reverend Sato, minister at the temple, describes how they were placed, two-thirds below ground level. This brings the right sense of harmony and calm to the garden. Beside the garden is a raised meditation area with a thatched roof and solid oak boards where one can sit and contemplate the arrangement of rocks. Being there, one feels deep calm and peace.

Spending time in such a place, perhaps meditating, perhaps simply looking at the stones, perhaps writing poetry or sketching, creates a mental image that stays with you. It can be recalled at other times, perhaps when you feel stressed or anxious. Images of huge rocks, two-thirds buried in the earth, solid and immovable, like the rocks in a Japanese Zen garden, create a bodily sense of calm. The rocks are well anchored in the earth and so provide an image of groundedness. Such images can help you feel more grounded because the body tends to mirror what it sees.

There are many images that can be used to help achieve grounding. If you listen to relaxation tapes, you will find that common themes recur. For example, you can imagine yourself growing roots, like a tree, that anchor you into the soil. You can imagine lying on a beach in the sunshine. You can imagine yourself in a beautiful place such as a woodland glade or beside a waterfall. It helps to work with such images, with which you can build up the associations of calm; either use a real scene, or use the same image in meditations or guided fantasy exercises repeatedly until you can call it up at will. Always be aware of the body state you are in while building these associations, since you will need to associate the image with a relaxed, calm body state.

Exercises of this kind increase your ability to enter calm states, but generally they work by building benign patterns of response; they create positive habit-energy but do not necessarily themselves bring you into a more direct experiencing of the world by actually breaking through the patterns of conditioning. Nevertheless, creating positive samskaras in this way can be a helpful approach, as it shifts the person into a more positive mentality. It is likely to help the person to become less defended in the long run, and it eventually paves the way for increasingly open contact with the world of the other. Such methods are sometimes described as "gradual path methods."

Taking the Attention to the Periphery of the Body

In developing grounding skills, it is useful to take your attention to the lower and peripheral areas of the body: your feet and the backs of your legs, your buttocks and lower spine. You can also be aware of sensation in your hands. This draws attention away from that central body area which is the seat of emotional activity. Grounding involves awareness of contact with the world, and this contact generally happens at the body's periphery. Later, work may be done to explore emotions through bodywork, working in the center of the body; but to begin with, grounding exercises are needed to build a container for this kind of work. Establishing groundedness before other work begins provides a secure refuge to which one can return if emotions threaten to become overwhelming.

Bringing Attention to Objects

An extension of the establishment of focus on the peripheral body is to focus attention on contact with material objects. This can be achieved through awareness of contact with the floor or chair. Detailed observation is crucial. It is important to train yourself to "look" carefully with hands and feet. It can be all too easy to imagine yourself making contact, rather than actually feeling it. You may base your perception on what you know intellectually rather than on the sensation.

Most of us are far more accustomed to using our intellects than to using our bodies. This is one of the reasons why bodywork is so effective. We have fewer old patterns of response and expectation to overcome with relation to our bodies, so we may be less defended against the work.

Another way to work with peripheral body contact is to hold something solid, like a round stone, in your hands, and focus on the sensation of contact. This particular technique is useful for people experiencing severe anxiety. If I am working with a person who suffers from panic attacks, I may give him a stone to hold in the palm of his hand while we do some grounding exercises, particularly focusing on that hand-to-stone contact. He learns to focus attention on the sensation of the stone in his hand, while at the same time achieving a calm mind state. I then give him a stone to carry with him in his pocket. The stone then becomes an *anchor* for the feelings of groundedness that we have worked to achieve. It can be held if symptoms start to return. Bringing attention to the feeling of the stone in his hand takes attention away from feelings of panic that are arising in his central body.

The stone, of course, also carries other significance—it is a reminder of the supportive atmosphere in which we have worked together—but in a simple way it acts as a physical aid to grounding.

Lowering the Center of Gravity

Grounding involves finding a low center of gravity. You can increase groundedness by deliberately directing attention downward. Such a shift of awareness creates subtle shifts in body position and the distribution of energy. You can see this effect by watching practitioners of martial arts. The basic stance intensifies the contact between the feet and the ground. Attention is deliberately directed to the hips, lower legs and feet, and to contact between the feet and the ground. In doing this, the practitioner develops strength and solidity in the lower body. The student of these disciplines spends much of his early training developing a solid stance so that he becomes able to maintain it unflinchingly, even when suddenly pushed or struck by an opponent. Cultivating this requires concentration of both mind and body. If the student is momentarily distracted, he may be caught off guard and knocked over. If he remains focused, he can resist substantial pressure.

Many of the images we use to help us feel more grounded involve objects with low centers of gravity. The rocks in the Zen garden described earlier are a good example—their bases are well buried so that they are immovable. In Japan, daruna dolls are made. These are said to be representations of Bodhidharma, the Zen master who, according to legend, spent nine years facing a wall in meditation and hence achieved considerable skill in grounding. These dolls have round bases, weighted in such a way that if they are knocked over, they rock back into an upright position. The figures have been copied as children's toys in the West. Many of us as children have played with a wobbly man figure that could not be overturned, without recognizing that in this play we were learning about being grounded. The dolls teach us that for stability we need our center of gravity to be low.

Meditation and Grounding

Meditation is a body experience that relies upon a low center of gravity. In meditation, good posture is of great importance. The body must be grounded. It is best to sit on the floor, literally in contact with the earth. Ideally the legs are crossed in the lotus position, but for Westerners coming to meditation later in life, some compromise must often be found. Whatever this is, stability is essential. So too is the expansion or "opening" of the abdominal area. The pelvis is tipped forward and the belly extended so that breath enters freely into this lower part of the body. Breath fills the lungs deeply, moving the diaphragm and the belly.

The body becomes still and quiet. During the time of meditation, there is no movement beyond the natural flow of breath and the gentle unfolding of autonomic (involuntary) body processes. The body becomes still, and the mind follows. Both become more open, allowing body processes and consciousness alike to flow more freely. At the same time, the meditator cultivates alertness. The spine is straight, the shoulders, arms and hands relaxed. Alertness of the body provides conditions for the mind also to become alert. Meditation begins in the body. Mind mirrors body, and body mirrors mind.

The space of the belly below the navel may provide the focus of attention during the meditation session. Awareness is held in the cradle of the pelvis in close contact with the ground. That contact is made through the triangle of the pelvic base and folded legs. The meditator's attention focuses on the subtle rising and falling of the abdominal muscles with each breath. It is slow and deep, not a big movement such as occurs in the upper belly or chest. With the awareness of this movement, breath seems to flow down through the lower body, right into the earth.

Grounding and Emotional Release

The connection between the somatic (bodily) and mental states is close. In deliberately adopting a body position, you provide the conditions for particular mental states to arise. By changing the posture of the body, you can relax mental tensions, improve levels of physical functions, and increase emotional expression and receptivity. Grounding takes attention away from the central body area where emotional energy often resides. Having achieved a grounded state, however, it is possible to move into more expressive work. The central body space often holds tensions associated with emotional experience. For those who habitually repress a lot of emotion, bringing attention to these areas can lead to emotional release. Such release can be useful and cathartic, but it can also sometimes feel overwhelming.

For someone in a crisis situation or with a history of traumatic experiences, understanding the difference between using body awareness as a means of grounding and using body experience for emotional release can be useful. As Buddhist psychology would suggest, contact with the external world, such as the grounding work described above, releases a person from being overly caught up in self-material. On the other hand, it is sometimes useful and indeed necessary to explore what patterns of conditioned response you are carrying in order to let them go. Using different body focuses, you may make a choice about which you do.

Self-structures are rigidities in the mentality, and similar rigidities develop in the body as a person defends against painful experiences. Rigidities prevent us moving freely and may create blocks to feelings or to particular response patterns. It is as if a person gets locked into a habitual way of defending.

Imagine that you have a sudden shock. Your body recoils. Maybe you pull your shoulders and ribs in and shrink back. The feeling of doing this is probably familiar. Now imagine that you have gone on feeling shocked for so long that the muscle tensions associated with pulling back in this way become established as your usual way of holding your chest and shoulders. The position will probably not be as obvious as it was when you imagined being exposed to the fresh stimulus, but it will have the same pattern of muscle reaction. Most people acquire habitual tensions of this kind at some time. The patterns of body defenses both dull their experience of persistent situations and reflect their habitual stance to the world. In other words, the body holds self-structures in a very similar way to the conditioned mind. When you look at others, you may see in their faces or their body language the habit-patterns that make up their physical identity.

So a person not only builds up a mental structure of defenses, which comes to be thought of as the self, but also creates physical body characteristics that are distinctive and reflect patterns of defense. Western theorists like the psychoanalyst Wilhelm Reich proposed that people build up systems of body armoring in response to painful childhood experiences. As a person works to release body tensions, the pain of old traumas may be released in ways that can be healing and cathartic. Buddhist approaches tend to advocate a more gentle style of working than that propounded by Reich, based on awareness and disidentification rather than primarily on emotional release.

This is not to say, however, that Buddhist approaches avoid emotion. Facing dukkha, in whatever form it takes, arouses strong emotion. The teaching of the Four Noble Truths suggests that you should face afflictions cleanly, not falling into habitual escape patterns and self-creation. Working with the body, you need to find balance.

Exploring old traumas can be important and may enable people to face past dukkha that has previously led them to escape into distractions. On the other hand, Buddhist approaches are more often focused on current experience. It may sometimes be more useful to develop groundedness than to work endlessly with past experiences. Grounding can help release old tensions without the need for cathartic expression.

Using Grounding on the Streets

Recently some members of our community have been working on the streets, talking with homeless people and building relationships with them. This sort of detached work involves walking around the town center, being prepared to sit and make conversation with anyone who is begging or seems in need. Building friendly contact is typical of an engaged Buddhist approach in that it is not specifically outcome-orientated. By giving the homeless person quality attention, we hope to create conditions for something to change. We cannot know what will happen, but in offering this kind of attention, we hope benefits will arise. We must trust that this will happen in the way it needs to, rather than trying to influence and control things too heavily. The contact we have may turn out to be a first step in moving the person with whom we speak out of the cycle of destructive behaviors that put him on the street—or it may simply improve the quality of his life there. There again, nothing may change. We have to value the contact in itself and not attach to outcomes.

Before going out on this work, practitioners find it useful to spend time doing grounding exercises. It helps to take time to sit and focus on grounding the body, then to be aware of groundedness as they walk. Walking has always been important in Buddhism. Begging for alms was a traditional part of the bhikshu's practice, and it was done by walking around the village holding a begging bowl. The image of the robed figure, simply walking, often barefoot, is still common today. If you are aware of your feet touching the earth at each step and you feel its solidity, you can use the act of walking to calm and center yourself. Each footstep is solidly placed, and the body is well balanced between them.

Earlier this year, a group from our community undertook a Peace Walk to London. We walked 180 miles by roads and footpaths over twelve days. In walking we bore witness to the need for action to bring peace in these troubled times. When we walk with grounded presence, our message of peace is all the stronger.

The Gift of Grounded Attention

If you can develop grounded attention, you not only feel calmer and more open to your own experience, you also start to be of more use to others. You become more receptive to what they are saying and more perceptive of the deeper meanings behind their words. You become more caring in your responses and create a calm space for those in distress, whether you encounter them through your work or as friends or family members.

Let us return to our original image, Jodrell Bank. The telescope's solid structure is essential for it to find small signals from distant stars. It relies on these to build up a picture of the universe. The structure must be flexible so that it can move and point in the right direction. If you are well grounded, you can turn your attention to the world in a way that is less likely to impose your mental flurry on your perception. If the grounding has been successful in taking you beyond self-preoccupation, you will feel less drag as you switch your attention from one aspect of your surroundings to another. If you develop both solidity and flexibility, you will be able to give full attention to those you encounter.

Encounter is outwardly focused: the aim is to give quality attention to those you meet. Grounding alone does not provide this. Grounding provides solidity in your interactions; but if you are simply grounded, your attention may be too caught up in your body sense and not enough in hearing the other person or experiencing the situation. You need to allow your grounded experience to drop into the background so that you can do the real job of listening.

The process of listening requires mind and imagination, but you also listen through your body experience. When someone needs to talk about their life situation, it is good if you can be with them in a grounded way. Sitting well grounded, you will be able to pay attention to central body experience. It is often possible to feel echoes of the other person's body experience through the process of contagion. If you can be open to whatever tensions and resistances that person experiences, you may learn more deeply what it is like to be in their situation. You become a sensitive receptacle, sensing feelings and noticing reactions that arise.

The telescope dish is strongly held on its girders, and is hollow in shape. You too can bring together solid, grounded presence with a spacious willingness to hear. The combination of solidity and openness operates not only at the level of psychological availability but also at a bodily level. You cannot separate mind and body, and you can initiate change through adapting body experience just as well as you can through changing your mental attitude.

When you give good attention to others, you pick up subtle changes of expression. Sadness comes into our friend's eyes when a particular place is mentioned. A moment of uncertainty is revealed by the hesitation when a loved one is close. A raised eyebrow accompanies doubtful thoughts. If you notice these changes, sometimes you may trust your observation and ask about them. "Your eyes look sad as you speak." "You look uneasy with him." "You look unsure about that." With experience, you learn to sense when it is best to share your observations and when it is best to remain silent.

In voicing your observations, you can show that you have noticed and offer the person a space to say more, without imposing your interpretations too strongly. Such observations bring you to a deeper level of understanding because they allow things to be said that would otherwise remain unspoken.

People often communicate important things with oblique references. They make a joke and watch to see if anyone has noticed the sadness buried in it. They talk about others, hoping someone will recognize that the troubles being described could equally be their own. They make cynical comments, hoping they will be taken seriously and the concern within them will be heard. Often people are not aware that they are giving out these signals. They are not aware of feelings evident in their faces as they talk. Many people, too, have had to hide their feelings. Showing that you see and respect their felt experience can be very important in helping another person to regain trust in life. As trust on the part of others grows, you too learn to trust.

Listening as Meditation

Buddhism teaches a great deal about attention. For many people, focused awareness is the primary Buddhist practice, whether in formal meditation or in everyday living. Through formal practice you can train the mind to remain clear and focused, resting on a wholesome object. The object of your attention can take a number of forms depending on the particular practice being used. It may be the breathing, an image, or simply the stream of mental process itself. The attention rests on its object in a way that is sharp but also soft. You should not grasp at the object, but you should hold it in central focus. When you hold an object in your attention in this way, you develop concentration.

Other Buddhist practices may involve keeping similar awareness in whatever task the person is doing. This may be awareness of the task itself, or it may be keeping the Buddha in mind throughout daily activity. When you listen intensely to another person in the way described above, that person becomes like the object of meditation, the subject of your central attention. If you can listen with the reverence you bring to your meditation practice, the person to whom you are giving this attention becomes as the Buddha for you, a symbol of enlightened relating.

During the Balkan wars of the 1990s, our organization made several visits to that area, taking food and clothing to people in the refugee camps. Although we were a small group, and the amount of material aid we were able to deliver was small compared with the provision coming from large aid agencies, the real value of the visit was in the person-to-person contact it allowed. Distributing clothes and food, the people who went with the vehicles were able to spend time talking with families who had been through terrible traumas of war, losing loved ones, homes and whole villages. Although language was sometimes a problem, nevertheless healing came from the caring attention that these helpers were able to give.

Many people in our world need opportunities to tell their stories. We all sometimes long to be heard. Buddhism does not expect us to live isolated lives, coping with everything on our own. As you take refuge, so too you learn to share personal burdens and feel the unconditional love that is available to us all if only we can be open enough to really contact others. To be so, you need to let go of some of your defenses. You need to stop seeking self-reference in everything you meet.

Emptiness

As it receives the radio signals emitted by far-off stars and galaxies, the telescope dish focuses them into the central point. Then its receptors transmit the information to the control room. To accomplish this, the telescope dish needs to be empty. If it does not have a clean surface, reception of signals will be distorted and data may be indecipherable. Similarly, if you aspire to be open and in contact with others, you need to create clean space in yourself.

Western phenomenology has a concept of *bracketing*—or, to use the original terminology, creating an *epoche* (Spinelli, 1989). Creating an epoche involves temporarily putting aside preconceptions and assumptions, and seeing or listening in a fresh way. Attitudes and ideologies are imaginatively put in a box while in the helping situation. They are put in brackets.

The term "emptiness" is well known in Buddhism. In Sanskrit the word for emptiness is *shunyata*. There are different interpretations of the teaching of emptiness. Some of them are somewhat complicated and metaphysical, and we do not need to address them here, but the common interpretation of the term suggests that to say that something is shunyata means that that thing is "empty of lakshana." When teachings say that all things are empty, they mean that things are what they are. They are not there to indicate something about us. They are non-self. Things are dharmas, not rupas.

When you listen to someone's story, you put aside your self-view and hear what is said better if you can be without investments of personal agendas. This does not mean that you should not sometimes share your thoughts or opinions, but you need to be aware when you are doing this. Putting aside personal perspectives is not easy, and one important focus of Buddhist training is to become more aware of the way in which self-material intrudes on one's encounters with others and more skilled in letting it go. If you are full of concerns and ideas from elsewhere, you will not listen well.

Let us use another image. When he goes out on his alms round, the bhikshu takes his begging bowl. He holds the bowl out to everyone, willingly accepting whatever is put into it. If you can live with that same openness and receptivity, you will live fully and contribute to a better life for many. The bowl is a symbol of the bhikshu. It is strong and able to contain food well; but it is also empty and open to receive whatever arrives. If you are truly empty, you will receive whatever people bring you with gratitude, for it is indeed an honor to be trusted by others. You will hear their stories without judging or rejecting parts. It is only when your self-material gets in the way and your bowl is no longer empty that you will start to discriminate unhelpfully.

THEORIES INTRODUCED IN THIS CHAPTER

- grounding as a method for achieving calm;
- giving clear attention;
- meditation method; and
- shunyata—emptiness of self.

· 10 ·

Conditions for Change

All things arise in dependence upon causes and conditions. This is one of the core teachings of Buddhism, specifically presented in the teaching of dependent origination. Certain things provide the conditions in which certain other things can happen. In order for those things to happen, other things must be in place first.

Creating Conditions

If I want to grow vegetables, I must first have a garden and seeds and spend some time digging. The garden, the seeds, and the digging provide the conditions for vegetables. They are not the only conditions needed. Sunlight and water and soil nutrients are also needed, for example. Nor are these necessarily the only possible conditions that could give rise to vegetables—I could grow tomatoes in a grow-bag on my balcony or sprout alfalfa on my kitchen windowsill. But the vegetables cannot grow without something to grow in, and a garden provides the best conditions for this.

On the other hand, having a garden, seeds and digging is no guarantee of vegetables, as anyone who has tried gardening will know. Seeds can be eaten by birds or rot in wet soil or fail to germinate because the weather is too cold or too dry. Even if they grow, there is no guarantee of getting vegetables.

I remember one summer watching our first melon slowly swelling in the garden of our center in France. Day after day I imagined the sweet orange flesh inside the tight green skin, which seemed to stretch before my eyes. I marvelled at this perfect sphere as it sat in the middle of the bed, surrounded by the tangle of leaves and stems of the melon plants. I imagined how I would serve it as a special treat for the community, the first melon we had ever grown ourselves.

It was only when I finally decided to pick the melon that I discovered that it was unnervingly light. Indeed, the melon was completely hollow: an empty shell with a neat round hole in its base. The flesh had been completely stripped out from the skin with neat little chisel-like teeth marks. The hole in the melon's underside had been invisible while it was on the ground, but it had just fitted over the equally neat, small, round mouse-hole in the middle of the garden. Friend field mouse had got there first. Since that incident we have sat our melons on flat stones while they are growing.

So, providing conditions does not guarantee an outcome— but it does make the outcome possible and even likely. This is the teaching of dependent origination in its broader form (the teaching also has a narrow, twelve-link form, discussed later in this chapter). It is not a theory of cause and effect in a narrow sense of "A causes B." More correctly, one could say "A makes it possible for B to happen"—and also recognize that some-times C could also make B possible. Some conditions are essential. Others are simply conducive. You cannot have chickens without eggs, but you can sometimes have vegetables without soil. Working with others is often about providing conditions. You cannot make people change, or bring peace to groups which have been in conflict for centuries, or force countries to adopt more humane policies, however much you might like to; but you can provide conditions that are conducive to these things happening.

In Chapter 9, we saw how it becomes possible to experience good contact and offer quality attention to others when we are well grounded. The groundedness and the attention both provide conditions for us to hear one another in depth. In turn, these factors are conditioned by a number of other factors. These include our ability to be flexible in our listening, and our not becoming attached to particular opinions about what is being said. These in turn depend upon our ability to put aside self-preoccupation, our ability to keep focus and our level of insight into human experience.

Dependent Origination

The Buddha understood the process of dependent origination on the night of his enlightenment. The realization of the way in which things are conditioned, and how this conditioning process creates and perpetuates much unnecessary suffering, lay at the basis of that great shift of understanding which constituted his enlightenment experience. He presented this understanding in many of his key teachings.

The teaching of dependent origination has a broad form and a narrow form. We have already discussed the broad form of the teaching, which describes the process whereby certain conditions create the possibility for particular outcomes. Particular conditions make particular events likely, and all things depend on particular conditions for their existence. We will now turn to the narrow form of the teaching of dependent origination. This will serve to summarize the theory presented in the first half of this book, as well as offer insight into how such theory can be applied in practical ways.

The narrow form of the teaching is more specifically known as the Twelve Links of Dependent Origination. This theory consists of twelve statements, each of which says that one particular element conditions another, which in turn conditions the next. The statements form a cycle, the last item being the same as the first. The cycle is presented in different ways in different contexts; often the element at the start and the end of the cycle is avidya, or not seeing, but because the twelve links are presented with different starting/finishing points in some texts, it is indeed a circular rather than a linear process.

The word *pratyaya* occurs in each statement. This word

means "conditions" or "provides the conditions for." Each statement takes the form *A provides the conditions for B.* The "pratyaya" statements thus describe the conditioning process that was elaborated earlier, but in the teaching of the twelve links give specific instances of it. This implies neither inevitability nor single causation, but it does imply a sequential process.

The theory of dependent origination needs to be distinguished from the later Buddhist theories of interdependent co-arising, which emerged in the Chinese world. These latter theories, which lie behind such concepts as Thich Nhat Hanh's theory of *Interbeing* (Hanh 1974), introduce a non-temporal view of experience. They seem to be products of an influence deriving from other Chinese philosophies and do not appear to go back to the Buddha's original teachings. (For further elaboration of this point see David Brazier's book, *The New Buddhism* [Brazier 2001].) The theory of dependent origination is time-related; that is, there is a direction to the process. A conditions B, but B does not necessarily lead to A.

The teaching of dependent origination is itself subject to a number of interpretations. Commentarial sources written by early Buddhist scholars viewed the teaching as a description of the unenlightened process of *samsara*, the process whereby a person creates conditions in one life that lead to a particular rebirth in the next life. According to this interpretation, the teaching of dependent origination describes three lifetimes. Construction of mental factors in a past life gave rise to the present life, and clinging in this life in turn conditions rebirth in a next life. This process keeps the person locked into the cycle of existence and thus makes them open to existential suffering. The person clings to life and so suffers. The three-lifetime interpretation of dependent origination is embedded in a set of beliefs that sees the ultimate goal of spiritual practice as being to escape from the cycle of rebirth into personal extinction.

Although these beliefs are common to the Indian tradition, they are not necessary to Buddhist understanding. The Buddha frequently declined to be drawn on matters of metaphysics and was generally concerned about how people lived in their current lives. His teachings were very practical and emphasized skillful behavior rather than the assertion of beliefs. The interpretation of the teaching of dependent origination can readily be seen as a description of the conditioning process as it unfolds moment by moment. This seems more in keeping with the tenor of other Buddhist texts.

This latter form of interpretation has been more widely proffered in recent times and is advocated by a number of modern western scholars. In the context of this book, it fits the same pattern of understanding as the Buddha's other teachings and so seems to reflect his general intent.

A "this lifetime" approach supports the theory that the teaching of dependent origination, and the other key teachings of Buddhism including the skandha teaching, the Four Noble Truths, and the omnipresent factors, all describe different facets of a single process—namely, the process whereby one escapes from affliction or dukkha through mental conditioning. People rigidify their mentalities and limit their perception of the world, and thus they cling to the idea of an enduring self.

The Twelve Links of Dependent Origination are as follows:

avidya pratyaya samskara
samskara pratyaya vijnana
vijnana pratyaya nama-rupa
nama-rupa pratyaya shadayatana
shadayatana pratyaya sparsha
sparsha pratyaya vedana
vedana pratyaya trishna
trishna pratyaya upadana
upadana pratyaya bhava
bhava pratyaya jati
jati pratyaya jaramarana
jaramarana pratyaya avidya

Although this formulation looks daunting in Sanskrit, do not be put off. You have in fact already met many of the terms in it earlier in this book. The teaching covers the same area of theory that we have already explored. It is a fuller version of

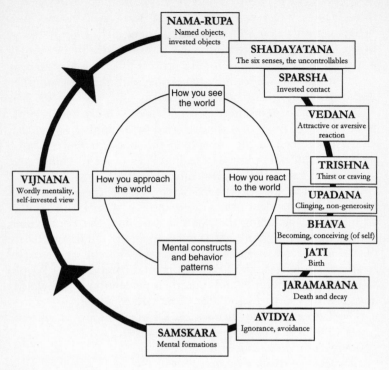

Figure 10.1

The twelve links of dependent origination, represented as a cycle

This representation demonstrates both the cyclical nature of this teaching and its comparison with the skandha process and other major Buddhist teachings. It is evident that this teaching particularly relates to the way in which one's approach to experience creates the self-invested mentality.

the same process theory as is described in the teaching of the skandhas. As such, this theory provides important additional information for understanding the skandha process, as well as confirmation of the process interpretation of the skandha teaching.

Let us look at the meaning of the phrases.

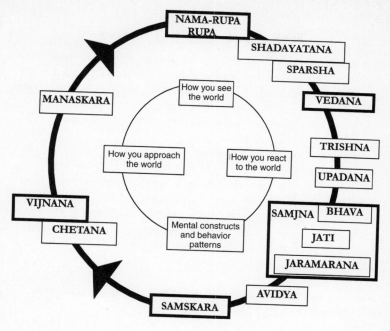

Figure 10.2

The skandha cycle with the twelve links and omnipresent factors added

This diagram shows all the elements from these three key Buddhist teachings, represented as a cyclical process.

Avidya Conditions Samskara

"Avidya" is often translated as "ignorance." Literally, it means ignoring or not seeing. Vidya means clear seeing. It is the enlightened view that sees everything. The prefix "a-" creates a negative form of the word. Avidya is deliberately not seeing things as they are. The distorting motive is self-concern.

Self-perspective is not really a single perspective. An individual may see things in different ways at different times. It is, rather, a limited perspective. It involves avoidance of certain other perspectives. People have an investment in not seeing certain things. They avoid seeing those things that are dukkha, and thus they create blinkers for themselves. These stop their seeing clearly.

Because people are in a state of avidya, they create samskaras, the proliferation of mental tracks that arise out of their unenlightened action. Samskaras are the constructions that people build in their minds as they try to make their experience yield evidence to support their self-construct. Because they hold on to the deliberately limited view, they build samskaras.

Samskaras Condition Vijnana

"Vijnana" means the self-invested mentality, the conditioned mind. The first two lines of the teaching of the Twelve Links, then, state that our motivated blindness to things as they are provides the ground for actions and mental formations that are fabrications. This in turn is ground on which a mentality centered on self can be sustained.

Vijnana Conditions Nama-Rupa; Nama-Rupa Conditions Shadayatana

The terms in these two phrases are already familiar. Vijnana, the conditioned mind, creates conditions for the perception of nama-rupas or named rupas. In other words, because your mind is conditioned, you label objects in particular ways. This labeling creates the conditions for the activity of the six uncontrollables (shadayatanas), which are the six senses. It conditions the process whereby they are drawn by certain objects. Recall the image of the senses as wayward forces, seeking out objects under their own volition. This teaching describes the process whereby the self-invested vijnana mentality maps out focuses of interest and encourages you to draw attention to certain objects. These processes involve grasping attention. The object you perceive is labeled. Your sense faculty then locks on to the sense object.

This first part of the cycle also includes three elements from the skandha process: samskaras condition vijnana, which conditions rupa. Notice too that in this sequence vijnana provides the conditions for nama-rupa. In other words, in this teaching the last skandha provides the conditions for the creation of the first skandha, corroborating the cyclical interpretation of the skandha process.

Shadayatana Conditions Sparsha; Sparsha Conditions Vedana

"Sparsha" means self-interested contacts, and "vedana" means positive or negative reactivity. Sparsha is one of the omnipresent factors, as is vedana, which is also one of the skandhas. Your senses grasp at the nama-rupa, creating contact. This conditions reactivity, in a process reminiscent of the image of the axe and block in the Ant Hill Sutra (see Chapter 7). That image described the sense locking onto its object. Sparsha is grasping contact. It is the product of unrestrained sense attachment. Vedana is the involuntary reaction that arises from this type of connection.

Vedana Conditions Trishna; Trishna Conditions Upadana

"Trishna" means "thirst" or "craving." The teaching of the Four Noble Truths suggests that trishna arises in response to dukkha. Craving or thirst drives the samudaya response. When you encounter dukkha, you experience craving which attaches to an object. In the context of the Twelve Links teaching, trishna arises in dependence upon vedana. It is the craving that follows the initial grasping response of vedana. You react to something by grasping or rejecting it, forming positive or negative attachments to that object; these provide the impetus for further grasping or attachment.

You can recognize this craving when it occurs in relation to strong reactions that you experience. When experiences arouse your emotions, you tend to get hooked by them. Buddhist theory also suggests that craving arises in smaller ways all the time.

A woman gets on a crowded bus. Someone else gets on who is smelly and unkempt. That person sits down next to her, taking up much of the seat so that she cannot avoid being in physical contact with him. The woman experiences a strong reaction to this unwelcome presence. It creates a craving to act. She wants to move, or perhaps even to get home and have a bath. Whether or not she is able to act on it, the reaction involves a strong physical impulse. At the extreme, such thoughts can become quite obsessive. She may not be able to put the urge to wash out of her mind. At this point she starts to cling to the thought of washing. This clinging is the next link of the chain.

"Upadana" is often translated as "clinging." Literally, it means non-generosity (Buddhists use the word *dana* to mean gifts, and specifically the gifts donated to support full-time practitioners). Thus, craving is the ground for an ungenerous attitude.

The elements of this part of the Twelve Link Chain are subject to the positive and negative valences which are presented as the Three Poisons, commonly known as greed, hate, and delusion (lobha, dvesha, and moha). In particular, vedana, trishna, and upadana are built directly on patterns of reactive grasping at, or pushing away, experience. These give rise to more persistent patterns of grasping, as bhava, jati, and jaramarana follow. Out of these, more generalized patterns of attachment arise to color the whole conditioned mentality.

Upadana Conditions Bhava; Bhava Conditions Jati; Jati Conditions Jaramarana

"Bhava" means "becoming" or "conceiving." As you cling to particular patterns of response and behavior, you start to create those mental structures that you think of as the self. "Jati" means birth. The process of conditioning creates a constellation of behaviors and perspectives to which you become attached. You identify with these patterns and think of them as "me."

Out of birth comes *jaramarana*, which means "decay-and-death-ness." Whatever self you give birth to, it will be the ground for jaramarana. On the night of his enlightenment, the Buddha struggled with Mara. Mara, whose name means Death, presented the Buddha with many terrifying and tempting sights. Plunged into the dark areas of his experience, the Buddha wrestled with temptations and fears. Facing these dark areas of experience provided him with the route to enlightenment. Such experiences can also, however, threaten to overwhelm you. Often you may try to hide your destructive aspects until they have grown to the point where you can no longer contain them.

There are parallels in the concept of jaramarana with the Jungian notion of the *shadow*. The public identity, or *persona*, it is suggested, is formed by rejecting certain aspects of the personality that are experienced as unacceptable. These parts of the personality Jung saw as creating a body of mental material called the shadow, made up of those aspects of experience that a person wants to disown. Jung considered that the shadow needed to be integrated for the person to achieve wholeness.

The Buddhist view is similar in that it suggests that you engage in a selective process, denying those aspects of experience that are painful. You experience dukkha and cut yourself off from it through selective perception and attachments. In favoring certain aspects of experience and identifying with them, you deny other aspects. These aspects of life do not go away, however. They always have the capacity to overwhelm and haunt you. They become distorted and compounded by your avoidance behavior. This is the experience of jaramarana. To break out of the cycle of self, you must face these dark forces. It is not easy. Yet, as much as you ignore these realities of life, they nevertheless come back and seem likely to destroy you.

Links between the Teaching of Dependent Origination and that of the Four Noble Truths

The teaching of dependent origination and the teaching of The Four Noble Truths are interconnected. Dukkha that is avoided compounds and manifests as jaramarana. This manifestation of destructive energy also occurs in the third level of samudaya. When destructive forces predominate, you fall into non-being.

The latter steps in the cycle of dependent origination reflect the different levels of the samudaya teaching. Samudaya represents the point of choice. When you experience dukkha, energy comes up in you and you feel craving (trishna). At this point, you have a choice. Either you face the dukkha and harness the energy—or else you retreat into the three levels of escape listed in the teaching on samudaya: sensory pleasure, becoming, or non-becoming.

In the teaching of dependent origination, these stages seem to be set out as a process. Trishna arises. From this, one may move first into upadana, which represents sensory clinging. The experience of the woman on the bus was a sensory response. She physically rejected the man and longed for physical distance from him and to get clean. In the teaching of samudaya, the next stage after the sensory response is bhava, or becoming. Bhava is also the next step in the cycle of dependent origination. Bhava is the creation of self-material or identity. The self is "conceived" and "born." This next step is jati. Finally, the creation of self condi-

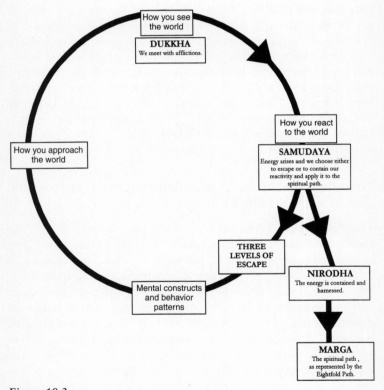

Figure 10.3

The teaching of the Four Noble Truths related to the basic skandha process

This diagram shows how, when one encounters dukkha, one can either be plunged into a cycle of avoidance or harness the reactive energy for spiritual growth.

tions the building up of destructive energy to jaramarana echoing the final stage of samudaya—*abhava* or non-being.

The cycle of dependent origination ends with the statement that jaramarana conditions avidya. Thus the cycle spells out a deep irony. An ungenerous attitude to life provides the ground for selfishness. Self-construction provides the ground for all the

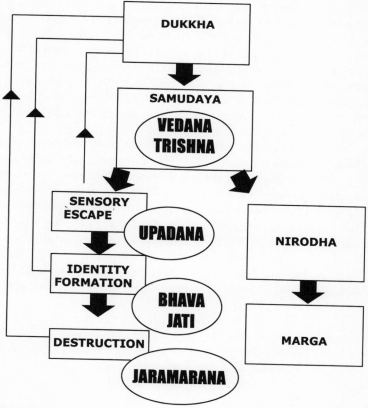

Figure 10.4

The three levels of samudaya and the teaching of dependent origination

The three levels of samudaya can be seen in the teaching of the twelve links of dependent origination. The whole cycle of the twelve links could be seen as dukkha.

misery covered by the term jaramarana. But it is precisely this misery that motivates people to shrink from seeing the world as it is and instead to build up false conditions (samskaras) that provide the ground upon which the ungenerous attitude rests.

Conditions for Change

Your mental states are highly dependent upon the conditions to which you are exposed. Buddhist psychology suggests that your mental process is far from being under your control. It has a way of running off into old thought patterns and behavioral tracks, one thought leading to the next and the next, until you are caught in quagmires of your own making. Depending on the life conditions that arise your mind will create differing levels of turmoil, out of which you create enough familiar behavior to feel a sense of identity.

You are exposed to conditions all the time, and these give rise to predominating patterns of response. Thus your mentality is conditioned. Some of these conditions you create, but there are many over which you have little choice. Some conditions are limiting and move you toward a narrowing of perception. Other conditions are enabling, encouraging you to open your heart in new ways. Enabling conditions are the precursors to change, and the creation of such conditions is an important aspect of engaged Buddhist practice. Providing the right conditions does not, of itself, create change. It *does* make change more likely.

The remainder of this chapter will explore particular examples of conditions that can be created. While you have little control over your mental activities themselves, you can exercise some choice about what conditions you expose yourself to. In particular, three types of condition are significant in their effects, and each represents a different area of experience. They are the conditions provided by significant interpersonal relationships, by the physical environment you inhabit, and by the story you tell yourself about your own life. The discussion here will necessarily be brief but will be expanded upon in future chapters. Later in the chapter, we will look at some more specific conditions that are necessary for psychological change to become possible.

Relationship as a Condition

The American psychologist Dr. Carl Rogers identified three core conditions which he saw as essential to providing an environment conducive to beneficial personal change: accurate empathy; congruence (i.e. straightforwardness, being what we appear to be); and unconditional positive regard. He concluded that a person in whose environment these conditions were present could be trusted to grow in his or her own way. Rogers saw human process as benevolent and the potential for growth as a basic human tendency. He applied these principles in many settings: in counselling, in education, in groupwork and in activism for peace.

Developing the ability to offer the core conditions involves developing trust in the process of change and willingness to let go of personal agendas. Spiritual practice can help you to engage in such a process insofar as its focus is on transcending self. Buddhism, with its emphasis on compassion and stillness, seems to proffer a similar view of necessary conditions and, in its aim of clear seeing (*vidya*), to share a vision of direct person-to-person encounter.

Buddhism has always seen relationship as of primary importance in the spiritual journey. Fundamentally, Buddhism is about your relationship with the Buddha. This relationship is seen as fundamental to the training process. The spiritual practitioner frequently works with a teacher to develop her spiritual training. The teacher–disciple bond is often an enduring and challenging alliance, continuing over many years, which supports the trainee and allows transmission of teaching in an experiential rather than simply intellectual form. The Dharma is transmitted from heart to heart.

As discussed in Chapter 9, the quality of your relationships depends upon your ability to let go of the clamor of self and to ground yourself in contact with your physical world. Your ability to let go of self-absorption can grow through a relationship of the kind offered by a teacher or therapist. As the deep encounter of such enduring and committed relationships occurs, so you start to move out of your attachments to self. You move into relationship with someone who is truly other, as opposed to being a player in your self-story. We will return to the theme of encounter as a manifestation of the teaching of non-self in Chapter 12.

Environment as a Condition

The spaces in which you live and operate condition your mental states. A space that is suitable for one sort of activity may be completely unsuitable for other events. Aspects of the space that on the face of it seem quite trivial may in fact have considerable influence upon your ability to do what is needed.

If you think, for example, about working environments, you will realize how much the aesthetics of a space influences our mood. Bright colors, fresh air, and good light quality all create conditions for lively thought. Dark, dingy conditions can depress you. Similarly, you are affected by levels of comfort. Too much comfort, and you may become too relaxed to focus on the task you are supposed to be undertaking; too little, and you spend much of our time avoiding work and complaining to ourselves and others. Other factors, such as the timing of events, the presence of other people, the sense of privacy or its absence, all contribute to the conditions that a work environment provides, and in consequence affect the quality of what you do. Many large organizations, especially where they are marketing to the public, put a great deal of energy into researching environmental conditions. In supermarkets and other stores, for example, psychologists are employed to suggest lighting arrangements, shelf layout, and color schemes to encourage customers to spend money.

At the same time, your view of any environment is selective. If your mind is conditioned in certain ways, you will see certain things. Two people entering the same room will have quite different views of it—just like the house-hunting couple in Chapter 4. Depending on your predominating mentality, you will be more likely to find any particular environment stimulating, depressing, pleasant, or ugly. It is therefore not entirely true to say that changing the environment will automatically have certain effects. On the contrary, to an enlightened being all environments will be beautiful. This is why we can talk of Buddhas living in the Pure Land (of which more will be said later in this chapter).

Having said this, we can consider the external environments we inhabit and look at ways to make them more supportive of good mental states. Creating calm and uncluttered spaces may offer oases of peace for yourself and those around you, contributing to quieter mental states. This subject will be addressed in more depth in Chapter 14.

The Story as a Condition

Everyone has their story. The personal story is a particular expression of the self-structures, closely related to self-image. It is a myth about how the current self has come into being. It may also be a myth about the person's present and future situations. The story of the self differs from the original lived experience in that it is always highly interpreted and selective. It is as if you take an assemblage of details from your past history and embroider them into a picture in which you are the central player, cast in whatever role seems to best fit with your current identity. The self-story is a creative and dynamic process. As your current mentality changes, so too, you write and rewrite your history, becoming perhaps the victim on one occasion, the hero on another. Events and personalities become significant markers in the tale. A single interaction may symbolize a relationship. A single day may represent a summer. You pass the images before your mind's eye and are in turn affected by them. That which is recorded in your personal history becomes larger than life, pregnant with implications. All describes, and ultimately creates, the self.

The self-story is a dialogue. It is the accumulation of images from which you construct personal meaning and thus insulate yourself from potential unexpected dangers. By telling the tale, you rehearse your abilities to cope with adversity and to fall on your feet in difficult circumstances.

The self-story and other personal mythology create powerful conditions. Through the story, you create and maintain identity. This may dictate how you anticipate experience, act, and subsequently interpret those actions. Becoming aware of the self-stories you are carrying allows you to review this situation. As you become more aware in this way, you may change the story or work to break free of its limiting aspects.

Creating a Working Container

To step beyond the limits you have created for yourself, you need to find an environment conducive to change. This environment acts as a psychological container: the stronger the container, the more powerful the experiences that can be contained within it. As in our earlier examination of the Ant Hill Sutra, the forces that lie near to the spiritual energy may be primitive and dangerous.

Nirodha, the third Noble Truth, is the truth of containment. If you unhook yourself from the objects of your compulsiveness, as the samudaya teaching suggests, energy arises that can be reapplied in positive ways. Containment is the key to spiritual and psychological transformation. It allows energy to be harnessed and diminishes your attachment to damaging patterns of behavior. Eventually you need to find that containment in your everyday world, but, while you are developing your capacity to do so, you need the help of a supportive environment.

Buddhist training provides a number of methods for containment. Through personal discipline, the trainee learns to contain reactivity and harness energy for spiritual growth. Containment is like the creation of a dam around an area of water. The walls must be strong enough to resist erosion and allow the water level to rise. As this happens, the water ceases being a raging torrent and becomes deep and still. At the same time, a dam will stand only if there is some controlled outlet for the water. If the pressure is left to build indefinitely, the dam will eventually give way. When the dam is well managed, however, its energy can be harnessed to turn turbines and generate electricity, or it can be directed into the places it is needed—through irrigation schemes or treatment plants, for example.

Working with a therapist, you can also experience containment. The presence of the therapist, if it provides sufficient intensity of attention and unconditional caring, offers an environment in which psychological transformation can take place. As this happens, on the one hand, defenses diminish and aspects of experience intensify. You feel emotion more keenly. On the other hand, as the therapist listens, responds, and reflects on what she has heard, you hear your own story told back to you in a different way. You see it as if you were listening to the story told by another, and consequently you come to question the tenor and details of your self-story. Having his words and feelings mirrored to you in therapy, you can come to see yourself as you are seen, in a less subjective way, developing *special objectivity*. In effect, you becomes *other* to yourself. You loosen your attachment to seeing yourself as a special case and see yourself and your process in the broader context of the world.

Structure and Containment

In the therapy situation, a great deal of importance is put upon the creation of boundaries. These might include having fixed time limits for sessions, regularity of meetings, and demarcation of the role the therapist will play. Some boundaries are ethical. Others are norms of practice that have evolved through time. When someone experiences chaotic or intense feelings, providing a structure within which to work can be helpful. Having an agreed limit to the time spent together can be reassuring, as the person knows that there will be a limit to the process. It also creates an impetus to use the time well. This creates the intensity needed for real psychological change to occur. Having a regular schedule for meetings of this type can provide further containment to the process, as the person will know that feelings that are aroused following any one session can be dealt with subsequently.

Spiritual training also frequently takes place in a structured environment. In a residential community or a monastic setting, time may be tightly organized, with set periods devoted to spiritual practice, work, communal meals, and even prescribed reading. The practitioner has little opportunity to fall into habitual patterns of escape and in consequence is constantly facing uncomfortable aspects of his or her reactivity. This kind of training has great value, not least in showing you just how much you still fall short of the ideal to which you aspire. Illusions of a comfortable identity fall away and fallibility becomes ever more apparent. These experiences can be uncomfortable, but they provide the potential for important growth points, at which old habit-patterns start to be relinquished.

Other settings offer less formal limits but may still provide circumstances in which caring interactions can take place. Such situations often require higher levels of self-discipline and ethical vigilance on the part of those who are in caring roles. In our community, we are frequently involved in work in informal helping situations. Here roles and boundaries can be a lot more complicated.

Often, we meet people who stay in our community for a period of time, or participate in projects or events which we support. Here, we may have multiple relationships. We may sit down to breakfast together in the morning, and talk about important personal or spiritual issues later in the day. In such relationships, a higher level of personal involvement and disclosure is likely than that which happens in more conventional therapeutic relationships. Time boundaries may not exist in the same way as they do in the formal therapy relationship, and observing confidentiality may be more complicated. At the same time, the transformation a person can experience in such circumstances is often every bit as deep as, or even deeper than, it is in regular therapy sessions.

When offering containment in such a setting, we try to be aware of the psychological impact of interactions that take place. The more effective the helping relationship, the bigger will be the impact of the behavior of the person who is in the helping role on the person receiving help will be. We keep a careful watch to try to ensure that our actions do not compromise the other person's psychological and spiritual growth. In other words, when living with others with whom we have a caring role of this kind, there is a level at which we always preserve awareness of the other person's psychological needs and the effect of our actions upon them. This is a discipline, and also it is part of our own spiritual training.

One aspect of this kind of work is simply our ability and willingness not to get drawn into patterns of avoidance. If we interact in a straight way, we offer the possibility for others to do likewise. Thus we do not get drawn into the kind of collective behaviors that avoid uncomfortable experiences and limit the intensity with which people live. Most social interaction avoids intensity, and people are well schooled in diffusing uncomfortable and embarrassing emotions. Jokes, platitudes, dismissive remarks, and changing the subject are all common ways in which people steer conversations away from what is psychologically meaningful. Often the person making these remarks is not even aware that a difficult topic has been avoided. People protect themselves and one another from facing uncomfortable subjects. Such responses are second nature. If you want to live more fully, you can allow yourself to experience intensity in communication. You can train yourself to notice when you are avoiding difficult feelings and cease doing so.

So creating conditions for change often involves creating a psychologically containing structure. This may be done through the external discipline of the spiritual community or within the boundaries of a therapeutic relationship. Within either structure, encounter takes place. Finding a structure within which to work is often a first step to change. The process may not be easy, but be wary also of too prolonged a search. If you are continually dissatisfied with what is available, it may be that you are simply seeking an environment that supports your existing self-structures rather than challenging them. On the other hand, it is important to be able to trust the environment you choose to work in—to trust that it will provide a safe and effective container, sufficient for you to let your habitual defenses go.

Faith and Trust

The most important condition for spiritual and personal change is your ability to trust. If you do not trust, you remain isolated in your self-world. You create barriers against others and build ever stronger defenses. When you start to trust others, you start to let go of these barriers and to open yourself to experience. In spiritual practice, faith and trust are of great importance. Trust is the first step in the process of acquiring faith. It involves tentatively reaching out from your self-prison to place confidence in another person or situation. Faith gives you confidence to step through the door of that prison into the world. It gives you the confidence to open yourself to whatever experiences life brings. Through developing trust in another person or situation, you develop faith. If you have faith, you live in confidence that the world is not basically hostile. If you have faith, you can trust that things will ultimately unfold in the way they will, and that this will be all right. Faith is not a bland assumption that everything is good in the world or that nothing needs to be done, but it is about having confidence that there is something fundamentally trustworthy in the unfolding life process.

Faith, for Buddhists, involves having specific confidence in the Buddha and his teachings. It also involves having faith in the vision of the enlightened world, what we call the Pure Land. The Pure Land is both the radiant world that a Buddha sees and the vision of what this world can be. It is the miracle of everyday life, which we miss because we are wrapped in our self-interests; and it is the potential world that will come into existence if enough of us can step out of our narrow perceptions into a wider perspective.

Faith is something that people support in one another. When you are with those who have lost faith, it may be vital that they see that you have not given up faith too. You can cultivate your faith in life through your vision of a better world. You develop your faith in the process of transformation that will bring a better world into being. To do this, you need to have made some progress yourself in psychological and spiritual work. Through this experience, you convey confidence to others that change is possible. You can cultivate your faith in the possibility of personal change. This faith grows through your experience of your own progress and that of others and through your coming to know others better and recognize the hidden strengths they have.

The process of growth is not an individual path. Offering a caring environment to others and following your own spiritual training are not different things. As you reach out to others, you are engaging in spiritual practice. Increasing your awareness of the needs of others, you discover and eliminate your own blocks and attachments. The engaged Buddhist path includes traditional practices, but the practices you evolve in helping others may well be those that change you most deeply. This is the point. Through engaged practice you mature spiritually and psychologically; and, as you do so, you create and inhabit a more beautiful world.

THEORIES INTRODUCED IN THIS CHAPTER

- dependent origination, broad theory;
- dependent origination, Twelve Links; and
- conditions for spiritual and psychological growth.

· 11 ·

Inspiration and Change

Creating conducive conditions is important to the process of psychological change. To move beyond the limitations that you have created through the processes of conditioning explored in this book, you must work with these conditions. You can change both the external circumstances of your life, and the psychological landscape to which you expose yourself.

There are many methods in Buddhism for training the mind, both through mental exercises and through practical activity. Such methods require effort and diligence. The path of such training is not generally an easy or fast route. It is what is referred to as the path of self-power. So far, Part Two of this book has been largely concerned with what would be broadly thought of as self-power methods—methods that rely upon the practitioner's willpower and commitment to training.

There is, however, a paradox in trying to overcome self-structures through self-power methods. If the aim is to reach a point of full engagement with the otherness of the world, to try to achieve this through working in isolation seems counterproductive. Even practiced in community, an approach that relies solely on self-power still places great emphasis on individual achievement.

In fact, self-power is only one side of the coin. It may prepare the ground and create conditions in which you are more open and receptive to opportunities that arise. To break out of self-absorption, however, you must allow yourself to be touched by something beyond yourself. You are reached by the other. You become inspired. This is the path referred to as "other-power." In other-power, the individual is seen to achieve change not through his own efforts but rather through the love of the Buddha, as manifested in the world. He is embraced by life.

Inspiration lifts a person out of self-preoccupation. When you are inspired, you feel appreciative and become purposeful. This chapter will look at inspiration and the way in which inspiration and aspiration work together to create energy for change. Inspiration and aspiration are intimately linked. Each leads to the development of the other. If you are inspired, you will develop higher aspirations. If you cultivate high aspiration, you are likely to open yourself to inspiration when it occurs.

Aspiration grows from longing. It is about the part of you that already yearns for a spiritually better life, a spiritually better world. It is about the deep impulse we all share toward whole-some connection with that world. It is about childhood nights gazing at faraway galaxies and reaching out in spirit across the universe. It is about gazing deeply into another's eyes and the wonder of making real contact. We all have deep longing in our hearts.

With this longing, there follows a sense of devotion and reverence. The thought of contacting the object of our longing is so precious that we feel deep gratitude as we imagine it. Our hearts soften and reach out. If we are lucky, at some point our longing finds connection. We are touched by something that inspires us. It may be a person or an idea, a scene or a situation. When we are so inspired, longing transforms into aspiration that flows out from us. We are no longer simply searching, but instead feel drawn to live in fuller, better ways. We feel drawn to seek a nobler path.

To understand the difference between aspiration and the grasping intention that seeks personal ends, return to the teachings of the omnipresent and the rare factors (see Chapter 6). As a person moves from the deluded to the transformed state, intentionality (chetana) becomes aspiration (chanda), and attention (manaskara) becomes reverence (adhimoksha). The word "chetana" suggests self-seeking intentionality, and the word "manaskara" self-interested attention; both words describe processes that are involved in the accumulation of self-material. They describe grasping intention and grasping attention. The corresponding rare factors, aspiration and reverence (chanda and adhimoksha) on the other hand, are responses that do not grasp. Indeed, they are not self-directed at all. They involve opening up the natural flow of our hearts. In developing aspiration, you allow your longing to be satisfied, and in developing reverence you allow your natural gratitude to well up.

There is a relationship between the omnipresent or common factors and the rare factors. Chetana transforms into chanda. Manaskara transforms into adhimoksha. In this, each common factor contains the seed of the corresponding rare factor, overlaid by layers of self-material. In the self-centered intentionality of chetana are buried the possibilities of higher aspiration. In the self-invested perspective of manaskara is buried the appreciative reverence of adhimoksha—and so on. It is only fear that causes one to lose faith and build defenses, blocking the emergence of these higher qualities.

Aspiration and the Unobtainable

Buddhism encourages you to aspire higher. The object of aspiration may be far beyond your grasp. In accepting this, you experience the failure of effort. You recognize how impotent you really are to effect what you set yourself to do. This experience is an important part of preparing yourself for the inspirational encounter. You have to recognize the limitations of the self. It is as if the practice calls your bluff. Secretly, the self wants perfection; so, in making perfection your aim, you test yourself. There is always a part of you that believes itself to be omnipotent. This primitive self is constantly ambitious and seeking aggrandizement. In setting impossible targets, this self strives to accomplish the unattainable and inevitably fails.

One example of a practice that creates this sort of deliberately unattainable aspiration is the bodhisattva vow. Common to many Buddhist traditions, it expresses the ideal of transcending self through service to others. This ideal is embodied in the image of the bodhisattva, who personifies good qualities, and is entirely devoted to the good of sentient beings. One of the best-known bodhisattvas is Avalokistishvara, bodhisattva of compassion, who in her Chinese form is the female Buddha Quan Yin.

Quan Yin is said to have toiled for many aeons, trying to relieve suffering in the world, but at the end of that time she was dismayed to discover that there were just as many suffering beings as when she started. At this point she was so distraught that she shattered into a thousand pieces. The Buddha Amida came to her rescue, putting her back together but giving her wisdom to accompany her compassion. Some images of this new, wiser Quan Yin are depicted with many heads. Quan Yin is no longer limited to one form, but takes whatever form is needed in a given situation.

The allegory in this story represents the giving up of rigidity of self, which comes when you set yourself superhuman goals, then fail to achieve them.

The bodhisattva is committed to the altruistic path and vows not to enter nirvana until all sentient beings are saved:

Innumerable are sentient beings, I vow to save them all.
Inexhaustible are deluded passions, I vow to transform
them all.
Immeasurable are the Dharma teachings, I vow to
master them all.
Infinite is the Buddha's way, I vow to fulfill it completely.

Taking the bodhisattva vow is an act of affirmation, putting into words the practitioner's aspiration. The vow is not intended to be literally capable of fulfillment. Rather, it touches the deeply felt longing which already lies in the person's heart and helps to create a channel for its expression through enlightened action.

Buddhist training creates conditions which lead to the development of faith and to commitment. It trusts that from these conditions, good outcomes will occur.

Buddhist teaching is sometimes described as a finger pointing toward the moon. You can see the direction, but you cannot touch the moon itself. Touching the moon itself is not the point. If you did touch it, you would find it was no longer the shining orb with which you are so familiar but a dusty, lifeless expanse stretching out to a far-off horizon. So too, the bodhisattva ideal is never literally attainable. Attainability is not necessary for something to be inspirational. The moon has been a source of wonder to many, yet to be inspirational, it needs to remain distant.

The bodhisattva vow creates vision despite, perhaps because of, its extremity. It awakens the potential for good in the practitioner and opens up possibilities for deeper engagement with others.

Always Going Beyond

Through holding an aspiration for the unattainable, one senses a direction of growth. In this respect, vision is important not as a goal, but as the source of inspiration. It is the spark that enables the moment of conception, not an end-point that will be reached. In other words, the importance of having vision is that it provides energy, motivation, and a sense of purposeful direction for you now.

If you are to progress, you must constantly be transcending your achievements. If you reach a point of feeling that you have arrived, complacency sets in; training ceases, and there is a danger that you may become convinced of your own skills and knowledge. You may stop being open to others, becoming caught up in self-congratulation.

Buddhism teaches you not to attach to your achievements. As soon as you feel you are getting somewhere with your practice, you need to become wary. When you think we have succeeded in doing what you set out to do, you need to get beyond that feeling and recognize the dangers of self-satisfaction. The end-point is always ahead. You can always go further. The eye must be on the horizon, not the feet. This is central to all Buddhist teaching.

In the Heart Sutra, the enlightened ones are described as those who have "gone beyond." The path to enlightenment means continually transcending self. Reciting the Heart Sutra, one is reminded of that need to go beyond all the common mind-states and even the key teachings of Buddhism itself. The concluding mantra summarizes this final state of complete transcendence:

> *gate, gate, paragate, parasamgate, bodhi svaha*
>
> *(Gone, gone, gone beyond*
> *Always gone beyond, awakened, Svaha!)*

Developing Aspiration

How do you develop aspiration? The teaching of the common and rare factors gives you some indication. Consider the difference between chetana and chanda. Chetana is goal-orientated intentionality, whereas chanda is aspiration.

Many people think they are developing vision when they set themselves goals. "I'm really going to go for that job." "I'm going to save up for a holiday in the Far East." "I want to go out with Mary." These goals often have more to do with maintaining the self-structure than transcending it. There are varying degrees of self-investment in them. They are part of a person's individual story. Yet the common factors contain within them the seeds of the rare factors. So, within these personal agendas, lie buried seeds of higher possibilities. There is potential for releasing locked-up energy through discovering buried aspiration.

Aspiration results from contact with a higher vision. It transcends personal agendas. It might arise through inspirational contact with a spiritual or religious tradition, or it might come from involvement in a social movement or contact with a great leader or teacher. Such meetings can provide the spark that lifts you out of the self-invested position and gives you the aspiration to make something of your life. This can happen in big ways, as you take on a completely new life direction, or in smaller ways, as you change some particular aspect of your behavior. When you are with people who are disadvantaged or distressed, helping them to find vision can be the route to change and healing. Try to listen carefully to their stories and hear within them whatever shreds of vision and aspiration remain. Find ways to water these shoots so that the person's inspiration grows. At the same time, in hearing their experiences and the courage that it has taken for them to come to the point of sharing them, you may be inspired yourself, fostering your aspiration to be of use.

Inspiration and Purpose

Inspiration creates a sense of purpose. To live with purpose is the enactment of higher aspiration. To understand the process whereby your life take on purpose, you can create a five-stage model.

We all feel longing in our hearts, but we often block it through our defensive patterns. If we allow it to grow, however, longing creates the channel through which we can allow ourselves to be inspired. The longing grows from within and inspiration comes from without. These two elements operate together cyclically to intensify one another. As longing grows, we search out and find inspirational experiences; and, as such experiences occur, the sense of longing increases. This is a common process in spiritual practice.

The process can be deliberately entered through, for example, adopting a particular inspirational image as focus for devotional practice. As the image becomes more meaningful, the feeling of longing for it increases. As the longing increases, your mind becomes more centered on that vision.

As the cycle of longing and inspiration intensifies, aspiration develops. Through watering the seeds of longing and inspiration, you discover aspiration. Aspiration is a higher state of mind—the "vow mind." From aspiration emerges the vow. The vow is the natural distillation of the spirit of longing. The energy

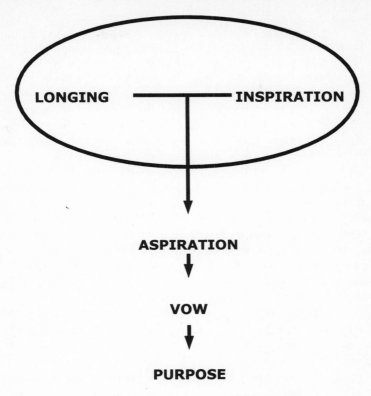

Figure 11.1: Developing purposefulness: a five-stage model

that has built up in the heart crystallizes into a decision to act. The vow is a decision taken with the heart. It becomes the directional force in a person's life. A formal example of this would be the bodhisattva vow referred to earlier, which may be taken by the practitioner to reflect the feeling of aspiration in her heart, but many vows are more personal.

The four elements—longing, inspiration, aspiration and vow—can be represented in relationship. Together they lead to purposefulness. Purposefulness is the dedication of the vow to action. It is the application of the vow mind in positive activity.

Primal Longing

Many people already have a strong sense of longing. It may be openly expressed or it may be hidden. When you are living comfortably, the self-structures are often well developed and it may be hard to detect any motivation for change or growth. Attention may be embedded in everyday interests and concerns and in fulfilling social roles and obligations. As in the Ant Hill Sutra in Chapter 7, the higher levels of socialization can be a long way from the spiritual heart of the psyche.

It is, ironically, at points when the comfortable life starts to go wrong that there may be opportunities to discover deeper longings and aspirations. Points of crisis can provide a window of opportunity. At such times, if a person seeks help from a therapist or spiritual counselor, it may be an indication that he is seeking a more meaningful life. For some people, the impulse is simply to rebuild the comfort of familiar identity structures, but others gain a glimpse of other possibilities. Such moments can be fleeting, the possibilities imperfectly formed. The longing is often expressed in quite limited terms. It is more likely to be expressed in a self-interested way, as intentionality, or chetana, than as aspiration, or chanda. Nevertheless, such intention has within it the seeds of that deeper transcendent longing, and there may at this point be opportunities to release higher aspirations.

Because the person who is in distress probably feels overwhelmed by life, it is likely that they are in flight. The flight response is the samudaya phase of the process taught by the Buddha in the teaching on the Four Noble Truths. At this stage the person may avoid the experiencing of dukkha on one of three levels. The longing that drives a person's intentionality may be at the level of sensual pleasures: a better house, a meal in a restaurant, a new car, a foreign holiday. It may be at the level of identity formation: longing for fame, recognition, or achievement of a certain career path. Or it may be at the level of longing for self-destruction and oblivion, whether through suicide, self-harm, or excessive use of alcohol or other numbing drugs. The problem with all these manifestations of longing is that their underlying motivation is concerned with avoiding experience. In this, they are all part of the self-prison. They involve a limiting of the life energy and a narrowing of life possibilities.

Underlying these longings and disguised by them, however, is a different and opposite, life-embracing force, which is directed outward and onward. This force is the *primal longing*. Though most of us have difficulty putting such a longing into words—and indeed, it is beyond verbalization—many people have some inkling of its presence. There are few people who are not moved by the natural world or by the most intimate sharing of human experience, whether tragic or loving. There are few people who do not feel some opening of the heart at the birth of a baby or in the presence of a great person. Even in popular entertainment, the soaps and tabloids trade on the fact that people are emotionally stirred by the great events of life. Birth, death, sexuality, marriage, human connection, natural events such as storms and volcanic eruptions, the beauty of the sunset, the drama of a solar eclipse are all subjects that catch the headlines. Such themes are not so different from those found in religious writing and imagery.

Cultivating Longing

Recognizing and fostering your sense of longing may help to create the conditions for change. The focus of the longing is less important than the experience of the longing itself. All longing is a distortion of the primal longing, which, as noted above, is itself hard to frame in words. Yet narrow expressions of longing lead into traps, establishing unhelpful habit-energies and creating more layers of self. Longing expressed through such a focus is often too contaminated with self or sensory elements to feed aspiration. Loosening your focus on ambition or acquisitiveness may help to intensify the helpful aspects of the experience and create space for a more aspirational vision to emerge. Exploration of the experiential aspects of longing, detached from such self-invested focuses, may bring you into contact with its primal levels.

Such an experience of longing can be very physical. A little while ago, I was sitting with a man who was in considerable distress, talking about his dissatisfaction with life. As I listened, I became aware of an intense hunger in my chest near to my heart. The feeling was very powerful, and at first I identified it as sadness. This did not feel quite right, so I asked myself again what I was feeling. This time I realized that it had a much more outwardly directed quality to it. I looked for an image. It felt almost like a hand reaching out from my heart—an open, begging hand.

As I sat with the man and with the image, I began to recognize a yearning in the sadness. The feeling was not directly connected with the subject he was talking about at the time, nor was it unconnected, so I shared my experience, describing what I had been feeling as I listened. This sharing did not come as a surprise to my companion. He recognized the feeling I was describing. We talked about the feeling of longing and the desire that he had to live a more spiritually based life. He had always had a sense of wanting something different, yet he had been driven by ambition and the need to meet goals which had more to do with his parents' expectations than his own. Letting go of these driving pressures felt frightening but also exciting. He longed for the faith to trust his dreams and let go of the way of life that was imprisoning him.

Many people lack vision. Although the feeling of longing may arise, it is hard to know what to do with it if there is no vision to direct it toward. Longing can easily become distorted into craving and can lead a person into seeking comfort from sensory pleasures. This is the pattern of addiction. It is not surprising, given the physicality of the longing one can feel. It is all too easy to try to satisfy the feeling of hunger, like that I experienced with this man, through food or drink.

Developing longing is a common Buddhist practice. The longing is generally directed toward an inspirational object or vision, for example a teacher, the Buddha, the Pure Land. Longing and its object go hand in hand. So how do you find suitable images to give direction to your longings, so that those longings become the fuel of transformation rather than a hindrance to change? How can you support other people in cultivating aspiration?

In particular, you need to bear in mind that an inspirational vision is rarely intended to be realistic. Inspiration comes more often from dreaming of the impossible than from planning the inevitable. There is therefore great value in expansive thinking and building dreams. In our rational, modern society, when someone starts to talk about travelling the world, or giving up his career to work with the homeless, or dropping out in order to become a rock star, others around him immediately panic and begin a process of reality testing. They soon conclude that the person is simply being escapist, unrealistic, and irresponsible, and put pressure on him to change his mind and settle down to a more realistic goal.

There is a place for reality testing and challenge, but there is also a place for dreams. Aspiration, at its root, is about the intention to act in certain ways. Dreams can provide a symbol for this intention. None of my teenage friends ever became pop stars, as far as I am aware, but some gained great confidence and enjoyed life a lot more fully by imagining they might one day achieve fame.

In Buddhist training there are often instances where aspirations are deliberately made that are impossible to fulfill. When a person takes the bodhisattva vow, she knows it to be unattainable. And yet, although aspiration is expressed in grandiose, global terms, it can still change the way the person who takes the vow acts. The application of the vow may take much more mundane forms than the wording of the original vow might suggest. A person vows to save all sentient beings—and begins to put it into practice by not being rude to her partner.

Similarly, a person may dream of backpacking around the world and, at the same time, work to tackle the agoraphobia that is preventing him from venturing out to the shopping mall. As the dream of backpacking becomes more vivid, he may come to the point where some of the fear drops away and he spontaneously feels more able to leave his house. There is, of course, a danger that a dream can become an escape rather than a true source of aspiration. He needs to guard against the image of the backpacking journey becoming an escape from reality. The aspiration must be felt as real, even though he recognizes that it may not happen. He must both hold the dream and tackle day-to-day living. Vision and effort need to be brought together.

The dreams that people have are often altruistic. It is not fashionable to make helping others one's life purpose, except in rather restricted high-status circumstances. Members of the British Royal Family or television celebrities may appear in the press with famine victims or war orphans; but giving up a comfortable lifestyle and career to work in uncertain circumstances often meets with less social approval. It can be easy to dismiss such dreams as unrealistic fantasy. Sometimes, however, such dreams do become reality. Who would have thought that a lone woman with little money and a bicycle could set up a health project in Zambia that would serve more than sixty villages? Yet a member of our community has done just that. Even if the dream does not prove realistic, in exploring such ideas we often find that our longing is for a better world and may find real ways to make a difference. The primal longing is outwardly directed. As it begins to become apparent, aspiration grows and reverence for life deepens.

Inspiration through Encounters

Inspiration arises out of encounters. You meet with people with situations or ideas that change your life. Such encounters can be very powerful, and their effects can stay with you for years. I have vivid memories of two encounters I had on different occasions in my teens. Each was with a visiting speaker brought into my school. Each meeting lasted less than an hour. I still remember both scenes vividly and recall the feeling that arose in me. Both occasions were completely absorbing. I was entirely lost in the experience.

On the first occasion, the speaker was a Theravadin monk. I remember nothing of what he said, but I do remember that he started off by chanting. As sixteen-year-old girls, we were, to my ongoing shame, overwhelmed with embarrassment and giggles. He continued chanting, unaffected by our bad manners. Some girls stuffed handkerchiefs in their mouths and others tried to sink down in their seats so that they would be hidden by the girls who were sitting in front of them. I was on the front row and couldn't hide my reactions so easily. I just sat there blushing and trying, with rather limited success, to hide the reaction that was threatening to well up in me at any moment. The little man just kept chanting. Here we were in complete emotional disarray, and he was unaffected. Gradually we all fell quiet. A deep feeling of peace descended over our classroom. The rest of the lesson we sat, silently absorbing we knew not what. The lesson ended and we came out into the spring sunshine changed a little. I cannot know if that first encounter with Buddhism was a step that put me on a Buddhist path many years later, but certainly the memory has stayed with me.

The second occasion was a couple of years later when, in the course of a senior class lecture series, we were visited by a speaker from the Teilhard de Chardin Society. This speaker talked about the ideas of the great theologian after whom the society is named. For the hour of the lecture I listened, transfixed. I felt connected to the speaker by what felt like a channel of direct heart-to-heart communication. Here the ideas being shared seemed to turn my mind inside out and uplift me on to a level of thinking I had not experienced previously. They brought together ideas and concepts that I had never thought could be brought together. Perhaps it was the idea of the evolution of the spirit that touched me so deeply. I had just been studying advanced level biology at the time, and had then, as now, a deep sense of the process of the natural world. At the same time, I struggled with the subject of religion, both longing for faith and doubting the beliefs I was expected to take on. This man's ideas took the process of life and elevated the evolutionary model into the sphere of the metaphysical. It took my mundane interest in studying the living world and within it found the seeds of a visionary model. That night I rushed home and in great excitement found a book of de Chardin's writings on my father's bookshelf. I tried to read it but, to my great disappointment, found it completely unintelligible. This did not, however, diminish my sense of inspiration, which stayed alive in me for years afterward.

Looking back, neither of these instances actually converted me to a way of thinking. I discovered in Buddhism, years later, some of what I had sought in those teenage years. Recently I have read and been thrilled by some of de Chardin's more inspirational writings. In those two experiences, though, I encountered something that touched me deeply at a level that brought together emotion and intellect. They awakened in me an experiential connection with a dimension of life that I hungered for. They fired me with a sense of almost overwhelming possibility, a powerful, clamoring longing for more.

Such points of experience do not come often, but their effects stay with us. Most of us have such moments in our bank of memories. As we think back over such encounters, we may uncover inspiration that has not been talked of for years and discover ways in which that inspiration is still working in our lives.

How do you recognize the inspirational? It is not always easy to tell, and that which inspires one person may be of little interest to another. Few of my classmates found either of the two occasions I remember interesting—far from it. No doubt, too, there were lessons that they remember as powerful which I have forgotten. We all, however, recognize the emotional intensity that such memorable encounters imprint on us.

Developing Inspirational Images

The inspirational experience does not always arise from encountering a person. Nor does the experience have to have been experienced as inspirational at the time for it to be meaningful in retrospect. The significant aspect of such an experience is its capacity to evoke a sense of longing and expansiveness in the present.

Tom came to a community center, but he struggled to make friends because he was very shy. He was overcome with self-loathing and embarrassment every time he thought of trying to do anything new in life. He often spent time talking with the workers about how incapacitated by his anxieties he felt and how he was too timid to have a social life or get a girlfriend. Then one day he shared a different memory.

"I wasn't always shy," he said. "Once I ran off on the beach and scared my parents silly. I spent half the afternoon playing with some other children in a pond, making dams. In fact I was really bossy then. I remember running along the beach with buckets of water, not a care in the world—I didn't half get in trouble when they found me!"

The worker was able to spend time with Tom, talking about that image of the small boy running along the beach. "I bet it felt really good running like that! Can you imagine . . . ?" Whenever she saw Tom, she would remind him, sometimes seriously, other times more lightheartedly, of the running child. It was an image they returned to many times. As this happened, Tom began to form a clearer image of himself as a child. He saw himself running freely down the beach, unencumbered by his adult self-consciousness. The image gave him inspiration, evoking in him the same feeling of freedom that he had felt as a child. Although it took time, gradually he began to let go of his preoccupations and feel more socially at ease.

Vows

Out of the longing and the inspiration emerges the vow—a spontaneous expression of the primal longing. In its ultimate form, the primal vow is that of the bodhisattva, encompassing the aspiration to save all beings. This is a poetic expression, a vow that, like the primal longing, can only partially be expressed in words. The primal vow is the ultimate expression of the altruistic mind. It is the vow that sees no other possibility than the universal good.

Restrictive Vows

The vows discussed so far are positive in their intent, growing out of the seeds of the primal vow. Some vows, however, can be restrictive. When a person is in what feels like an impossibly painful or difficult position, he or she frequently responds with a vow from the heart. This vow may be altruistic; but often, particularly if the person feels powerless, perhaps because he is a small child, it takes a restrictive form. The child may have vowed never to trust anyone again, or to take revenge on all men, or to become so rich he will never again be without basic resources. Such vows give the child a sense that he will achieve justice or become happy one day.

Restrictive vows are rarely remembered in adulthood, but they may still exert a power in the person's life. In adult life, the person may compulsively act out behaviors dictated by the childhood vow without understanding why he acts in that way. He may follow a path of distrust, aggression, or avarice, without realizing that his behavior is being driven by a vow made in response to a childhood event.

Identifying and letting go of childhood vows can be important work. It is not always easy, because the origins of these vows are so often forgotten, but recognizing the powerful grip that such a vow can have may help you to spot it and explore its history. Just as with self-seeking intentionality, restrictive vows contain within them the seeds of more altruistic motivation, and unlocking this can be healing.

Ethics and Precepts as Inspirational Vows

Buddhist practitioners often mark their commitment to the spiritual path by taking precepts. Precepts are a form of vow. They are a series of statements that form the basis of the Buddhist lifestyle. At the simplest level, common to all schools of Buddhism, the precepts are guiding principles. The five most basic ones are not to kill, not to steal, not to behave in sexually inappropriate ways, not to speak unwisely, and not to take intoxicants. They not only provide guidelines for ethical living but also are said to describe the lifestyle of the enlightened person. Transmitted through a ceremony that emphasizes the inspirational power of the words, these precepts form the aspirational vision that holds the practitioner in her training.

Although in Buddhism vows are often framed in traditional forms or words, if they are to be meaningful the words must echo something already heartfelt. At the same time, taking the precepts is itself intended to be a source of inspiration which will in turn strengthen a person's practice and intensify her commitment. Taking a vow and using it as a central part of training may be an expression of a practitioner's deepest longing and also offer inspiration. Taking formal vows or precepts represents a significant step in a person's practice, but the practitioner needs to be in touch with the primal vow and to feel its connection to those formal vows if she is really to work with these aspirations.

It is interesting to reflect on the Buddhist precepts in the context of this chapter and the previous one. As guidelines, they provide a set of limits for the practitioner. Such limits form a structure which can offer a container for the process of transformation. At the same time, in offering a vision of the enlightened life, they also provide the inspiration that can help you to reach beyond self-interest toward higher aspirations.

Living and being with others in a practice community can of itself be inspirational. When people are inspired, they act in purposeful ways. They become a source of inspiration to others. Life has meaning. Purposefulness is the application of aspiration, and living with others who are purposeful is inspiring. Shared activity that arises from such community is the embodiment of the primal vow in practical ways.

THEORIES INTRODUCED IN THIS CHAPTER

- inspiration and aspiration;
- the primal vow;
- enabling and restrictive vows;
- ethics and precepts as enabling vows; and
- behavioral codes for practitioners.

· 12 ·

Experiment and Encounter

As we saw in the last chapter, meeting an impressive person can be inspiring and create conditions for you to experience substantial, often sudden, change. Such meetings come rarely; but they can shape your life direction. All the same, meeting an inspirational figure can, in one sense, remain a remote experience.

Discovering the Feet of Clay

Neither of the two meetings I experienced in my teens, described in the last chapter, involved me in getting to know the people concerned at a personal level. In the second meeting, my encounter with de Chardin's ideas was even mediated by the woman giving the lecture. I am really not sure, looking back, whether it was she or de Chardin who spoke to me. Certainly, she was animated with her enthusiasm for the great thinker, and this conveyed itself to me. At the same time, I did not feel that it was her, personally, that held my attention so raptly. Somehow, she seemed to embody the man and the ideas she was describing. In her, I saw the great theologian come alive.

Inspirational meetings can often be of this kind, in which the person one meets in effect stands in for another figure who was, in turn, inspirational for them. In some spiritual practices, this process, whereby a living person "stands in" for the religious founder, can be explicitly intended. Some Buddhist schools encourage devotees to see their teacher as "Buddha." This is not because the teacher necessarily claims enlightenment, but rather because, as a human presence, he can dramatically represent the spirit of the inspirational figure behind the tradition. Other schools rely heavily upon the idea of transmission, in which the direct handing down of the teaching goes from teacher to disciple in a lineage, with ceremonial recognition of the passing on of the Dharma thread. In this way of thinking, each generation embodies the wisdom of previous generations.

Some aspects of Buddhist life are actually intended to diminish the interference of individual characteristics with what is being transmitted. The wearing of traditional clothing, such as the Buddhist robe, creates a kind of anonymity that allows us to be a channel for the teachings and thus for the presence of the great teachers of the past. It is a reminder to us not to think of ourselves as clever or talented in giving the talk, but simply to realize that we are passing on what we have learned from others. Nothing we say will be original. We become an instrument for the teachings. It is rather like the masked player in the Greek drama, who presents a persona that is untainted by his personal expression and thus can represent the archetypal heroic characters without detracting from their presence.

The power of the meetings that I experienced in my teens was probably in part a function of the psychological distance in the relationships. I saw the person, in each case, in a limited way, not needing to see their more "flawed" aspects, which no doubt existed. It was not so much the people I saw as the quality they displayed at the time of our meeting.

While both meetings were deeply significant for me and felt profoundly like heart-to-heart encounters, it is also possible that I was able to create and retain my own stories about these meetings. I encountered these inspirational people but did not actually converse directly with either of them. There was nothing to challenge my perspective, except perhaps my uninterested classmates.

To say this is not to diminish the significance of such meetings. As is evident from the degree to which they still remain so clear in my mind after all these years, they touched me in significant ways. In large measure this was probably as result of my not knowing either person personally. Each was able to represent important qualities for me in just the way the Greek actor might. At the same time, getting to know either of the people more fully might have brought a different kind of learning.

In meetings of the kind I have described, where no interactive encounter takes place, a person may form an image of the encounter purely from his own viewpoint. Other people involved might or might not recognize this, as it is likely to be based on the personal meaning the individual himself attached to the meetings. The other people's experiences of the meeting may not be taken into account at all.

The inspirational relationship, though powerful and valuable in one respect, can be limited in other ways. It has a one-way quality to it. Like reading a book or watching a film, it can be highly emotive and can have a big impact on a person's life; however, it does not generally invite direct encounter.

Getting to know the people who inspired me in a more rounded way might well have been both difficult and a further opportunity for growth, as my idealization was challenged by the emerging reality. It is not easy to realize that one's hero has normal human failings. Such people are not supposed to belch, have smelly socks, or wake up in a bad mood. Yet most inspirational figures do, at least sometimes. We often experience an uncomfortable jolt in relationships with such people as spiritual teachers at the point when the "feet of clay" become apparent. Yet these points are also spiritual growth points. They are certainly essential to the creation of the type of working alliance necessary for spiritual work. Similar points of insight are also immensely valuable in many other relationships, such as that with a therapist or celebrity. They can even occur when you meet an older relative whom you have not seen since childhood, or when you see work acquaintances outside the office.

When you encounter others through direct interaction, their

clay feet become more obvious. This can be a healthy process. Retaining an idealized view of the other allows you to play all kinds of mental games. You can avoid responsibilities, expecting the other person magically to take them away. You can imagine them always to have the answer you need, always to love and accept you, always to be ready to comfort or be wise or be protective. You may invite them to be a sort of parent figure for you. This can be very attractive, as it allows you to be child-like and feel safe. It restores the sense of permanence and security that some people were lucky enough to feel as small children. God's in his heaven and all's right with the world. As the relationship goes on, if this pattern is not challenged, the strength of these childlike longings may well increase. Many people approach spiritual teachers, or others who are in supportive roles, in this way and then feel very angry when the teacher turns out not to be such a perfect parent.

Recognizing the other person's human side can be an invitation to grow up. Meeting them in a more direct way opens up the possibility of a new dimension of the relationship. The inspirational or parental relationship, while valuable in some ways, is still in danger of being rooted in delusion. Breaking through the gloss of idealization makes it possible to encounter the other more directly.

Thus the spiritual teacher questions and challenges the trainee, discussing possibilities and suggesting practices, but expects the trainee to take responsibility for life decisions. In this way, a spiritual teacher has been likened to a sports coach. He may give observations or advice; but, like the athlete, the student must integrate his advice into practice.

This is not to say that the person on whom you choose to rely as a guide or teacher should not have good qualities. You need to choose carefully whom to put faith in. At the same time, you should look for an adult relationship in which to train. You need to accept the other person's human side and make intelligent rather than unquestioning use of their teaching. This enables a different sort of relationship in which enquiry and experimentation replace passive dependency.

As a therapist, I have often been aware of times when others have viewed me in unrealistic ways. This happens quite commonly in the early stages of therapy and can be part of a person's attempt to feel safe. The person may elevate me into a parental role or overestimate my knowledge or wisdom. Sometimes it is appropriate to leave a person's view unchallenged for a time, but often there is a need for a more open process in which the other person gradually comes to see my humanity. This does not mean that I share all my personal history with them, but it does mean that I am willing to show when I am uncertain, uneasy or just plain wrong.

In practice, as I live in a community, much of my life is somewhat public, and those who come to see me often stop for a cup of tea with other community members or ask about community events. Even before I lived in community, few who visited me for therapy sessions could have failed to know I had teenage children when the sound of thundering feet on the stairs and the slam of the front door announced a late departure for college. These things always seemed to help the process of the therapy relationship. They made me human.

For some people, though, such events did not seem to disrupt the idealized image they had of me. The tendency to idealize can be very strong. What is important is that I do not start to believe the idealized image that others may have of me, and I do not invest self-energy in maintaining attractive identities.

A Spirited Group of People

In Buddhism there is a tradition of enquiry and experiment, which goes back to the Buddha himself. The Buddha did not expect his disciples to follow his teachings without question. He encouraged his followers to approach his methods with what we might think of as healthy skepticism.

This approach was pragmatic and respectful. The Buddha was forthright and spoke his mind to his followers, but he also expected them to test out what he said and draw their own conclusions. He expected them to learn through their practice and experience, and he taught methods by which they could do so. This way of operating created a group of followers who were able to take the initiative. These people went on to spread the message of the Buddha's movement across much of India, often operating alone or in small groups, apart from their teacher for much of the time. They needed to be able to stand on their own feet.

The pattern of life for the early Buddhist community, or sangha, was that the Buddha and his followers would assemble during the rainy season to study and practice together. The Buddha gave his teachings at this time. During the rest of the year the group would disperse, its members going out into the cities and countryside to teach and to travel. This lifestyle required people who were strong and inspired and had integrity. It also required people who were not simply copies of their teacher, but who had internalized his teachings in an integrated way. We can see from the descriptions of the early disciples that the Buddha's followers were indeed a group of strong individuals with different characteristics and personalities, who were able to operate cooperatively or singly. They were a group of adults.

This chapter will look at the way in which fostering honest, adult-to-adult relationships can create conditions that are challenging and facilitate growth, but which allow people to develop in different directions. We will look at how we can create a balance of responsibility in relationships. Encountering others involves letting go of self-preoccupation. The element of encounter in a relationship is an important transformative element in itself.

Supporting Change

Just as the Buddha trained his disciples to test and develop their practice, so too you are more likely to discover unanticipated capabilities if you approach your interactions with others in a spirit of open enquiry. Every encounter has the potential to teach you both about your patterns of reactivity and also about the other person and their unique experience and attitudes. This is true whether the relationship is a friendship, a working relationship, or a caregiving one.

Too often, you may approach others with assumptions already formed in your mind about them. Before you even speak, you will have attributed all sorts of qualities and characteristics to a new acquaintance. Your mind approaches encounters with expectations, and you place labels on what you see (nama-rupa) in order to maintain your view of the world. This process happens at subtle as well as gross levels in meetings between people. You not only fit others into stereotyped categories according to obvious things like age, gender, or appearance; you also catch subtle similarities, importing into new relationships dynamics from earlier ones. If you can let go of your assumptions about the other person and really listen when you meet, there may be an opportunity to really encounter one another. The other person may be of a different culture or from a different part of the country. They may be a different age or sex from yourself. Certainly, they have had their own experience, and they live in their own circumstances. You need to be willing to listen to them and explore the possibilities and limits of their world without assuming you know them in advance.

If your life seems to have been similar to theirs, there is even more reason to be careful. It is even harder to really listen to another person's story when it is similar to your own. You are too ready to picture their situation through the scenes and characters of your own drama, and you may not hear the special aspects of their experience at all. You may use the elements in their story to reinforce your own self-story, missing the opportunity really to enter their world.

On the other hand, you should not be overly dismissive of your first impressions of others. When you are meeting someone for the first time, you may see things about them that you later cease to notice. You may pick up particular nuances of manner that you later blend into your general sense of John or Mary, but which actually reveal significant aspects of character. Before the relationship is established, you may be viewing the other person in ways that are limited by your own preconceptions, but you are not yet caught in a shared story. Later you may create a joint world-view that covers up certain aspects of each of your behaviors. This process is commonly called collusion. It is the formation of a shared skandha process.

In some situations, I am called on to play a professional role. It may be that I have just been invited into a work team as a consultant. It may be that a new client has just arrived in my therapy consulting room. It may be that a new student has just joined the course I am teaching. In such settings, it can be especially tempting to assume we have answers. But how can I know the story behind this meeting? How can I make assumptions about what is best for this other person?

As someone who has been approached for help, I probably do have things to offer. I have my own knowledge and experience. This may derive from my training or my understanding of mental and social processes. We all have situations where we have expertise. It may be knowledge of practical systems, such as how to get benefits or register with a doctor. It may be intuition, based on experience of working with many people over the years. We can use these things to help others. We also all have the experience of being human. If nothing else, we can be willing to listen and to respond.

When two people meet in this way, both parties bring something to the process from their past knowledge and experience. At the same time, both people are on new ground, inasmuch as they do not know what will arise from their encounter. As they talk, they may discover what perceptions each is holding about the situation and about the other. There may be specific difficulties or processes connected with the situation itself, or relating to its history, that they need to understand better. This requires a shared exploration. In exploring these things, they become engaged in a kind of co-research project. Taking an attitude of co-researching is respectful.

When you engage with another in a shared task, you are wise to acknowledge your limitations and respect the knowledge and intelligence of the person working alongside you. You may also help the other person to develop new skills that will give them the personal tools to continue work when you are not together. You cannot know in advance what these will be, and you will probably have to work together to deepen your understanding of what is needed. It is as much a question of discovering the means of working together as of one person teaching the other to use specific methods. Together you learn to learn.

Buddhist psychology is practical and experimental. We are all fellow travellers on the spiritual path. We will not necessarily share formal practice, but we will share a process that can change both of us. The path is unpredictable, and together both of us must use whatever methods we have to figure out a route.

Experiment and Avoidance

Thinking of psychological and spiritual growth as a research project offers a number of useful conditions. First, it encourages experimentalism. You are encouraged to discover practical strategies for change and to try them out without feeling pressured to make them work. In this way, some of your patterns of avoidance and distraction can be bypassed.

You can also take a more playful attitude to changing your habit-patterns. If a person wants to make changes to their behavior, for example by giving up eating too much, it is often easier for him simply to experiment with making the change for a while. If he anticipates that the change he has made will be permanent, he may feel pressured to continue it, even if it becomes unbearable. He will never be allowed sweets again. Experimentation is often a useful first step. He can play at eating healthily for a day and see how it feels. This will probably not result in him breaking the habit completely, but it may be a useful dress rehearsal for the real thing. He will learn about his cravings and maybe be able to foresee trouble spots for the future. Later, there may come a time for a person to make an absolute decision to stop an unhelpful behavior, but such decisions are often more effective if taken at a later stage in the process.

Sarah was struggling to keep her smoking under control, having been advised by her doctor to cut down on it. Every time she tried to stop smoking, she would find herself getting through two days and then being overcome by unbearable cravings. As they increased, her mind would become a whirl of resentment, self-pity, and frustration. Inevitably, after a few hours she would end up giving in to the feelings and soon be smoking more than ever.

Working with Mark, Sarah discussed the problem.

"Perhaps you need to just look at the process a bit more closely," Mark suggested. "There's no point in just going around this pattern again and again. I wonder what would happen if you tried not smoking for a day and just watched what happened. That way you wouldn't get caught in the difficult feelings that come up later, but you could find out something about the process of not smoking. You could maybe keep a diary and notice what goes on—things like what you are doing and how your thoughts and feelings come and go. What do you think? I don't know what you'll learn, but it would be interesting to see what your life is like for a day without cigarettes when you are not getting caught up in all those feelings of resentment."

Just observing a process in this way can be very helpful. By taking attention off the part of the process where Sarah was failing, Mark encouraged her to approach not smoking as an interesting and positive experience. The aim was not so much to help Sarah give up smoking immediately as to encourage Sarah to take a more experimental attitude to the problem, thus becoming less emotionally invested.

When a habit is deeply entrenched, it has often become part of our self-structure. You are no longer using the behavior as a sensory escape, but are maintaining an identity through it. You are not just smoking, you have become "a smoker." It feels much harder to give up. By observing the behavior, you step back and reduce your level of identification with it, thus returning it to the level of sensory escape. It is much easier to start to let go of it at this level. You also diminish emotional investment and thus create disidentification, since emotional energy of this kind tends to build self-structures.

Mark did not tell Sarah what to do. He suggested the experiment in an open way, so that Sarah was able to think about whether to try it and what aspects of the experience she needed to explore. She increased her sense of responsibility, staying in a more "adult" style of operating. Mark avoided encouraging her to become dependent on him. Telling her what to do might have carried the risk of making him seem like a parental figure. Encouraging Sarah to take responsibility for her own process in this way, he reduced the risk that she would later avoid responsibility for the process through either uncommitted compliance or rebellion. Sarah and Mark had already developed a good working relationship that included quite a bit of good-natured give and take. This enabled them to be generally straightforward with each other.

Being experimental has a number of benefits. It encouraged Sarah to try out stopping smoking without creating the necessity for the changes to be permanent. It did not even place relative value on being a non-smoker. Although both she and Mark knew that giving up smoking would be healthier, Mark avoided allowing the matter to become a moral issue. Sarah did not need to stop smoking to get Mark's approval. He defined the choice in practical terms and left the responsibility for making it with her. They both knew that Sarah's health was being affected by the smoking. They also knew that Sarah was finding giving up very hard. It was Sarah's job to choose the best way of reconciling the factors.

Your actions condition your mental state. In trying the experiment, Sarah experienced adopting a more adult, objective manner in relation to her smoking. She experienced observing her actions and reactions, and through this created a simpler relationship with the habit of smoking. Her identity was no longer tied up with it. She did this for one day, during which she experienced feeling calm, present-centered, and thoughtful without smoking cigarettes. She did not anticipate the increasing feelings of deprivation that she had experienced when trying to give up smoking altogether, so she could experience being a nonsmoker in a positive way without feeling conflicted.

Because of the limited time of the experiment, Sarah did not experience giving in to her craving. She did experience going through a day without cigarettes in a positive frame of mind. This experiment gave her experience of doing things differently. It lay down new patterns of habit-energy. It created conditions that might help her change her smoking habit in the longer term, if this was what she decided to do.

As Sarah experimented in this way, she developed a more experimental attitude to her experience and a curiosity about her own process. This spilled into other aspects of her life, enabling her to see other difficult situations as opportunities for growth.

This experimental attitude has some similarities to what in Buddhism is called "developing the mind of training." As the spiritual trainee progresses, he begins to see more and more experiences as possibilities for training, recognizing the opportunities that each situation provides for him to explore and overcome patterns of attachment. In this way he is able to train more and more effectively.

A Different Sort of Helping Relationship

The relationship that develops through the sort of co-researching approach Sarah and Mark had may be rather different in style from that which develops in some Western therapeutic approaches. One characteristic of this relationship is that it encourages interaction to take an adult-to-adult form. This can feel more like the kind of relationship that a Western therapist or other practitioner would expect to have with a supervisor. It is also more similar to the kind of relationship that a Buddhist practitioner might have with the teacher or spiritual guide. Sarah began to regard life as an experiment and to explore new ways of seeing and acting. She reported back on these in the sessions, working with Mark to understand her psychological process and to refine the methods of experimentation. Such a relationship offers support and advice, but it demands that the student or disciple take responsibility.

The emphasis on helping others to take responsibility for their actions is just as relevant in groups and in community settings as in a one-to-one therapeutic relationship. Having worked in various different community work settings over the years, I am very aware that, although ideologies of empowerment and local consultation are common, they can in many instances mask the imposition of ideas by workers on service users. This problem is often exacerbated because workers are expected to move toward particular outcomes, which have often been decided by higher authorities and which espouse value systems very different from those of the user group. Empowerment then risks becoming coercion, and local people becoming mouthpieces for views that originated in the council offices or in classroom discussions on community work courses.

Real equality requires honest sharing of views and a respect for difference. Sometimes this means being firm about your bottom line. Sometimes people do not have a choice and must accept an option that they do not want. Sometimes you need to state your views on the matter but also give space to the opinions of others. You listen to other people's perspectives but may decide to take a different course of action. Trying to avoid confrontations of this kind can be inauthentic. It may allow you to retain the self-image of being a caring person whom everyone loves, but it is not honest. Even if you are primarily protecting other people's feelings more than your own, you are in fact encouraging just the kind of flight from reality that Buddhist psychology suggests is so unhealthy. Facing real limits is often the opportunity a person needs to grow.

Some years ago, I worked in a neighborhood learning center. If, as sometimes happened, the majority of people who attended a project preferred bingo afternoons to computer courses, it was not necessarily acceptable to the project's funders and did not fulfill its aims. Sometimes we just had to make a decision to offer computer classes for the few who wanted to attend them. This approach felt more honest than trying to persuade people to advocate things they do not really want or believe in. Clearly, in an ideal situation, everyone's ideas are incorporated; but sometimes the worker needs to take an overview of a situation and propose solutions that are not popular.

Encounter and Challenge

The process of encounter is important to psychological growth. It involves making contact with the world beyond the self.

Someone who is deeply caught in self-preoccupation can have a very distorted world-view. It is clouded by self-invested perception, by rupa rather than dharma. In most relationships, without feedback from the other person you quickly build up false views. If the person you are interacting with is straightforward and open, this distorted perception is challenged. When someone is authentic, their human presence is apparent. Otherwise, a person may simply become a player in someone else's script. It is all too easy, especially when, dealing with people in professional or functional roles, to fall into perceiving them as a facility or service. When real meeting takes place, distortions become evident. The mud that is on the windshield becomes more visible, and there is an implicit invitation to remove some of it.

In social relationships it is often quite possible for a person to go on believing that their perceptions of other people are accurate. Politeness prevents people from questioning what is said or revealing enough of their real feelings and experiences to demonstrate wrong perceptions. It is easy to hold onto delusions because nobody challenges them. Living in this kind of situation, you can build up a false sense of things and, in your social circle, find shared norms that confirm your false perception of reality.

When real encounter takes place, it offers a greater degree of authenticity than most social settings allow. This is valuable, even though the experience is often less comfortable than adhering to social niceties would be. Honest encounter requires both parties to be clear with one another, and often to be assertive and self-revealing. It allows them to see the ways in which they distort the world through their patterns of assumptions, as well as helping them to establish new behavioral patterns by the experience of interacting in a more direct way.

Buddhist psychology puts the highest premium on transcending self and experiencing the world with clarity. This means seeing the world as other. To do so is to give up the skandha process and live the enlightened life, free from the self-prison. Encountering another person fully provides an opportunity to break out of the cycle of self, at least in that moment of meeting.

Counterpart Roles

Against the background of honesty and direct communication, patterns of habitual behavior emerge. These take two forms:

- First, some behaviors are part of a person's general pattern of habit-behaviors. These are common to most of his interactions and are connected with his sense of identity and the ways he has learned to express it.
- Second, in addition to this background of generalized habit-behaviors, certain behavior patterns occur that are specific to the dynamics of each particular relationship.

Feelings can arise within a relationship which seem to have nothing to do with its reality. Such feelings may trigger behaviors that follow old habitual patterns. A person may start to become dependent or challenging, may become argumentative or bossy, may crack jokes or regress. These patterns may be ones that he has played out many times with different people, but always in a similar situation. The similarity that exists between past and current situations that trigger particular behavioral responses may be clear. For example, the person may always be defensive and irritable with older women. But it may not necessarily be so obvious that an old pattern is being played out. Many people in second marriages import dynamics from their first relationship. It can often take years to unscramble the influence of old expectations and reactions on behavior towards the new partner.

Discovering the roots of such patterns and the aspects of the other person's presence that trigger these reactive responses can be very helpful. There may be quite specific things in the other person's behavior or appearance, or in the situation, which activate a response pattern. These aspects of the other person's behavior may create a powerful rupa, triggering a particularly strong samjna response and so creating the conditions for habitual behaviors to arise.

Some western psychology relies upon theories of transference and countertransference. The process described above, in which some habit-energies are triggered by contact with particular people or situations, can be seen in terms of these theories. Buddhist psychology, however, generally takes a broader interpretation of such patterns of response. Conditions in a relationship replicate past conditions. Patterns of behavior arise in response to the new conditions that mimic the patterns that arose in response to the old conditions. Many such patterns grew up in association with parents and other significant childhood figures. Buddhist psychology recognizes this but does not put as much emphasis on the special importance of parent–child patterns as transference theory does. It sees them as one source of habit-patterns among many. Samjna entrancement occurs in response to a variety of triggers.

Buddhist theory also differs from western models in that it emphasizes the conditioning effect of what the child did. Action is seen as more important than feelings or the dynamics of the child's relationships. Buddhist psychology suggests that the frequent repetition of the pattern of action causes a pattern of behavioral energy to persist in the mentality and to be re-enacted.

Patterns of relational behavior tend to persist because, when they are played out, other people become hooked into playing supporting roles. If a person tends to be dependent, he finds people who are dependable to associate with. If someone tends to be angry, he finds people who will share a fight with him or those people who will be submissive and easily coerced. This leads the person to be selective in his choice of associates. He seeks out friends and partners who will play roles that are complementary to his own. In this way his habitual roles become persistent. Pairs of people who habitually play out roles that fit together often form strong relationships, and indeed this pattern forms the basis of many marriages. Both people have their self-worlds reinforced.

At the same time, we are all programmed with the potential to play many roles. We know how to play most parts either because we have played them before in the past or because we have observed others playing them. A person who has a strong pattern of habit-energy gives out subtle messages about how he wants to be responded to. When another person presents you with a role, the likelihood is that you have its counterpart within your repertoire. Only occasionally do you meet someone whose pattern is completely new. This process of playing out roles and counterpart roles happens all the time in ordinary interactions. People are generally unaware of the ways that they are hooked into the programmed responses. We all have a range of potential samjna responses.

When people are facing difficult and painful situations, strong habit-patterns are likely to be triggered. When you encounter dukkha, you are likely to fall into habitual forms of escape. This means that all the processes of conditioning are likely to be operating particularly strongly. Habitual patterns are more likely to be repeated, and the self-structures are likely to be more strongly activated.

This process occurs particularly strongly in encounters that take place in contexts where one person is a professional, such as a teacher or therapist, and may seem relatively anonymous. The uncomfortable emotional intensity of such a situation can also create the potential for habits to be triggered. At the same time, the presence of a supportive but somewhat remote figure creates the likelihood that those habit-patterns will be expressed through the relationship. The professional helper may be treated as a counterpart rather than being encountered directly. While some therapies deliberately encourage such patterns in order to explore transference, a Buddhist therapist would probably not deliberately seek to work in this way. Nevertheless, where such a situation does arise naturally, exploring the patterns can be one fruitful option.

Staying within the Counterpart Role—or Rejecting It

When role and counterpart role patterns seem to be operating, you can act in several different ways. One useful approach can be to simply experience the counterpart role. If your partner is speaking to you in a demanding way, how do you feel yourself drawn to respond? What pulls are being exerted on you? What reactions are being invited? In keeping awareness of your own experience of the interaction, and observing reactions and behavior that arise with the kind of objectivity described earlier, you may come to understand more of the patterns in your partner's life. You may be able to talk about them and track down where they originate, so that the patterns no longer need to intrude on your relationship. It may also allow your partner to ask more directly for the support he or she needs.

Often, though, it is not helpful to be drawn into playing out parts in other people's games. Avoiding this requires sharp awareness, but it can be very helpful. Encountering a person who does not allow himself to be drawn into counterpart roles or other conditioned behavior patterns can be deeply disconcerting. It is often the mark of a good spiritual teacher that he or she does not play our games.

To be in the presence of someone who has freed himself sufficiently from self-material that he is no longer hooked by his own samskaras in response to our behavior patterns disturbs our own patterns of response. Meeting such a person can be like crashing up against a wall. It unsettles you because suddenly your own patterns become exposed.

If you begin to dance, but your would-be partner does not move, then you suddenly find yourself standing alone on the dance floor feeling a little foolish. Meeting someone who does not engage in the kind of role and counterpart games which most of us play out all the time can be a bit like this. If one person starts to play out a pattern and the other person does not respond with a corresponding move, the first part of the pattern is left exposed. At this point, the first person may have a moment of insight that can transform their mentality so that a large area of self-material is released.

THEORIES INTRODUCED IN THIS CHAPTER

- co-researcher styles of working;
- encounter and challenge; and
- counterpart roles and shared samjna experiences.

· 13 ·

Working with the Other:
Other-centered Approaches

The experience of direct encounter breaks you out of self-preoccupation. If you can treat people as "other" rather than imposing self-view on them, you move to a more enlightened way of living. Achieving such contact is not necessarily easy, though, as people all look for self-confirmation in most of their interactions. Even when you think you are being authentic, you may be subverting the process in subtle ways. Nevertheless, the work of understanding other perspectives offers a route to a less self-preoccupied way of being and may free you from a more rigid state of mind.

An Other-centered Approach

Western psychological methods generally focus on the client or patient himself, bringing his attention back to his own perceptions, feelings and experiences. If a man arrives for a session with a Western therapist, for example, and talks at length about what his mother thinks or does, that therapist is likely to keep bringing his attention back to his own viewpoint. She may say: "But what about you?" or "How do you feel about this?"

A therapist working from a Buddhist perspective is much more likely to encourage exploration of the reality of the other person's perspective. This might involve asking questions such as: "But does she really think that?" or "And I wonder how this looks to her?" Far from discouraging discussion of the other person's perspective, Buddhist therapists may well encourage such exploration. This is because by experientially understanding the other's point of view you start to break out of self-preoccupation and see that this other person is existing in his or her own right. When you can really understand how someone else sees the world, as opposed to how you think their way of being reflects upon you, you realize the limits of your own perspective. Getting into another person's shoes is revealing.

It is not uncommon for someone who is seeking relief from personal problems to talk at length about others. There may be an element in this of not taking personal responsibility for their own situation, but it has a healthy aspect too. It often represents a genuine desire to relate better to and care better for others. You may want to know why the people you love behave as they do, what their life experience has been like, and what their history is. You may want to understand why they hurt you, or why they are so unreasonably sad. Exploring these things may give you insights that can help you to relate better.

Often, however, the process of talking about others has more to do with your own agenda than with the actuality of the person being discussed. In other words, when a person talks about his mother, he may be trying to understand her in her own terms, but he may be simply reinforcing his view of what she means in his life. He may be creating a rupa. He sees his image of "Mother" and fails to see her as the person she really is, or was. You could say there is a lot of mud marring his vision.

Object-related Work

The mind is conditioned by its objects. This means that your mental process is determined by what you give attention to. Object relation theory provides a mode of working that can be very revealing of your conditioned patterns of association. If I pay attention to an object that has powerful meaning for me—such as my grandmother's rings, described in Chapter 4—feelings arise. I give my attention to a powerful rupa and experience samjna. Samjna responses involve a level of entrancement.

In object-related work you deliberately bring to mind an object that is a powerful rupa. If you are imagining the object, you can intensify your sense of it by looking at it in detail. What color is it? Are there variations of color? What does it feel like if you touch it? If the object is in front of you, you can imagine it in other contexts. I might see my grandmother wearing her ring, perhaps on her wedding day, perhaps in her old age. Sometimes it can be powerful to ask yourself questions, such as: "Where would I like this object to end up when I no longer have it?"

Sometimes the object that is brought to mind is a person. Once again, it is useful simply to focus on the rupa and to make the image as clear as possible. This might involve describing the person as he or she appears. What is Mother wearing? Where is she sitting? What expression does she have on her face? You are creating a sense of rupa. For this reason, in object-related work the attention is often kept on the visual aspect of the person, which is thus transformed into something rather like the Greek mask discussed in the previous chapter. This visual aspect becomes the receptacle that will hold your perceptual habit-patterns. You do not need to ask: "What is she thinking?" at this stage.

As the rupa becomes more powerful, the other aspects of the skandha process also become more obvious. You slip into the entrancement associated with the samjna response. Emotional reactions will increase and you may feel impulses to act in habitual ways.

Object-related work provides a valuable method for exploring the process of conditioning as it operates in particular relationships or situations. It facilitates emotional expression and catharsis, which may be helpful to people who find it difficult to contact and express feelings. It can also help a person to bypass the more controlling aspects of the psyche, since it avoids rational patterns of discussion.

A therapist may encourage the client to see his or her personal world more vividly through responses that increase the pictorial aspect of the story. This will intensify rupa experience and deepen the samjna response.

"So you grew up in a mining village. Lots of small terraced cottages. I guess it was pretty dirty in those days."

"Your Dad was a miner? I can see him coming home after his shift, still pretty grimy, wearing his working clothes."

This mode of working creates a vivid, pictorial style of interaction, which also has the effect of inviting a person to relive experiences, increasing the intensity of samjna. In this way the subtle patterns of response become apparent and can be explored and understood. It can also be a very moving way of working, as treasured scenes from the past are shared. It can be very touching to work in this way with someone who has been bereaved, for example. At the same time, emotions that are evoked can be very strong and may feel overwhelming, so you may sometimes need to be cautious in inviting others to work in this way.

Differences between Object-Related and Other-Centered Work

Object-related work involves exploring a person's responses to a powerful rupa. It may involve helping a person to intensify their experience through descriptive or imaginative methods. It allows a person to become more familiar with the responses that habitually occur or to experiment with new behaviors.

Other-centered work involves swapping places with the rupa. In other words, if, say, the powerful rupa that is being worked with is a person, probably represented by a symbolic object such as a cushion or photograph, you will physically swap places with object that represents the person. Doing this, you effectively enter their viewpoint and see the world, including yourself, through the other person's eyes. This shift of perspective brings surprising insight. After building an image of Mother, you might imaginatively step into her shoes. How are things for her? How does she see her life? How does she see you? How does she feel when you telephone, or when you don't? This time you are not just seeing her, you are getting inside her thought processes, as far as you are able.

Psychodrama is a western psychological method developed by Jacob Moreno in the early to middle twentieth century. In psychodrama there is a technique called "role reversal." This is a dramatic method in which a person steps into the shoes of someone else who is significant in their life. In this reversed role, he sees the scenario that is being enacted through the other person's eyes and speaks with their words. He experiences being that other person. In a psychodrama, the protagonist (the word "protagonist" is used to describe the person who is exploring his psychological issue in the drama) is encouraged to swap places with significant others in his story. He might enact being his mother. He might experience being her, walking around her house or workplace. He might experience her feelings about speaking with him on the phone. In role as her, he might even talk to someone else who had been placed in role as him.

The process of psychodrama is such that, in the creation of the scene, the protagonist becomes deeply and experientially immersed in the reality of the other person that is to be enacted. This is a form of deep samjna entrancement. The scene ceases to have the "as if" quality of much therapeutic work and temporarily becomes, for the protagonist, present reality. In this state of psychological immersion, the protagonist moves from the self-perspective into the other-perspective.

The role-reversal technique can provide dramatic new understanding of another person's perspective and often brings about cathartic release. It not only allows the person to deliberately act and speak as the other, as an actor might in playing a theatrical role, but also facilitates spontaneous experiencing of the other person's thoughts, emotions and body experience. Of course, this is not necessarily historically accurate, and involves a large element of interpretation, but the effect can still be a big change of perspective. A person may experience feelings of reconciliation, love, and appreciation.

Other methods for working from an other-centered perspective can enable similar shifts of perception. It is possible to use the imagination to perform role reversal. This can be done by a person working alone. Sometimes a person will use a cushion to represent another person. As with psychodrama, it is useful to start working in an object-related way, imagining the person in great detail. Once the image is well established, the person can then take up the position on the cushion and "become" the other. In this reversed position, active imagination or writing can be used to explore feelings and attitudes and to recall life events.

Seeing the other-perspective does not necessarily require complicated techniques at all. Even in conversation, you can explore the other-perspective. You do not always have to dwell on "How is it for me?" but can consider the other person's point of view. Talking about the other person's perspective on events and issues can be very helpful in clarifying our thinking and giving you space to explore differences and recognize your own rigidities of view.

Breaking Out of the Self

While object-related work can help you see and understand the nature of your conditioning and the patterns in your mental process, other-centered work attempts to take you out of the limitations of the self-perspective into a new relationship with that which is other. It creates the possibility for new viewpoints and different experiences. Methods such as role reversal provide insight into the limiting effect of the self-perspective.

One effect of this method that many people find surprising is that, in the other-position, a protagonist often has access to knowledge that he did not consciously have in the self-position. A typical scenario might be a confrontation with a parent.

"Did you really love me?" asks the protagonist at the height of the scene.

The psychodramatist asks him to reverse roles and be the parent.

At such points a shift of knowledge takes place. Before reversing roles, the protagonist did not know if the parent loved him. He longed to know and desperately sought reassurance, but could not find it. As soon as he reverses roles and becomes the parent, a change happens. Suddenly he knows and answers spontaneously.

"Of course I loved you. I just wasn't very good at expressing it."

Or, perhaps: "No, I never could love you as I wished."

To watch such a scene can be both moving and baffling. How can such a switch take place, as if by magic? Yet the protagonist seems deeply satisfied by the answer he has received. It rings just as true for him as if he had heard it from the actual parent in person.

In fact, we all know a lot more than we think we know. Our minds cling to certain perspectives and avoid others, limiting the information they allow us to "know." This is part of the process of maintaining the self. In the psychodrama, part of the protagonist's self may have been built on not knowing if he was loved, or maybe on believing that he was not loved. To allow in the knowledge that his parent did in fact love him would destroy part of his sense of identity. Even though he longs for the love, at some level he cannot let himself know it because that would mean letting go of the identity that protects him. Feeling the parent's love would bring the self into question. Thus the knowledge remained hidden from view. The self is maintained through a habit of taking a particular perspective on the world.

Moving to the other-centered view provides a means to bypass the censorship that operates to maintain the self. This censorship has limited your view and created the self-prison. In temporarily stepping out of this prison, you may loosen the rigidity of this perspective and see the world differently.

Working with Other-centered Methods

In addition to the methods offered by psychodrama, other techniques can be helpful in exploring the other-centered perspective.

Living Out Another's Story

People are not isolated. They live in family systems. These systems create conditions for particular interconnections to arise. Exploring your family story using narrative or other methods, you can begin to understand how your experience is embedded in a bigger story, that of the family. Family myths can have powerful effects in shaping lives, and it is often only when you start to explore the psychological conditions of your family of origin that you see how the different parts of the picture fit together.

Sometimes the story of another member of the family has played a significant part in shaping your particular mentality. A parent or grandparent's story may have provided the conditions that in turn have led to behavioral patterns that are still being played out in your current life situation. Sometimes a whole personal or family mythology has grown up around one particular person, labeling them as the cause of all the family's troubles.

Asking questions about your life and experiences can be greatly liberating. "What did Father do in the war?" "Did Grandmother grieve for the children who died?"

A while ago I worked with Jane. Jane's father had been a prisoner in the Far East during the Second World War. Jane experienced severe anxiety, which manifested as agoraphobia. She was often terrified to leave her house. Jane was also locked in anger at her father, who she considered had ruined her childhood with his depressions and outbursts of rage. At length, however, she was persuaded to tell his story.

Her father had been taken prisoner early in the war, in Burma, where he had experienced awful living conditions. She did not know exactly what had happened. He had never spoken about these events. I invited her to create a story using her imagination. Immediately she became very emotional. She realized that her father must have witnessed terrible atrocities. She knew enough about the history of our times to know the kind of thing to which he might have been exposed. She began to understand how it must have felt for him, being locked up for years and witnessing friends dying of disease and ill-treatment.

She and I spent some time exploring the detail of what life in a prison camp must have been like. Jane's father had not been very old at the time of his imprisonment, about the age she currently was, and she imagined the contrast between this life and his previous experiences back in England.

Jane began to realize that her feelings of agoraphobia were somehow linked to her father's wartime experiences. Previously, she had not let herself know his story. Perhaps this was to maintain her anger against him, or perhaps her anger was a response to the fear his experiences evoked in her. At the same time she had effectively mirrored his experience by making herself into a prisoner in her own home. She had re-enacted his story. Jane understood the way her life and that of her father had become linked. In recognizing this, she released some psychological tie with his story. She began to see how hard his experiences had been and feel a great deal of pain and anger—anger not at him but on his behalf, for his situation. She also began to experience his story as different from her own experience and was able to forgive him for his difficult moods. She began to let go of her agoraphobic patterns.

Family secrets are powerful forces that shape people's lives. When something remains unspoken, each person within the family is isolated and silenced, yet each knows at least something of the story. Hearing the family story from the perspectives of others can liberate us from the hold it has over a person.

Biographical Work

Telling another person's story can be healing. Creating a biographical record of that person's life can extend this work. You can do this in many ways. You might generate written narratives or create a scrapbook of memorabilia. Taking on the researcher role is helpful in establishing a less self-invested, less childlike way of looking at things. It encourages you to adopt a more adult mode of operating, and so may take you beyond your most entrenched views of the people who have been involved with you since childhood. The material that is produced through such a piece of research is easier to view in a neutral or positive way than the self-stories to which most people usually cling.

Creating a biographical scrapbook about a significant person offers a new perspective. It might start by recording the details of the person's birth, childhood and early life as far as they are known. It can include pictures, photographs, or other mementoes, as well as materials relating to the time in which these events happened: pictures of historical events, the clothes people wore, the houses they lived in. The biography might include details from accounts written by contemporaries of the person. It might also include imaginative writing.

Making such an account may be a solitary activity, but it might involve you in talking with other members of your family and even with the person who is the subject of the study. This is likely to have benefits for the whole family.

My own mother was recently encouraged by her brother to write about her childhood experiences. This engaged her in a process that took place over several months as she collected memories and sent several draft copies of her account to my uncle to be typed. The process thus became a shared enterprise, and different members of the family became involved. The result was a moving account of a village childhood. It impacted not only on her, but on others of us in the family. It showed me a new facet of my mother's life and gave me closer understanding of her early experiences.

It can be difficult to see the life of a relative who has been significant in our childhood, such as a parent, through different eyes. You probably have powerful associations and images of your parents. They are strongly rupa for you. Yet sometimes, spontaneously, you do glimpse them through someone else's eyes. Meeting a person who knew your parents as contemporaries and who comments about them, may suddenly present you with a very different image from the one you previously had. My father is a Methodist minister, and I remember one day in childhood being somewhat taken aback when, in a church where he was visiting preacher, a woman from the congregation came up to our family group after the service, looking very misty-eyed, and crooning about how lucky my brother and I were to have such a wonderful Daddy. My younger brother and I looked at one another in some bemusement at this display of emotion.

Nevertheless, many years later, I was deeply moved by the tributes given to my father on his retirement by so many people in the college where he had been chaplain for much of my childhood. Someone had created a beautifully bound and illustrated book out of a collection of memories from staff, students, and others who had worked with him. Poring over this, I saw how others experienced my father, and the impact he had had on so many people. This was not new knowledge for me, but seeing it recorded in the words of those others brought it to life in a new way. I did indeed feel proud and lucky.

Invocatory Work

Invocatory work involves using an object to represent something that is significant to you—something that is rupa for you. It allows you to explore your relationship to significant others, ideas, places, or things through the transfer of associations. The object that you choose to use for this kind of symbolic work becomes invested with the constellation of associations and reactions that you have for that person or concept. Thus you invoke the symbolic presence of the other. These symbolic objects or images can represent things that themselves are abstract or imaginary. By doing this, you create the possibility for interaction or exploration at a level that may not be possible simply through speech.

Drawing is a simple and useful form of invocatory work. Creating an image, you give form to something which otherwise remains in your imagination or purely verbal descriptions. You can draw diagrams to understand things and explain them to others. You can draw images of things to show how they were. You can draw spontaneously to explore feelings and associations. When you have drawn something, you can show your picture to others. You can explain how it was. Looking at a drawing is different from imagining an image. The picture becomes concrete and is not so amenable to the subtle adjustments that you constantly make to maintain a self-view. The image is still a representation of "you view," but putting it on paper offers you a greater degree of separation and objectivity.

Once you have created an image, that image is an object. What was previously part of your mentality, part of your self-structure, now becomes something that is other. You can now relate to it and respond to it in an object-related way. This may evoke strong emotions. You can now even reverse roles with the image, imaginatively becoming it. This latter kind of work can be extremely valuable. It is often when you make this kind of perceptual leap that new understanding comes.

Joan is helping Andrew to explore a drawing he has done. The drawing shows his brother standing outside the house where they grew up. Joan asks Andrew to place the picture on the floor in front of him. She asks him to describe what he sees. At this point, Andrew is doing object-related work.

Andrew talks about his brother. He tells Joan that Ian is two years younger than himself. He talks about the house. He recalls memories of playing with Ian in the garden. He describes a day when they squabbled over a football and both ended up in trouble. As he talks, Andrew becomes more animated. Initially, the account is simply factual, but, as he continues, Joan can see that Andrew has a lot of feelings about his relationship with his brother.

At this point, Joan suggests that Andrew stand in the place of the drawing. This means that Andrew has to physically move from the chair he is sitting in, so Joan puts a cushion on Andrew's chair to mark his place. She also puts the picture behind her, out of sight. Taking the place of the picture, Andrew experiences another point of view. He experiences being his brother, standing outside the house. This is a kind of role reversal. In this new position, it is possible for Andrew to discover how his brother felt on the day they quarreled about the football. He may also discern deeper patterns of resentment, affection, jealousy or pride that Ian had felt. In this way he might start to understand his relationship with his brother better, and to appreciate why his brother was currently responding to him in a rather ambivalent way.

The spatial relationship between positions is important in this sort of work. Although it can be done imaginatively, the work is much more effective if a person actually moves between the two points in the room, occupied by the self and the other. In this example, Joan marks the two points by symbolic objects (the picture and the cushion), creating the possibility of experiential shifts.

By spatially fixing the different positions, it becomes possible to leave the self-position and explore other perspectives. Marking the self-position makes this possible. The symbolic object, in this case the cushion, holds the person's "self" and protects it so that he can experience other viewpoints. Stepping into other perspectives undermines the myth that the self-view is the only reality.

Similar principles to these apply to other forms of invocatory work. You can use stones, small objects, cushions, or chairs to represent the other-position or positions. You can even explore a number of relationships simultaneously. If there are many objects, a number of other people can be represented. Groups or family networks can be investigated. Complex interrelationships can be explored from several different people's perspectives.

The Outsider Position

In the interaction between Andrew and Joan, two basic positions were created—the self-position and the other-position. These two positions were in relationship.

There is a third position that is possible in this scenario. This position is outside the scene altogether. Up to this point, Joan has been holding this place. She has played the role of neutral observer. An option that Joan could have offered to Andrew would have been for him to stand beside her and look at the scene from where she stood. He could have replaced the picture on the floor and stepped aside, so that he could look at both the cushion (representing himself) and the picture (representing his brother in the garden).

Introducing the observer role can open up access to new parts of a person's mental faculty. These might include his wiser parts. It can sometimes be useful to make this explicit. Rather than simply offering him her place, Joan might suggest to Andrew that he step into the shoes of his "therapist" or "wise adviser" and from that position tell "Andrew" how he should handle the situation with his brother. Sometimes this device will indeed bring wise advice about how to handle a difficult situation.

Group Work

Groups offer situations that challenge our attachments to particular positions and encourage you to see the points of view of others. Whether formal or informal, groups provide settings where you are constantly exposed to other people's perspectives.

At different stages of the group process, members may be more or less open to seeing the real qualities of others in the group. In the early phases of a group, there is often resistance to acknowledging difference. Members are preoccupied with finding common ground and creating shared identity. Processes that unfold in the group are similar to those you see in the individual. The group responds to its insecurities by creating a group "self."

The formation of group identity creates a danger that the members either are coerced into false positions or have their individual identities reinforced inasmuch as they are reflected in the group identity. This can be particularly problematic in support groups for people with similar problems. Individual identities, built, say, on being alcoholic or on being a survivor of sexual abuse, may simply be reinforced by belonging to a group of people who have created similar identities. In this case members will be subtly coerced into building stronger self-positions and distancing experiences that diverge from this image.

As the group grows in strength, however, the possibility for members to encounter one another grows. By skilled facilitation during this phase, the practitioner or therapist may enable people to appreciate the otherness of the other group members. When you empathize with other perspectives, self-views become less entrenched. It can be much harder to hold onto the self-position in a group than when working one-to-one. The extent to which this relinquishing of the self-position becomes possible does depend on the style of interaction within the group and the extent to which the creation of a group-self has been avoided. Nevertheless, in this respect groupwork provides a valuable method for applying Buddhist psychology.

The Threatening Other

A particular difficulty can arise when using other-centered methods if the "other" is a person who has been threatening or abusive. People who have experienced abuse may live with terrifying memories of things that were done by parents or other powerful adults. They may be haunted by images and dreams and may experience "flashbacks" in which scenes become so vivid that incidents of abuse are re-experienced as if the abuser were actually present. In these situations the question arises whether it is helpful to make the person who committed the abuse appear more real or not.

Although it is not helpful to increase the vividness of a flash-back experience, at other times increasing reality is valuable. It has been my experience that, far from being unhelpful, other-centered work can be extremely useful in these situations, but that the method of work needs to be chosen skillfully. Other-centered work is relevant in these situations because, as the person who perpetrated the abusive acts becomes more real *as a person*, the power of the rupa diminishes. He is no longer perceived just as the abuser. Other-centered work allows a person to move into a more exploratory mode of interaction with the other. It helps him or her to operate in a more adult mode.

When abuse is explored from the self-position, as happens when a person is reliving the experience either in discussion or through flashbacks, the perpetrator is perceived as he was perceived by the child. This is object-related work, which increases the rupa-ness of the perpetrator. He is huge and frightening. The person feels as she did in childhood because she has locked herself into a role which is counterpart to the image of the abuser. As she talks, her image is intensified and her terror increases. Getting out of this role into the observer role can be very helpful.

Other-centered work offers the possibility of shifting from a narrow, childhood self-view into an objective position. The perpetrator may then be seen as a person. This does not condone his actions, but it does reduce their overwhelming power. He may now be seen as rather pathetic, or a dirty old man. He may be seen as misguided or selfish. He may be seen as locked in his own destructive patterns. He is no longer a threatening monster.

The important point is that as the person starts to see the perpetrator of abuse through adult eyes, she starts to see him in the context of the range of human behaviors. She will certainly not approve of what she sees, but she is no longer the victim of it. She also sees the complexity of human motivation and action. She may understand him and even feel some pity or forgiveness. Most importantly, though, she feels free to let go of the haunting memories and move on.

Self is maintained by preserving the other as a self-indicator. Change the image of the other, and the self loses its supporting condition. When the self is painfully negative, as in the belief or statement "I am a victim," this can be liberating. Even when the self has been built on being a survivor, there is a time to let go and find broader perspectives.

The work that will diffuse the power of such a rupa image is often lengthy. Achieving distance and separation requires sensitivity and containment. If there is a likelihood of flashbacks and other under-distanced responses, it is important to avoid retraumatization. This means trying to avoid situations in which the other is perceived most powerfully as rupa. You could try using methods like drawing, but make the image very small, or use small objects to represent the abuser. You could talk about events that happened but keep your discussion in a rational, adult mode, only gradually allowing more emotional responses to arise. Finding a suitable mode in which to work, so that a person is neither under- or over-distanced from traumatic material, requires skill. It has been written about in articles by Mia Leijssen and by myself in *Beyond Carl Rogers* (Brazier 1993).

Mediation

Appreciating and understanding the other is not confined to situations in which the "other" is absent. Some circumstances involve deliberately bringing together, with a mediator, people who are in conflict with one another. The role of the mediator is to help both people involved to see each other's perspectives and respect each other's positions.

A friend of mine, who worked for many years as a mediator, went into some of the most difficult conflict situations in the world, in areas such as the Balkans and the former Soviet Union. His careful work is testimony to his skill in helping groups of people who are frightened, angry, and living with the after-effects of terrible conflicts. Often the people he brought together had been locked in their differences for generations, alternating between uneasy co-existence and bloody confrontation.

For each side in such situations, the people in the other faction have become identified as the enemy. They are invested with such negative associations that it is often hard to get beyond the imagery of hatred. Both sides present their own versions of events, colored by the stories each holds about the other. Views, understandably, are shaped by each side's experiences and by their self-perceptions. It is often hard to find any common reality. Images of atrocities are presented. Rapes, mutilations, and killings are described. Each powerful image creates another focus for the frightened and hurting people to identify with.

Yet, for healing to take place, common ground must be found between those on opposite sides of the conflict. Dialogue and understanding must be encouraged and nurtured. The two groups must start to see each other's reality, and get beyond the constructed images. Such work often begins with ordinariness. When you see someone as enemy, you construct an image of a monster. Just as the perpetrator of child abuse is seen as all-powerful and all bad, so too, the enemy of an oppressed group is generally perceived in wholly negative terms. Discovering that "the enemy" has a full range of human qualities and experiences breaks down the construction of the enemy-rupa and allows dialogue to start. Working with groups of young people, common interests in music or sports may be found; working with groups of women, common concerns for family and home. Ordinary interests provide the bridges that enable the "enemy" images to start to drop away.

From these beginnings, seeds of trust may be planted.

Although the situation may be finely balanced, the two sides can be invited to share more. How did it feel to be living with the fear of attack? How did it feel to lose friends, family, children? How did it feel to live through starvation and see your home destroyed by bombardments? As the two groups are invited to hear each other's experiences, the images of "the enemy" diminish and the common human experience enables trust to begin to grow. Reconciliation is not easy, but if it is to have a chance, the hurt on both sides has to be transcended, and this can happen only by such letting go.

THEORIES INTRODUCED IN THIS CHAPTER

- object-related work;
- other-centered work;
- observer perspective;
- groups and other-centered work;
- other-centered work with those who have experienced abuse; and
- mediation and other-centered work.

· 14 ·

Working with Environmental Factors

Your mind is conditioned by the things you expose it to. Nobody exists in isolation from a context, and that context contains the objects that you use in building a mentality. Your perception is colored by your pre-existing mentality. It can impose radically different interpretations on events depending on its predominating qualities. Nevertheless, the environment you inhabit and the activities you participate in condition your mental state. If you are aware of this, you will look at the effects of your lifestyle on your mentality and may make changes.

This chapter will explore ways in which you can use our environment and the daily activity you carry out within it to help you break out of conditioned mental states. Since Buddhist training is very much concerned with setting up environments conducive to such mental transformation, the earlier part of the chapter will deal particularly with the spiritual training context. The second part of the chapter will look at how spiritual training methods can be adapted to ordinary life situations.

To start with, consider a practice that the early Buddhists used. It roots the spiritual experience directly in the practitioner's experience of the body and of the physical world.

Work with the Elements

The body is not isolated from its surroundings. You are a physical being, made up of physical constituents, just as your environment is. Your body is not unique or special, as you might like to imagine. It is made of the same material elements as everything else. In this sense it is non-self.

Early Buddhists used practices that focused on the non-self nature of the body. In particular, they practiced meditating on the elements. Recognizing the elements of earth, air, water, fire, and space both inside and outside the body, they gained an experiential knowledge of the continuity of matter between the person and the world.

These meditations began with an exploration of the earth element. The practitioner meditated on the earth element within the body. This was its hard, substantial parts: bones, skin, hair, stomach contents, and so on. They would then meditate on the earth element outside the body. This might be ground, stone, wood, and so on. In meditating on these, the practitioner would contemplate the continuity of elements within and outside the body and would develop awareness that none of these constituents could be experienced as self.

In the Mahahatthipadopama Sutta, the Buddha's disciple Shariputra talks of the practice of meditating on the elements. He describes observing the elements "inside oneself" and "outside oneself." The aim of this practice was to reach a point where the common understanding of inside and outside broke down. "I am aware of the earth element in me. I am not the earth element. I am aware of the earth element outside me. I am not the earth element." The practitioner arrived at an experiential knowledge that the physical elements are continuous. There is no boundary between the person and the world. Both are made up of the same elements. Both are non-self.

Friends, just as when a space is enclosed by timber and creepers, grass and clay, it becomes termed a "house," so too, when a space is enclosed by bones and sinews, flesh and skin, it comes to be termed "rupa." (MN 28.26)

The practice of meditating on the elements was commonly used at the time of the Buddha. It seems to have been used particularly by the women's sangha. Meditating on the elements can still be a very useful practice, especially in situations of uncertainty or danger. It is reassuring to feel one's continuity with the rest of the material universe.

As discussed in Chapter 9, you can use grounding exercises to develop your experience of the continuity between the world and your body, and of the material nature of both. Doing this, you gain confidence in the solidity of matter. You recognize that you are not special and separate. Through such exercises you also gain a stronger experiential contact with the other, even coming to experience your physical being in this way. Through doing so, you come to fully inhabit your environment, loosening the restrictions which the self-perspective imposes.

Conditions for Spiritual Progress

The physical nature of your body and your environment provides one focus for training. Another focus is the pattern of activity in daily life. This also creates an environment for change, one that you can adapt to create healthier ways of being.

In the Akankheyya Sutta (MN 6), the Buddha talks about the conditions that are necessary for someone to make spiritual progress. He teaches that it is by living an ethical and committed lifestyle that this is achieved. In particular, he teaches that change is brought about through keeping precepts, keeping a serene, uncluttered mind, meditating, seeking insight, and living simply.

Here is a methodology for living. This prescription for a life of spiritual growth provides you with a list of five practices for refining your training. These provide a practical framework for thinking about your life; general principles that can be translated into everyday terms.

Keeping Precepts
The precepts are a behavioral code followed by Buddhists. They provide an ethical framework for a practitioner's life. Taking

precepts involves making a commitment to the life of training, and is generally done in a formal ceremony. There are different levels of precepts; the first level that people take is generally considered fundamental to the Buddhist lifestyle. These five precepts concern not taking life, not stealing or misappropriating property, not being sexually irresponsible, not speaking unwisely, and not using intoxicants. There are higher levels of precepts that describe more spiritually committed lifestyles, varying in different traditions. Often they are elaborations, reflecting the spirit of the first five. Some higher precepts also involve renunciation of various things to which a person might feel attachment, such as luxurious surroundings, cosmetics, or even personal ownership of possessions.

Keeping precepts is a fundamental practice, both because in a broad sense the precepts define a life that is ethical and not harming to others and also because precepts offer a benchmark against which a practitioner can develop awareness. As you progress in practice, you may become increasingly conscious of how you constantly fail in subtle ways in your attempts to keep the precepts. For instance, it is impossible to avoid being impli-cated in many acts of killing that happen in the world. You cannot walk across a field without treading on small creatures or eat a meal without knowing that some animal has probably died in its production, even if you are vegetarian. You cannot prevent mice getting caught in big harvesting machines or insects falling into grain hoppers. Dukkha is inevitable. The precepts thus become a means by which the practitioner both modifies her behavior and increases sensitivity.

Although there is no reason why a person who is not living a Buddhist life should choose to take Buddhist precepts, everyone's ethical behavior conditions their mental states. Ethical questions are therefore very relevant to psychological growth.

The Buddhist precepts provide an ethical code that is not very different from the values most people hold. If you live in ways that go against such values, you are probably creating a lot of misery for yourself and others around you as a result.

Keeping a Serene, Uncluttered Mind

Establishing calm provides a basis for living effectively. You saw in Chapter 9 how grounding can help to create a calm mind. Finding calm, however, is as much a function of your overall mentality. If you are caught in cycles of obsessive thoughts, or compulsively search for comforts to distract yourself, you will not be at peace. By increasing your awareness of these patterns, you can start to release yourself from your internal knots. You may find other practices that help in this. They may include mindfulness practices, which will be discussed later in this chapter.

Meditating

Meditation is probably the best-known aspect of Buddhist lifestyle in the West. Although it is not as universally practiced by Buddhists in the East as one might suppose, it does provide methods for calming the mind and gaining insight. Meditation can take a number of forms. An important aspect of all meditation is the development of concentration. Different meditation techniques take different focuses for this concentration.

Some approaches involve observing mental process. The practitioner simply sits with awareness, allowing the stream of thought to pass by without interfering. This form of meditation has been likened to sitting beside a river watching the flow of water. As the practitioner sits, the thoughts gradually settle and the mind becomes calm and clear. Observing the stream of thought, you learn much about your mental process and the habit-patterns that keep you trapped. This kind of meditation is sometimes called "choiceless awareness."

Other meditation techniques involve deliberately focusing the mind on a *wholesome object*. This might mean following the breath or holding an image in mind. It might involve looking at an actual object, such as a candle flame or a flower. This kind of meditation aims to quiet the mind. Sometimes the "object" of such meditation is the Buddha. At other times you may choose some other inspiring image, such as a picture of a bodhisattva or a religious phrase or mantra. The focus of your meditation symbolizes the spiritual dimension of life in whatever way you conceive it. When you sit in the presence of such a wholesome object, you allow our mind to be conditioned in positive ways. You also open your awareness to the inspirational object and, in this way, allow yourself to connect with an experience of the inspirational *other*. In doing so, you increase your capacity to open up to the world and to the miraculous.

Meditation is generally a regular part of the Buddhist practitioner's life, practiced on a daily basis. This regularity of practice maintains a process whereby the mind is continually exposed to positive sources of conditioning. It both lays down benign tracks in your mentality and clears away compulsive ones.

Many people meditate to relieve stress or gain awareness. This can be a useful practice. The activity undertaken does not even have to be formal meditation to be helpful. Sometimes I suggest to someone who does not have a meditation practice that she simply sit quietly for five minutes each day and note down all the thoughts that run through her mind. For someone who tends to become caught up in compulsive thought patterns this can be a useful exercise. It brings insight, and the daily practice of sitting quietly itself has a calming effect.

Seeking Insight
Much psychological work involves seeking insight. You can seek insight into your own process, and you can seek insight into wider spiritual meanings. Personal growth work often centers on gaining insight into the self, but the insight that the Buddha talks about in the Akankheyya Sutta is insight into what is beyond the self. This means breaking out of your conditioned thinking and experiencing your surroundings more fully. This type of insight involves spiritual breakthrough in which a deeper relationship with the world is found.

Living Simply
Spiritual practitioners live simply. Many people find it difficult to understand the ability of the person living a religious life to live happily without the things modern society thinks are essential. How could someone relax knowing that they do not have a pension plan? How could I do without a new kitchen this

year? Don't you get fed up with wearing the same clothes all the time?

Possessions complicate people's lives. Many of us seem to have an endless ability to accumulate things, and these get in the way of our getting on with life. You want to do things, but you are prevented by all the baggage you would have to dispose of first. This happens at a psychological as well as a material level. The alaya is our accumulation of habit-patterns. It is psychological baggage. Many people are often only too aware of how these old tracks prevent them from living effectively. You should not overlook, however, the physical level of accumulation and the way in which material clutter also slows life down.

In our community, because you have an engaged practice, you try to live a simpler life. As we work in ways that often require us to travel at short notice, this may be particularly important. Limiting possessions may include having fewer clothes or making do with a smaller range of toiletries. When a member of our community went to join the rural health project in Zambia for six months she took little more than the clothes she stood up in. She needed the luggage space for essential medicines and other medical supplies for the center. When one lives with others in relatively small spaces, possessions become something of a liability. They have to be stored, and when space is at a premium, one is constantly tripping over boxes of miscellaneous stuff. A few things, of course, are immensely useful, but so many of the trappings of modern life take up a lot of room and contribute little to essential requirements.

Accumulated possessions often restrict people's lives quite severely. I feel sad when I meet so many young people who are burdened and trapped by their affluent lifestyle. I remember a young woman in her early twenties who was desperate to find a new, well-paid job, so that she could keep paying her large mortgage and manage the loan repayments on her car. She said that she really wanted to travel and see the world, but though she was single and had no ties, she could not do so because she could not envisage a life that did not have the luxuries she had grown used to.

Possessions provide an illusion of security. Just like the mental accumulations of self-material, they provide means for sensory indulgence and for furnishing image and status. For this young woman, the house and car provided an illusion of security; but in reality they prevented her embarking on the things she really wanted to do in life.

Mindfulness Training

The five areas of practice considered in the previous section provide a framework for bringing training into daily life. Another practice that is commonly used by Buddhist practitioners in daily life is mindfulness training. Mindfulness training involves developing awareness in all that you do. It encompasses several of the principles underlying training listed above. In mindfulness training one develops three particular areas of awareness.

Keeping Buddha in Mind

The first aspect of mindfulness practice involves keeping awareness of your spiritual purpose. In Buddhist practice, this is particularly done by *keeping the Buddha in mind*. The Buddha symbolizes the heart of our aspiration. As the founder of the Buddhist faith, he represents the inspiration that fires our practice. You can keep the Buddha in mind by having images of him around your house and workplace. You may think about your mindfulness practice through the day and bring your awareness back to whatever you are doing at that time. You may recite a mantra or phrase to yourself.

For Pure Land Buddhists, holding an image of the Pure Land in mind is an important aspect of practice. The *nembutsu* practice is an example of this. This is the repeated recitation of the phrase *namo amida bu*, which roughly translates as homage to Amida Buddha and expresses our continuing gratitude to the Buddha Amida. Amida Buddha is a personification of the Buddha's continuing teachings in the world.

These are traditional ways of doing the practice, but the essence of all these practices of keeping the Buddha in mind is the act of keeping your focus on higher ideals. You can each therefore find an image or phrase that works for you. The aim is to keep your attention on inspirational images and reconstrue phenomena as indicators of enlightenment instead of indicators of self.

Being Present

The second aspect of mindfulness practice is to have awareness of what you do. This means being present in your actions. When you wash dishes, you wash dishes. Feel the hot water in the bowl, enjoying the sensation as it runs through your hands and the colorful bubbles as they catch the light. Handle the cups carefully, enjoying the smooth texture of the china, and appreciating the skill of the potter who made them. When you make the bed, you make the bed. Feel the smooth expanse of the sheet as you lay it across the mattress. Appreciate the warmth of the blankets and the colorful pattern on the counterpane. Think of the needs of the person who will sleep in the bed. This aspect of mindfulness practice involves being present in the moment and opening your mind to an appreciation of all the things that have come together to enable that moment. It also reminds you to give your attention to the physical world, thus creating opportunities to become more grounded and more in contact with real things.

Noticing Habit-patterns

As you develop mindfulness, you become aware of the processes that get in the way of your mindfulness. You notice the habitual thoughts that crowd into your mind as you work and prevent you from just getting on with the task. These are the manifestations of self-energy. You become aware of them—how they arise, how they are maintained, and how they fall away. You try to let them go and return to mindfulness.

These three aspects of mindfulness practice are not separate. The Buddha is the enlightened one. Enlightened perception sees everything with appreciation and gratitude, just as it is, in the moment, free from self-view. This means seeing everything as dharma. When you see dharma you live in the Pure Land, home of Buddhas. In this way, being present in your actions and in the world is keeping Buddha in mind. Conversely, when you really keep Buddha in mind, you are fully present in all that you do.

Whether or not a person is committed to a Buddhist path, the basic principles that lie behind these mindfulness practices can be adapted to create a healthier attitude toward life. These practices are practical applications of theories this book has already explored. They involve allowing your mind to be conditioned by positive and inspirational rather than compulsive forces and moving out of self-focus and into relationship with the world.

Intensity of Training

Intensity in practice enables change. For someone who has embarked on a life of training, the demands of living without habitual distractions can itself create extra pressures. When you are really interacting with others, or living in a way that is more fully engaged with important work, you live with emotional and physical intensity. This intensity itself can bring you directly into contact with your patterns of habit-energy. As you become tired or emotionally drained, you may encounter old triggers that can lead you into old compulsions. The temptation can be to withdraw into your personal world; but this is often just the time when you need to work hardest. You need to tackle these patterns of behavior while at the same time continuing to live in a way that is engaged with life. If you can continue to be available to others and undertake whatever daily occupation you have, you will prevent yourself from slipping back into the old patterns of escape.

It is the intensity that a particular trainee brings to the Buddhist life that shapes the progress, or lack of it, which she experiences. The greater the awareness you bring to your work, the greater the possibility for your own spiritual and psychological growth, and the more useful you will be for others. Intensity often comes when you immerse yourself in your work and at the same time keep awareness of the process you are going through in doing it: of the patterns of thoughts that arise, of the reactions you experience, of your willingness or unwillingness in the task, and of what you are actually doing. In this way, intensity of spiritual practice comes from sustaining mindfulness while choosing activities that are intrinsically worthwhile.

Developing Awareness

Mindfulness practices are concerned with fostering awareness and keeping attention on things that will have a positive effect on the mind. So far, you have looked at these activities primarily in the context of Buddhist practice. The remainder of this chapter will describe practical approaches that anyone can use to develop these qualities.

Journaling

It is common in many forms of psychological work to keep a journal. This may be used in a free-flowing way, or for specific exercises, or with particular structures. Buddhist psychology suggests that people have a tendency constantly to reinforce their self-structures. This needs to be taken into account when undertaking journaling work.

Keeping a free-flowing journal has mixed value. On the one hand, it can provide a place where experiences and thoughts can be recorded and reflected on. This process allows you to put feelings and intuitions into words and clarify them, which may provide emotional relief. It also externalizes subjective experience, which may provide distancing and objectivity.

On the other hand, it can also reinforce the self-view and create a stronger attachment to a particular identity. In a journal, you have free rein to construct a self-story, with no outsiders present to challenge your assertions. Anyone who kept a diary as a teenager knows what excesses of melodrama or vitriol can be used to justify a fragile identity. Journaling exercises that provide a degree of structure and challenge may therefore be more useful in avoiding too much self-indulgence.

One therapeutic method that makes considerable use of journaling exercises is Morita therapy. This method, developed by Japanese psychiatrist Shoma Morita early in the twentieth century, has been brought to the West through the work of

David Reynolds. The Morita approach draws heavily on Buddhist ideas. It puts a lot of emphasis on action and lifestyle. Reynolds has developed his own combination of this and other Japanese therapies, which he calls Constructive Living.

In particular, the Morita method focuses on moving a person into purposeful action and away from a state where they are at the mercy of crippling emotions. It places a lot of emphasis on the distinction between action, which is under the control of the person, and feelings, which are not. Unlike many Western approaches which emphasize waiting until something feels right before acting, the Morita approach emphasizes putting the attention into whatever activity needs to be done and allowing feelings to flow in their own way. The aim is not to eliminate feelings but to accept that they are just part of your experience. You do not need to become fixated on them.

This approach accords with the Buddhist model of the mind. Most feelings arise as a result of your habitual thoughts. They are responses to self-indicators. Giving them excessive attention simply allows those response patterns that support the self-structure to be maintained and rigidified. Action, on the other hand, takes you into direct contact with the physical world and with other people. Morita therapy takes the focus of attention away from the flutter of self-thoughts to a broader engagement with life.

> *Morita therapy does not suggest that we live life as automatons regardless to our wishes—far from it. We should examine our lives carefully, living each moment effectively and well. Every small action—the way we climb stairs, open a door, enter a room, wash our hands—should be done purposefully and thoughtfully in concert with our deepest long-term needs.*
>
> *Awareness of, and sensitivity to our inner states are essential to Morita therapy; such awareness and sensitivity allow us to be properly directed by our ultimate concerns, and not just pushed around by momentary whims or feelings.*
> (Reynolds 1980, p. 18)

In Morita approaches, journaling exercises are introduced as a way of directing a person's attention toward their actions. A person is asked to record what they do during the day. The therapist highlights the difference between attention that is directed toward action and that which is preoccupied with feelings. He annotates the diary, providing interpretations and comments along these lines. In this way the therapy has a strong educational aspect. The diary provides a means of reviewing actions that provides (a) insight into the relationship between actions and the natural flow of feelings, and (b) a broad view of how actions together create purposeful living.

Reynolds offers his own form of the Morita diary. He suggests creating two columns. In one of these are recorded the actions of the day and in the other are recorded the feelings that were experienced alongside them. The message here is that while thoughts and feelings come and go and can be left to take care of themselves, you can make deliberate choices about your actions. I have used variants of this myself, both in reflecting on my own experience and in helping others. I have found that the emphasis on recording what is actually done is extremely useful in reducing the power of obsessive or depressive thoughts.

Time

Morita-style journaling methods can make you aware of the way you use time. Focusing on what you have done creates a picture of the balance of different activities through the day. The way you use time often reflects your priorities in life. Some tasks are unavoidable, but most are to some degree chosen. In a broader sense, the lifestyle choices you have made create the demands on your time, which you then tend to see as beyond your control. Creating a record of time usage can often bring surprises. You may discover that you spend far more time on some activities and less on others, than you had imagined. You can also notice your reactions to these observations. What activities do you value, and which do you view as a waste of time?

Journaling that pays particular attention to the way time is used can also reveal longer-term patterns of time use. Keeping a log in which notes are made at regular intervals through the day reveals patterns of activity or changes in mood. You may become aware of natural cycles of energy and mood and learn to live with them, either by adapting your activity or by carrying on in spite of the feelings. Such logs can be maintained over a long period of time, revealing yet larger cycles, which may be hormonal, weather-related, seasonal, or related to particular memories or associations.

Sometimes, structuring your time can provide a framework for change. It can be useful to make active decisions to do certain things at regular times—time to meditate regularly, to sit down and eat meals, to meet with friends, to relax. Living in community at our center we live by a structured schedule, incorporating such activities on a regular basis and creating an ordered day in which work, formal spiritual activities, and social time are planned. This provides opportunities for a greater degree of communal activity and eliminates much of the mental energy that is otherwise spent in deciding what to do next.

Living Environments

The space in which you live conditions your mental state. If you live in bright, clean surroundings, you are more likely to feel happy. If you live in a dirty, cluttered space you are more likely to feel depressed. Some people seem more affected by physical surroundings than others, but most are affected to some degree.

Making changes in your living environment can have powerful effects upon your mental state. This might mean moving to a new house or apartment, but it probably requires less drastic change. It might simply mean redecorating or rearranging furniture. There are a number of reasons why the process of changing one's living space may facilitate mental change.

- The space acts as a rupa for you, conditioning particular mind states and behaviors. If you have experienced particular events when living in a place, the place may act as a reminder of them, and the mind state associated with the events may persist.
- Changing the environment directs your attention toward action rather than introspection. This is good Morita-style therapy.

- Creating a clearer space can symbolically represent creating a clearer mind. It will condition quieter mind states.
- New associations can be created with the new space. Colors and furnishings can be chosen to support a healthier lifestyle.

Particular things may be introduced into the living or working environment that support present awareness or spiritual practice, or that condition particular mental states. These might include inspirational images, pictures or mementoes of loved ones, or natural objects.

Shrines

In Buddhist households it is common to find a household shrine. People may create a special place where they can sit and meditate, or a place where they can be reminded of people who have died. Even for people who profess no spiritual background, creating special places that commemorate important aspects of their lives is common. When I was working on a housing estate in Newcastle, I met a woman who had a special shelf in her living room on which were photos of all the members of her family who had died. She told me that whenever she opened a bottle of wine, she always put a full glass on that shelf for her relatives. This woman's belief system was not Buddhist, yet her shelf of photos was not very different from the ancestor shrines found in many Buddhist houses in the East.

Creating a special space within your home brings your experience of the sacred into the heart of your life and gives space for it to grow and flower. This may have different meanings for different people. It may be a space of calm, of reflection, of remembrance, or of inspiration.

Ritual

Creating a special space within the house provides a focus for small degrees of ritual, so often lacking in daily life. Ritual anchors awareness and develops your capacity for feeling respect and appreciation. Modern society tends to avoid ritual and bring increasing levels of informality into most areas of life. There has been a move against any form of ceremony or even formality.

Though there are some signs that this trend may be reversing, most people live without even the simple family rituals that were taken for granted in the past.

By valuing formality, you can bring a sense of order back into your life. This may be as simple a change as sitting down to a meal with the family rather than allowing each member of the household to eat separately in front of the television. Living in community, I have come to appreciate the opportunities that shared meals give for conversation and for building a sense of common ground. Because you are a Buddhist community, you generally start the meal with an offering. This provides a focus to the beginning of the meal—the expression of gratitude—but also offers a silent space in which you can be aware of the company and the food. Some groups like to sit in silence holding hands or light a candle before a meal. Such actions provide a separation between daily life and the act of eating. They bring the group together. Creating such rituals, you establish a more grounded approach to life.

Watering Good Seeds
There is a Buddhist practice that the Vietnamese Buddhist teacher Thich Nhat Hanh calls *Watering Good Seeds* (Hanh 1992). It involves giving attention to those aspects of your life, particularly your behavior, which are positive. It means building times into the day for activities that are replenishing and calming, such as walking in a park or listening to music. It means placing yourself in environments that promote positive mind states. This practice is based on the principle that by your present actions you create the conditions for future actions. By evoking positive mind states, you create the propensity for future happiness.

Spiritual Friends
The people you associate with condition your mental states. Your patterns of behavior reflect the patterns of those with whom you spend time. You have already seen how interconnected people are and how their moods and attitudes rub off on one another. The Buddha made much of the concept of spiritual friends and of the importance of associating with those

who would support your practice and not undermine it. Being surrounded by people who are caring and who appreciate whatever changes you are trying to make can make a tremendous difference to your lives. If a person has problems with alcohol, it is unlikely they will manage to change their drinking habits if all their friendships revolve around evenings in the pub.

THEORIES INTRODUCED IN THIS CHAPTER

- lifestyle as a condition for change;
- precepts;
- meditation and meditative exercises;
- mindfulness training;
- Morita approaches;
- watering good seeds; and
- spiritual friends.

· 15 ·

Catching Snakes and Riding Dragons

At the bottom of the ant hill, the bhikshu found the Naga serpent. "Do not harm the Naga serpent," the brahmin advised.

The Naga serpent represents spiritual energy. Coiled within you, it lies sleeping under the layers of conditioned mind that you think of as your self. Your energy is sapped by the habit-patterns you are caught in. It waits to be rediscovered and used.

At our center in France, you sometimes come across snakes. Mostly harmless, they like to coil themselves under the loose stones of walls and paths. As the summer sun heats up the stones, the snake basks in the warmth, hidden and safe. Lift a stone, and sometimes you will see the smooth dark coils of a *couleuvre*, the common snake of the area.

Take care though. Not all snakes are so harmless. Sometimes you find adders. Two summers ago, walking on the road at dusk, you came upon five or six young adders enjoying the residual heat of the day that the tarmac surface provided. Knowing these could deliver a poisonous bite, you took care to avoid treading on them as the light faded, and watched for them on subsequent evening walks. Adders need respect.

Encountering snakes provokes a strong reaction in many people. It has even been suggested that humans carry an instinctive, genetically determined fear of snakes. Yet snakes have also been used in healing since prehistoric times. Snake venom can be used to make potent drugs or to create antidotes to the poisonous bites. The person who knew how to catch and milk a snake of this venom had the potential to be a healer. Thus snakes have been the symbol of healing and wisdom in many cultures, including your own. You are all familiar, for example, with the symbol of intertwined snakes that denotes the medical profession. The Buddha used the image of the snake to represent this combination of danger and healing.

The Snake Sutra

There is evidence that the early Buddhists may have had a role as healers. Certainly the image of the snake is used a number of times in the sutras, and the association of snakes with healing is clearly implied.

In the Ant Hill Sutra the image of the Naga Serpent represents spiritual energy. In the Alagaddupama Sutta (MN 22), or Snake Sutra, the Buddha uses the image of the snake to represent the Dharma or Buddhist teachings. He describes how the person who tries to catch a poisonous snake must approach it carefully and catch it in the correct way, using a forked stick to pin it to the ground by its neck so that it can be grasped by the back of the head. In this way it can be milked of venom without danger that the person holding it will be bitten. If a person grasps it wrongly, say by its coils, the snake will turn around and sink its fangs into that unfortunate person's hand. If the man grasps it correctly, however, even though the snake may writhe and twist around him, it will not be able to deliver its poisonous bite. The Buddhist teachings are here presented as medicine that may be either powerfully healing or destructive.

As your spiritual practice deepens you may encounter the darker sides of yourself, previously hidden by social habit. In the Ant Hill Sutra in Chapter 7, the more superficial layers of conditioning are highly socialized defensive structures. Most people smooth over life's vicissitudes by avoidance or pleasantries, which create tenacious habit-patterns. Socialization both enables people to live comfortably and creates a barrier to real spiritual change. As a you begin to address your spiritual side, these layers may start to dissolve and the deeper layers of conditioning emerge, which have their roots in your more primitive aspects. As the Ant Hill Sutra shows, these are both the most dangerous aspects and those closest to the Naga serpent, which represents pure spiritual energy.

Spiritual training can lead you to look into those parts of yourself where these energies lie. It breaks down your common patterns of escape and distraction and leads you to fall back upon other aspects of yourself. These parts are both a source of greater spiritual energy and a potential source of danger, as, if the energies released are not contained through spiritual practice and ethical rigor, you can go badly off the track.

Those who work with people who have been very disadvantaged or abused often come across individuals whose lives are driven by these more primitive forces. This is not through spiritual training, but because normal socialization has broken down under stress, or because they have never had that level of socialization in the first place. For such people, a lack of spiritual containment is likely to create dangers of spiralling distress and pain as lustful or aggressive energies play havoc with their lives. Nevertheless, you should be aware that these energies, albeit difficult to handle, are closer to the spiritual core. They therefore offer the potential for transformation. This explains why those who make most spiritual progress in life are often not those who have lived quiet, conventional lives, but those who have, in some sense, lived near the edge.

The Snake Sutra, then, suggests that you need to take care how you approach spiritual teachings. Any teaching can be misinterpreted and used to justify the wrong sort of thinking.

The Sutra begins with the account of a certain bhikshu who wrongly believed he could act as he pleased as long as he purified his thoughts. The Buddha is quite forthright with him, emphasizing the importance of right action and the impossibility of separating the mind state from the effects of what one does. Ethical behavior and discipline create the container in which the training can be put into practice. Taking on training requires commitment, and it is important that it is taken on in the right spirit.

They do not learn Dharma for the sake of criticizing others and for winning in debates. (MN 22)

Motivation and the right intention provide a basis for spiritual growth. If you have these, you will make progress even though at times your training can feel tortuous and painful. If you struggle to face the turmoil that comes when you try to break your habit-patterns, you will recognize the image of the snake. Psychological change is not always easy, and at times facing your darker aspects can feel like wrestling with a large and ferocious serpent; but if you can hold onto your basic faith and keep your sense of reality, the writhing coils will not throw you off course.

That which is potent can be used for good or ill. In Buddhist thinking, the energy that you have is all good energy, with the potential to be used for spiritual purpose. The crucial thing is how you harness your energy and to what purpose you use it.

Working with Your Own Darker Feelings

When you make a commitment to spiritual training, you may discover aspects of yourself that are difficult and painful to acknowledge. Sometimes these dark parts are all too familiar; at other times they can surprise you. A serious engagement with training creates circumstances that confront you and that are likely to provoke your reactivity so that you can become more aware of it and overcome it. In addition, as you let go of the socialized defensive levels, you may find less socialized ones emerging in their wake.

If you are involved in helping others, it is particularly important to be able to recognize and contain these responses, since the work is often personally challenging, and is of itself likely to confront you with your inner demons. It is also, however, better that you are familiar with your areas of sensitivity and reactivity so that you do not find yourself reacting inappropriately when you are with someone you are trying to help. Containment should not mean repression, but it should mean not acting out your worst impulses.

You must develop the ability to recognize when you are about to fall into negative patterns of reaction. This recognition will give you the opportunity to use that reactivity as an occasion for training rather than be carried away by your feelings. If you can do this, you will not only increase your ability to cope with your own demons, but you will also be able to listen to other people who are distressed without being drawn into their turmoil.

Primary and Secondary Feelings

So how can you work with your darker responses? How do you integrate those aspects of your experience which seem most frightening and destructive? First, you need to recognize that there are different sorts of feeling that can arise.

As you saw when you looked at the teaching of the Fyour Noble Truths, there are responses that arise naturally in response to dukkha. They include feelings such as sadness, anger, grief, and regret. These are direct reactions to affliction. Call them primary samudaya reactions.

The primary reaction at this stage of the samudaya process is uncomfortable, and the impulse is to escape. Energy wells up, and gets redirected. It hooks on to an object. This is the secondary reaction. Such responses are concerned with escaping the pain. You build up habitual patterns of escape of this kind. Such patterns have been the focus of much of this book.

Primary responses are direct expressions of suffering arising from afflictions. Secondary responses avoid the reality of dukkha and build habit-patterns. In practice, a person experiences a combination of primary and secondary responses. Both sorts of response are fuelled by the energy that arises from encounters with difficulties; both potentially provide the means for spiritual training. Releasing energy caught up in dark, destructive feelings generates the possibility of change.

Both sets of responses are part of the samudaya process. Raw feelings arise and attach to an object. Spiritual training is about breaking into the samudaya response. In his teaching on nirodha or containment, the Buddha told his followers to unhook from the object of samudaya. The process of unhooking interrupts the patterns that have been created, freeing the energy for training and purposeful action. You harness the energy of your reactivity for the spiritual path instead of being swept into patterns of habit-reaction. This is containment. This is nirodha.

So when you experience difficult, dark feelings or when you meet others who are in such states of distress, you can see that the feelings with which the person is struggling will be a mix of primary and secondary responses. Some of the feelings will be straightforward responses to suffering; others are reactive patterns. The secondary samudaya response involves attachment. In extreme situations, this may operate in primitive ways, as described in the images found at the lower levels of the Ant Hill Sutra—as raw lust or hate attachments.

Anger

Buddhists are generally thought of as peaceful people, slow to express anger. The Buddha taught that his followers should abandon anger and hate, yet anger and hate still arise in most of us, and for many people are a frequent and understandable response to terrible or oppressive circumstances. Repressed anger can lead to depressive states—the despair due to anger of which the Buddha spoke. How, then, do you work with feelings of anger as they arise and neither break into inappropriate outbursts nor fall into destructive repression?

If you try to get rid of anger without a real change of heart, you risk simply repressing it and deluding yourself. You do not in this case truly overcome your anger, but only divert it. This can be unhealthy and destructive to all around you. Repressed anger has a way of emerging indirectly. The Ant Hill Sutra presents the image of the grumpy toad, representing despair due to anger. A person who represses their anger may act in ways that can be labeled passive–aggressive, letting resentment slip out indirectly through remarks or actions that sabotage or undermine others.

In the Kakacupama Sutta (MN 21), the Buddha tells the story of a woman who had a reputation for being kind, gentle and peaceful. This woman's maid set out to test her mistress's patience by deliberately provoking her. Eventually her mistress lost her temper and hit the maid with a rolling pin, cutting her head. The maid then complained to neighbors, and soon her mistress's reputation was in tatters. No longer seen as peaceful, she was labeled a rough, violent and cruel woman. From this colorful account you see that the Buddha understood the dangers of suppressing your anger. Impulses towards anger and revenge need to be rooted out completely, not soothed over by easy circumstances. Anyone can be nice when the sun is shining.

Those who live or work with people who have suffered greatly have special reason to root out angry reactivity—and many opportunities to practice, too. People who have been badly treated may be harboring a great deal of anger, and when you expose yourself to their conflicted and angry emotions, that anger can get passed on to you. It is easy then to be swept away by your own responses. Feelings can be very contagious, and if you have not made some progress in controlling your anger, it may erupt at the wrong times.

So what can you learn from the Buddhist teachings about how to work with anger? How can you develop steadiness in the face of others' reactions, and how can you help others to work through their angry feelings?

Anger and Identity

If you look at the examples of anger given in the sutras, you find that when the Buddha talked of giving up anger, most of the references are to anger that arose out of personal pride or attachment to identity. This anger creates a strong resistance to criticism, making it difficult for a person to change. People caught in anger and resentment are described as being unwilling to be corrected. A number of the sutras refer to anger making it difficult for a person to be admonished and thus to make any progress in the spiritual life. Unwillingness to look at one's own part in something, or to change, means that this kind of anger feeds itself. It then leads to a pernicious cycle of anger and despair.

The Buddha's view of anger offers a good example of the

self-prison. The emotion arises when one feels the self under attack. Pride or feelings of entitlement get the better of them. The anger wards off others, and justifies patterns of thinking and action that create the self-image. Anger is often a means of protecting the self; yet to overcome this kind of anger one must get beyond self.

The view of anger as a form of self-prison is reinforced if you look at the Buddha's suggestions for working with anger. In the Cetokhila Sutta (MN 16) he speaks of overcoming anger through ardor, devotion, perseverance, and striving. In the Cula-Assapura Sutta (MN 40) he speaks of overcoming it through cultivating loving kindness. Both these strategies break down self-preoccupation by encouraging outwardly focused concern. You break anger by reaching out to others. Cultivating ardor and devotion builds higher aspiration. You go beyond self by aspiring to something better. Increasing perseverance, and striving overcomes preoccupation with personal discomforts or irritations so they cease to hold your attention. Developing loving kindness creates a concern for the people around you.

Anger and Grief
Anger is often a secondary emotion. Frequently it arises on the back of other emotions such as fear, hurt, or grief. Anger protects the self, and the self protects against experiencing grief and pain associated with dukkha. If you live in troubled times, you build identity as a protection against the feelings that arise from unavoidable events. At the same time, those very uncertainties of life make it inevitable that your identity feels threatened. When this happens you may react angrily. Much anger is defensive in this way.

When working with anger, you may need to discover and face the primary emotion that is hidden by the anger. If you can do this, you do not need to cling so tightly to identity, and you can release the energy tied up in it.

A person who has recently been bereaved may express a great deal of anger. This is generally regarded as a normal part of the grieving process. In fact, however, it is often an attempt to escape the overwhelming sadness. Anger reinforces the self-construct.

It says: "I don't deserve this." The process is quite understandable. It provides psychological strength for someone struggling without many resources. At a time of bereavement the normal structures of identity may be in collapse. If the one who died was very close, a person may suddenly feel devoid of identity. They cease to be the other half of a partnership: the husband, the wife, the father, the daughter. Identity has been the psychological protection against life's traumas. To lose it just at this point when life is most painful can feel overwhelming and may lead to psychological breakdown.

The reconstruction of the self, though spiritually problematic, is the normal response to dukkha. Becoming angry is part of this process. What Buddhism teaches is an exceptional response, often requiring a context of training and support. The possibility for spiritual breakthrough is ever-present, but for most people facing a sudden bereavement, the gradual construction of new identity brings relief.

On the other hand, a person who expresses more sadness and less anger may create less rigid self-structures. Facing primary emotional responses leads to greater spiritual change and growth through the experience.

Recently, a good friend died in tragic circumstances. In the days after I heard about his death, I found myself repeatedly feeling irrational waves of anger. How could the accident have happened? Why was life so unfair? Why had he not taken greater care? I knew that most of the anger was not founded on reality, so I observed it more closely. As soon as I did so, I realized that I had been subtly avoiding facing the horror of what had happened. As long as I was angry, I did not have to see the unpredictability of death; to acknowledge that life could be extremely precarious and that what seemed cozy and permanent could be utterly destroyed in a few moments.

Anger often accompanies tragedy. There is clamor for guilt to be apportioned. Accidents happen, and frequently today litigation follows. As a society you grow less and less able to live with the knowledge of impermanence. You want to preserve the illusion that bad things do not happen to good people like ourselves.

Anger and the Skandha Process

Anger that is driven by many experiences of fear and pain creates a pattern of reactivity that becomes part of the continuous process of maintaining the self. A person who has felt much pain may be a very angry person, apt to react to the slightest provocation. Working with anger may involve working with the primary feelings that give rise to it. It may also involve observing the continuing pattern of reactions and learning to interrupt it before the anger is expressed in a damaging way.

Awareness of skandha process is helpful. The process begins with a perception. This perception provokes the angry reaction. This reaction leads to patterns of association. The person is by now swept into an old pattern of thinking and responding and acts on the basis of the patterns that have been laid down by past actions, which in this case may be unwise. In this way, the seeds for future angry outbursts are sown.

The angry outburst appears to arise from seeing a particular situation. Someone who gets angry easily may see many things as provocative. This is because perception is conditioned. Their mentality seeks out things that confirm their world-view. Their senses lock on to objects that attract their attention. For a person who has a lot of anger, sources of irritation will catch the attention, and things that other people would not notice will catch the eye. Perhaps he only notices how noisily that man eats. Perhaps he only sees how often that woman interrupts people as she talks. Perhaps he only sees that other woman always puts the hot pan down on the work-surface where it causes burn marks, or always makes a silly laugh as she speaks. A person feels angry and then seeks aspects of other people's behavior to justify feeling angry. The mentality always watches for those things that confirm its view.

The practice of guarding the sense doors can be helpful in identifying the processes that feed anger. You can learn to notice how your attention is caught and how you seek out particular rupas. You can then deliberately challenge these self-perceptions. You can do this, for example, by using metta practice, which involves deliberately cultivating loving kindness for the other person. You imaginatively see their perspective and stand in their shoes. How does it feel for them to experience your anger all the time? What might they be feeling to cause them to act in the ways they do? New perspectives can loosen the hold of anger.

Another way of working is to develop awareness of body responses to anger. Vedana response is a body reaction, preceding the stage of samjna entrancement. By becoming aware of the physical symptoms, you may catch an angry response before it leads you to act angrily. Noticing the hot rush of indignation, the tension of rejection, or the cold sweat of rage may help you avoid conflict, just as, in Chapter 5, Sharon was helped to recognize her anger as it arose and so avoid losing her temper at work.

Avoiding Reinforcement

There has been a vogue in some youstern therapies for the idea that anger needs to be "gotten out." Happily, this approach is now being questioned in many quarters as practitioners discover that anger can be a bottomless pit and that thumping cushions increases rather than decreases aggressive traits. This understanding is completely predictable from the perspective of Buddhist psychology. What is enacted creates the propensity for future action. The Buddhist practitioner should therefore be wary of encouraging angry speech or action in the helping context.

On the other hand, there are occasions when such exploration is useful. There are a number of reasons why anger may need to be expressed in psychological work.

- Repression of anger is not helpful, and it is generally better for a person to be authentic in their emotions. Sometimes a person needs to express anger in order to know its depth or to release a head of steam built up over time. This sort of outburst of anger may be important in getting to a place of honesty.

- Expressing anger in a space that offers containment may help a person recognize the destructive potential they are carrying. It may help them to appreciate the need for working through the impulses to harm others.

- By expressing anger, the person may get beyond the anger to the primary emotion. It is not unusual for a person to become angry before reaching a point where they can express grief or hurt. Exploring the depths of anger may reveal repressed grief or other emotions.

- A person may go through periods of anger as part of the self-reconstruction process in order to emerge from depths of despair and grief that they are unable to face in other ways.

So you must consider these factors but also to weigh against them the problems of creating habit-energy that will feed future angry responses. There will always be a trade-off between the immediate benefits of gaining relief and of reaching understanding of the roots of the anger and the longer-term problems of reinforcing patterns of angry behavior through the process of expression. It is certainly questionable whether there is any value in repeatedly expressing anger in this way.

Useful Anger

As a therapist, I have sometimes experienced anger arising when I am with a person whom I am helping. This can be unnerving. I do not like to think I can be angry with those I am supposed to be helping. Acknowledging such responses may reduce my complacency.

Recognizing anger can also provide insight into the psychological process of the helping relationship. It is therefore useful to recognize angry feelings and step back from them, regarding them as helpful information. Perhaps the response arises through contagion and the other person is repressing angry feelings, which are emerging indirectly. Perhaps their behavior invites anger as a counterpart to their own role as they re-enact a pattern of playing the victim or provocateur. Or perhaps the feelings are simply an indication that the practitioner has areas of repressed anger that need to be addressed.

Some anger is not self-motivated at all, however. (Though this occurs less often than you would like to think, since you all, almost certainly, project anger from time to time as part of your self world-view.) Although the Buddha spoke frequently of eradicating strong defensive emotions such as anger, he did not decry all forms of sharp response. Indeed, in the Snake Sutra, he expressed himself in very strong terms to the mistaken bhikshu. In the Aranavibhanga Sutta (MN 139) he also suggests that there is sometimes a place for sharp speech.

> *When one knows overt sharp speech to be untrue, incorrect and unbeneficial, one should on no account utter it. When one knows overt sharp speech to be true, correct and unbeneficial, one should try not to utter it. But when one knows overt sharp speech to be true, correct and beneficial, one may utter it, knowing the time to do so.* (MN 139.10)

This extract shows that the Buddha saw a time for judicious expression of criticism, but that this expression should arise out of the needs of the situation rather than the lack of containment on the part of the person expressing it. It needs to be for the general good, not for self-serving reasons. Overall in this sutra, the Buddha advocates an unhurried, open way of being, in which responses are not driven by personal preferences or agendas.

Fear and Dread

Anger arises as a defense against painful emotion. Recognizing and facing the primary emotion that lies behind your anger may release you from the hold of angry feelings. Facing the primary feelings, however, is not easy. You may be afraid of your emotions, which is why you repress or divert them. But also, your mind creates and amplifies negative states. Fears and anxieties are often rooted in mental constructs that ultimately arise from a longing for permanence. At root, your fear is fear of impermanence. There is a strongly compulsive element in anxiety. This is the product of its role in self-formation.

In the Sutra on Fear and Dread (Bhayabherava Sutta, MN 4), the Buddha talks of his understanding of the way the mind creates and amplifies fear. He describes how the bhikshu, going into the jungle, might be beset with anxieties. Hearing the crack of a twig or a bird in the undergrowth, he might interpret the sound as an indication of evil spirits.

Most of us can identify with such experiences. I remember spending a few nights sleeping out in the woods in our center in France. I did not take a tent as it was summer and I liked being in the open under the stars. The first night was wonderful, and I slept soundly, but the second night I heard a rustling in the undergrowth nearby. I am not generally worried by the noises of the woods at night and feel little fear being in the open, but for some reason, on this occasion fear arose.

Quite suddenly the thought entered my mind that I had heard a local person talk of wild boar in the area. I knew that it was extremely unlikely that any wild boar would venture near to our land. We are several miles from the forest, and even there boars are shy and rarely seen. In the darkness, though, my mind started to race away. The rustling increased. I felt my body reacting with fear, my heart pounding and my ears searching for more clues as to what was in the vicinity. I told myself not to be silly, but for a few minutes my mind was filled with images of a large, tusked boar pounding out of the brambles and trampling me underfoot.

For a few minutes I lay holding my breath. Eventually I convinced myself that I was being silly. The creature went its own way. I never saw it, but most likely it was a hedgehog or some other small animal. Even mice can make a lot of noise at night. So, the mind plays tricks, and our fears about impermanence surface in crazy ways.

The Buddha uses the Sutra on Fear and Dread to describe the practical methods he used for working with his own fears. During his spiritual journey prior to his enlightenment he would deliberately evoke fears by going into dark places in the forest where shrines full of skulls and other frightening images were situated. Here demons and harmful spirits were believed to lurk.

While I walked, the fear and dread came upon me; I neither stood nor sat nor lay down till I had subdued that fear and dread. While I stood, the fear and dread came upon me; I neither walked nor sat nor lay down till I had subdued that fear and dread. While I sat, the fear and dread came upon me; I neither walked nor stood nor lay down till I had subdued that fear and dread. While I lay down, the fear and dread came upon me; I neither walked nor stood nor sat till I had subdued that fear and dread. There are some . . . who perceive day when it is night and night when it is day. I say that on their part this is an abiding delusion. But I perceive night when it is night and day when it is day . . . tireless energy was aroused in me and unremitting mindfulness was established, my body was tranquil and untroubled, my mind concentrated and unified. (Bhayabherava Sutta, MN 4. 20–2)

This account describes a process remarkably similar to modern cognitive-behavioral methods involving repeated exposure to the focus of the fear and deliberately facing feelings until they subside. When you see things as they are, you are no longer haunted by your fears of what they may be. Achieving this clarity, you release the energy that has been tied up by your fear.

Riding Dragons

In his book *Zen Therapy*, David Brazier used the image of riding dragons.

These days . . . we are apt to seek out a therapist to . . . help us get the dragon back into its cave. Therapists of many schools will oblige in this, and we will be returned to what Freud called "ordinary unhappiness" and, temporarily, heave a sigh of relief, our repressions working smoothly once again. Zen, by contrast, offers dragon-riding lessons, for the few who are sufficiently intrepid. (Brazier 1995, p. 14)

This image of dragon-riding has drawn comment from many who have read David's book. It has clearly caught people's imaginations. Why should this be?

Perhaps it is because all of us, deep down, know that the dragons are friendly. You have a sense that while returning to ordinary unhappiness may be a comfortable enough option, it is, in some way, less than you are capable of. Within your sorrow is your energy. That energy is tied into your struggle to hide your nature as ever-changing, impermanent beings. It creates the myth of a substantial self. But that energy can better be applied in other ways. If you can release it, you can use it in living to the full, in encountering the world and in helping others to do likewise.

THEORIES INTRODUCED IN THIS CHAPTER

- the Snake Sutra: teaching as powerful for good or harm;
- primary and secondary anger;
- anger and grief; and
- harnessing anger and other negative emotions.

· 16 ·

Facing Impermanence

Leaves fallen
Dark and dank, under the oak
Decaying into soft brown loam
I do not need to know how grass will grow next summer.

This short verse came to me during a period of meditation last Easter. It was just a week since my close friend had died. She had been ill for several years with cancer and for nine months had known she was dying. It was the previous July when she told me that this time she would not take any more treatment. Treatment could only prolong her life by months, and she felt more ready to go with the process of dying that was already unfolding.

I spent those summer months at our retreat center in France and so was unable to see my friend for a time; but she was often in my thoughts. Although we exchanged letters, I did not know at that stage how long she might live. I did not know if she would even be alive when I returned to England. Before I had left, we had had long talks, sitting in her garden, as we had done so often when our children were small. We shared memories and talked about the times we had spent together. We had been friends for many years. We had met through a common interest in working with women's health groups. We had run workshops together. We had trained as therapists together. We had sat up late many evenings together talking about our lives, our plans, our ideologies. In recent years we had seen less of each other as our lives had taken different directions, but we had never lost contact. It was a time to catch up and to look back, to say the things we would regret leaving unsaid, to decide what did not need to be said after all. As I left for France, we said the first of many goodbyes that we would say that year.

In fact, it was April when my friend died. All through the autumn and winter I spent time with her, first sitting in her living-room and occasionally venturing out for walks on the days she felt stronger. Later, when her failing lungs prevented her making even the short journey to the stair-lift which had been specially installed for her, I sat with her in her bedroom.

Those last months I remember her room as a place of great peace. Her daughters had redecorated the walls in a deep lilac over the summer before, knowing she would spend her final weeks there. As winter gave way to spring, early sunshine flooded through the windows. I sat, sometimes on a chair by her bed, sometimes on the floor by the window. The room was full of the smell of spring flowers, daffodils, and white lilies. Sometimes we talked. Often we remained in silence. There was nothing more to be said. She would doze, and I would meditate. Or maybe we would meditate together.

It was a time that I remember for its sharp reality. On the edge of life and death, we knew each time we said goodbye that it might be the last. Yet in the time we spent together, there was no hurry; there was nothing we needed to do.

There were moments during those months when I felt more alive than I ever had. In that time when there was no certainty of future and the past was left behind, there was nothing left but to be alive in the here and now.

During her last week, my friend slipped into a different place. The last time I saw her was the day before she died.

As I sat with my sadness that April morning, images of the past year flooded my mind: the garden, the room where I had spent so much time. My mind went back to time spent in France and the woods there, where there is a meditation hut. The hut is situated under a large oak tree. The tree is old and has been coppiced in the past so that its low-growing branches could provide fodder for cattle. There is a flat stone by its roots on which I sit to meditate. I had spent time in the hut on solitary retreat during the summer. During that time, my friend's imminent dying had often been in my mind.

Sitting in woods, one is constantly aware of the processes of life and death. Fallen branches and even dead trees lie rotting on the ground, home to a host of insects and fungi. Yet on these branches often small plants grow, finding a rich holding for their roots in the crumbling wood. Moss invades everywhere so that branches, stones, and earthy banks are covered with soft green growth. Small creatures rustle through the undergrowth. Butterflies and other flying insects flit between the fringed branches of the leafy canopy. The floor is covered with last year's leaves and the seeds of next year's trees.

These images returned to me. One of the benefits of meditation practice is that through it one can create mental images that then become anchors in times of sadness or difficulty. The experiential understanding of birth and death that came from that time in the woods came back to me in images now as I sat facing my grief. The decaying leaves, creating the rich woodland soil. The glimpses through the trees to the field beyond, bright in the sunshine, with grasses waving, wild flowers, and tall, tall thistles. Here was life unfolding in its own way. Things growing, things dying. Processes so interconnected that you could not look at anything and truly say whether it was in the process of birth or death. More than this, though, the processes carried on of their own accord. I did not need to do anything. I could watch the scene. It was just as it had been when I sat with my friend and the process unfolded in its own time.

Buddhist psychology suggests that people spend much of their lives in flight from the processes that are inevitable. Birth, sickness, old age, and death are all dukkha. They are also a Noble Truth. Dukkha is an inevitable part of life yet people often spend their energy trying to defend ourselves against it. They create mental structures and defenses so that they do not need to think about it. They try to reassure themselves of their permanence by creating a sense of identity. Yet life is much simpler than this. The miracle of the wood is that life continues and flows in an interconnected way. New trees replace old ones. Young birds hatch each year as old ones die. Only we humans have such difficulty in letting go and allowing ourselves to be part of this greater dance of life.

Impermanence and Control

As a therapist, I am often in the position of helping others at times of crisis. These times have frequently involved some kind of loss. Whether there is bereavement or whether a person loses other important aspects of life—a job, home, health, maybe— there is a confrontation with impermanence.

Experiencing the death of someone close is a particularly strong reminder of the uncertainty of life and may provoke a spiritual or psychological crisis. It brings you into certain knowledge that the world is not predictable. It is not controllable. It is not under the influence of your will. It is non-self.

Many psychological strategies are concerned with helping you feel in control. The processes of self-creation are basically strategies in the war against impermanence. You create the illusion of a substantive self, and you impose your view on the world so that you can feel in control of it all. Buddhist psychology presents another possibility—that if you can let go of your self-investment in the world, you will see everything in different ways. You will be open to the radiance of life and the miracle of being alive. You will truly encounter the world and the other people whom you meet.

Working with Loss

When you are experiencing a loss, it is often hard to hold onto any sense of the miracle of life. My friend's death, though painful to those who loved her, was in some ways a gentle process. There was a sense that she gradually let go of life. She was able to tie up loose ends so that she died with a sense of completeness.

Deaths are not always so gentle. Sudden accidents, violent killings, or agonizing suffering do not make death easy to bear. A Buddhist approach is not to smooth over the unpleasantness of such things. Even the gentlest death is unlikely to occur without some suffering and indignity. To meet someone who is struggling to come to terms with sudden loss, you need to be able to contain many emotions.

A Buddhist approach is a middle way. It suggests that you need to allow your feelings to flow but not to get swept away by them. It is natural for feelings to arise, but you should not allow them to push you into those grasping behaviors that serve only to create illusion and build up more trouble in the future. Helping others, you can encourage them to face feelings that come up in them without rushing into distractions. There are times when comfort is very much needed, but it should not be simply a denial of the pain. In modern Western society people tend either to hide feelings or to let them rule despotically. It is better to accept that feelings naturally arise and are not something shameful or harmful to be hidden away.

So there is a need to talk and to let feelings flow, but also within this to find stillness. Being with someone who is experiencing loss, you may need simply to provide a quiet space. If you can be with someone with stillness and reverence, your groundedness will provide the containment that they may not be able to cultivate in themselves. Grounded presence communicates something of the trustworthiness of the world, despite the tragedy that is currently unfolding. Just as the image of the wood returned to me in my meditation at that time of grief, so too, the presence of someone who is not swept away by tides of feeling can bring calm, comfort, and confidence to the person who is struggling. The Buddha saw the sadhu walking across the town square at that time when his encounters with sickness, old age, and death had so disturbed him. That image of a spiritual practitioner's presence in a world of suffering provided the vision for his subsequent search.

As you provide a calm presence, you may also encourage the person to talk. Talking directly about the loss can be important and healing, but you need sensitivity to what a person is ready to bear at any point. Most people who are in grief have a sense of what they need to do. The process of coming to terms with a loss can unfold over time and have different stages. You can support by helping the person move through the process, by listening and enabling the sharing which is at the edge of what is bearable. You should not intrude by forcing the process beyond the point it has already reached.

In addition, you may help the person to find reconnection with life. Connecting with the universal processes, as I did through my meditations in the woods, can place the loss in a broader context and bring resolution. The places and images that provide this wider context may vary from one person to another, but most people have a sense of life beyond individual survival, even if this sense is unformed. Helping someone to find their own images of the life process may help them to turn grief around.

Impermanence as an Opportunity

In facing loss, you are faced with the truth of life. When someone dies, those who are close to that person experience an irrevocable change in their lives. They also see in the other's death that their own death is inevitable and may come at any time. Buddhism has put much emphasis on contemplating death and impermanence. This is not because it is morbid but because it recognizes that in holding on to the illusions of immortality you take a lot of energy out of your life and avoid really living for the time you have. Facing death, you have the opportunity to face life.

The following passage is from a letter written by the Japanese teacher Rennyo. It is commonly read at funeral and memorial services. The text expresses powerfully the Buddhist injunction to live fully and use the opportunity life provides to seek enlightenment—in other words, to live fully and encounter reality while the opportunity is available.

In silently contemplating the transient nature of human existence, nothing is more fragile and fleeting in this world than the life of a person. Thus we have not heard of a human life lasting for a thousand years. Life swiftly passes and who among people can maintain his form for even a hundred years?

Whether I go before others, or others go before me; whether it be today or it be tomorrow, who is to know? Those who leave before us are countless as drops of dew. Though in the morning we may have radiant health, in the evening we may return to white ashes. When the winds of impermanence blow, our eyes are closed forever; and when the last breath leaves us, our face loses its color.

Though loved ones gather and lament, everything is to no avail. The body is then sent into an open field and vanishes from this world with the smoke of cremation, leaving only the white ashes. There is nothing more real than this truth of life. The fragile nature of human existence underlies both the young and the old and therefore we must, one and all, turn to the teachings of the Buddha and awaken to the ultimate source of life.

By so understanding the meaning of death, we shall come to fully appreciate the meaning of this life which is unrepeatable and thus to be treasured above all else. By virtue of true compassion let us together live with the thought of Buddha in our hearts. ("White Ashes," in Rennyo's Letters, 5.16, translation from Jodo Shinshu service book)

When you experience a loss, you are forced to reorganize your sense of life, and this process of reorganization can provide a window of opportunity for spiritual growth. Many people turn to the spiritual at times of crisis and bereavement, and although this can be viewed as a kind of escapism, it can also be an opportunity for real spiritual change. The support of friends and others who are around at the time of the bereavement may help a person make that difference between a superficial turning to religion for comfort and real engagement with its life-changing potential.

Saying Goodbye

An important part of the grieving process is that we say goodbye to the loved one. The process of saying goodbye may begin before a death or separation occurs. With my friend I was lucky to have many months in which we could say our goodbyes. During this process we went through a number of stages. We shared good memories. We talked about unresolved matters. We got to know each other's sense of life and death and our respective beliefs and feelings about it. We shared our perspectives on things that had happened, sometimes surprising each other with our different views of the same events. We talked about how my friend would like to be remembered and how I could help in the process that would unfold after her death.

Our initial conversations happened while my friend was still well enough to talk at length. Later, we said goodbyes in shorter ways. The last time I saw her, on the day before she died, she was not able to respond to me. I do not even know for certain if she heard or understood what I said. Yet I sat with her and shared a few brief glimpses of our friendship, thanked her, and said goodbye.

When there is not the opportunity to speak with the loved one before the death, and even when there is, the funeral and other ceremonies of memorial play important parts in the process of letting go. Such occasions provide a focus and a vessel for containment, encouraging the grieving person to bring together and face feelings, as well as to reflect on the life of the one who has died and bring some psychological closure.

Ceremony and Ritual

It is at the time of a death that people frequently turn to ritual and ceremony. This is common to most societies. The need to mark such events as a death with some form of symbolic activity or communal expression seems so universal that it may be intimately linked to our instinctive natures as humans. Ceremony and ritual provide a vivid way of expressing those aspects of your life experience that are hard to express in other ways. The dramatic enactment of a ritual conveys grandeur and authority that words alone cannot. Ritual provides opportunities for multilayered symbolism that need not be explicitly interpreted and allusions to beliefs and processes that are important but not easy to define. It brings communities together in shared activity and, as traditional ceremonial is re-enacted, provides continuity between the generations.

Although the Buddha refuted belief in rituals as magic, the Buddhist world has created a great many rituals and ceremonies to mark the different facets of life in a sangha or community. As a Buddhist practitioner, it is not uncommon to become involved in helping others create rituals to say goodbye to loved ones. This may mean taking part in funeral or memorial ceremonies, or it may involve helping a person to plan and enact smaller, more personal rituals.

Personal ceremonies may be as simple as writing a letter to the dead person and placing it in a special place or floating it down a stream. They may involve creating a shrine or other sacred space in which the person can be remembered. They may involve planting a tree or laying flowers, making a gift to the wider community, or dedicating an event or book to the person. They may involve cleaning the room the person occupied and giving away or disposing of possessions. All these actions can take on ritual qualities if they are approached in a way that allows the drama of the situation to unfold, and if they are given sufficient respect and planning so that they can be carried out in a full and meaningful way.

Ritual and ceremony rely upon tradition but are also a living form. A good ritual always requires a combination of formal structuring, often drawn from time-honored sources, and space for spontaneous responses. There is a language to ritual that is made up of common elements, but it is also a form of communication that allows for inventiveness. It can be simple or elaborate. Sometimes the ritual element is introduced simply in the manner of speaking—the use of poetic language or a slightly raised tone of voice. These things can enable simple words to become vehicles for a deep expression of feelings that are otherwise hard to put into words.

Ritual requires the ability to use the dramatic with respect and dignity. In learning this art, you need to immerse yourself in the forms that are available to you. Performing ritual is an act of non-self expression. To do it well, you need to move beyond ego and take on the performance role for the wider community. Much as the shaman allows himself to be the channel for the spirit world, so too the performer of rituals becomes a channel for the collective expression of feelings and beliefs within a group. This is true even when the ritual is only for one participant. It is in the nature of ritual that it is an opening to the collective level.

Facing the End

In the autumn, when my friend was sick, my thoughts often moved to the processes of life and death. One day I was walking in the local park, a beautiful landscaped valley with a river running through it, overhung by tall trees. The water of the river plays over rocks, in places forming small waterfalls, with sheets of churning, shimmering water. At other places it lies in shallows where ducks waddle about, scrounging bread from local children.

As I stood watching the water with its dancing reflections, a leaf fell from one of the overhanging trees. It was autumn, and many leaves were falling, but this leaf caught my attention.

Many people were dying, but my friend was also holding my attention.

I watched the leaf as it span and tumbled in the water, down over the waterfall and on, downstream and out of sight. Just one leaf, gone in a moment.

I looked up at the tree. It was early in the autumn, and not many leaves had fallen. The branch still looked well covered. In fact it didn't really look as if it had lost any leaves. The tree was still perfect.

I thought some more. Soon the tree would lose all its leaves. A good wind and they would all go chasing up the valley, leaving just the bare dead branch. What then? Come spring, the tree would grow new leaves. It would still be a perfect tree, doing what trees should do.

But what if the tree blew down? Trees do not last forever. A winter storm might send it crashing into the stream, where the park attendants would cut it up for burning. What then? Last year the park lost several trees, yet the wooded banks still look just as fine as ever. If that tree fell, there would still be others.

Yes, but what if they cut down the whole forest? What if they decided to build on the land? So many beautiful woodlands have already been lost to developers. What if the woods disappeared? What then? But there are other woods. Despite pessimistic anxieties about the environment, there are still plenty of beautiful woodlands around. If these woods go, we will still find woods where we can walk.

But will there always be woods? There are so many environmental catastrophes today; we seem bound to destroy this planet. What if we really mess up and the whole earth gets wrecked or destroyed—what then?

Look. There is a whole universe out there, perfect just as it is. If this little planet blew itself to kingdom come, that universe would still be there, galaxies on wheeling galaxies of it . . .

Often we look too narrowly at life. We become caught in our small part of the story and construct our self-world to the exclusion of the bigger vision. We invest in our own stories and miss the big picture. Buddhist psychology invites us to let go of our personal agenda and embrace the whole. This does not mean that we should lose sight of the details. We still need to care for the individual leaves and trees and parks, but we need also to have a sense that there is a big, big world available. Our own stories are important, but they are not special just because they are ours.

Buddhist psychology invites us to release ourselves from the limitations of the self-perspective. When we can do this, we touch the universe. We develop faith in the process of life. We embrace life more fully.

> *A leaf falls*
> *Onto the surface of the water*
> *Then tumbles over the waterfall.*
> *But the tree is still perfect*

CREATING CONDITIONS

Next spring
The tree will have new leaves
Dancing in the summer breeze
It will be perfect still

If I should die tomorrow
Think of me with love
But do not grieve too much

Glossary

Buddhist Terminology

abhava   Non-becoming.

adhimoksha   Reverent appreciation. The attitude that leads to liberation.

ajjhosana   Holding.

alaya   Originally meaning possessions or accumulation, hence clinging, this term later came to be used to describe the storing of karmic residues or mental contents. Eventually it became reified into the part of the mind used to store these things.

anunaya   Personal attachment.

avidya   Not seeing, ignorance. The opposite of enlightened vision.

bhava   Becoming.

bhikshu (fem.: bhikshuni)   An ordained follower of the Buddha who keeps the full set of vinaya precepts or rules. Literally the term means sharer, i.e., one who is not attached to possessions. Often referred to as a monk, though mendicant rather than monastic. The term was used in the Buddha's time to describe his ordained disciples and is still used. Not all ordained Buddhists are bhikshus/bhikshunis.

bija   Literally, seed. The term is used to describe units of karma.

bodhisattva Originally, one destined for Buddha-hood. A person or mythical figure who embodies positive, helping qualities. In particular, one who has vowed to forgo nirvana for the sake of saving others. The bodhisattva vow expresses this wish.

chanda Aspiration, desire, will.

chetana Intention; literally, chitta-ness. The mind that is chasing something.

chitta The attentive mind, the heart.

commentarial tradition An understanding of the Pali sutras built up as commentaries by scholars during the period 500–1000 CE.

conditions All things arise dependent upon conditions, so everything is said to be conditioned. Buddhist psychology emphasizes working with conditions to create the possibility for positive change to arise. Things that are conditioned are not determined.

dana Generosity, donations, generally to the ordained community.

deva A celestial being.

Dharma The Buddhist teachings.

dharma Reality, the objects themselves.

dhatus Foundations, bases.

dukkha Affliction; literally, a bad space.

dvesha Hate, one of the Three Poisons.

jaramarana Decay-and-deathness.

jati Birth.

karma Action, the continuing effects of action; hence natural law of moral effect.

klesha Negative mental factors; *see also* kushala.

koan A question to be struggled with in order to reach a point of spiritual breakthrough. Sometimes koans take the form of traditional questions, such as "What is the sound of one hand clapping?" But they can also be seen as arising naturally in daily life; hence a life issue that recurs can act as a koan for us. Koans are not soluble by direct reason. They require spiritual growth for the solution.

kushalas Benign mental factors; opposite of kleshas.

lakshana A sign; often used to mean a sign or indicator of self.

lobha Greed, one of the Three Poisons.

manana-vijnana The part of the mind that orders or moderates experience.

manas *See* manana-vijnana.

manaskara Attention. This factor functions to "yoke the associated states to the object" (Bhikkhu Bodhi, *A Comprehensive Manual of Abhidharma*).

mano-vijnana The mind's eye, or imagination; thought. One of the six senses.

mantra A short phrase, usually of ancient, contracted words that are difficult to translate, that is repeated in order to focus the mind on the positive and to protect the mind from negative thoughts.

marga A path or track.

metta practice A Buddhist practice that involves imagining sending goodwill to others.

moha Confusion; one of the Three Poisons.

nama-rupa A phenomenon, a named object, an object that is perceived.

nirodha Containment (often translated as cessation).

nirvana The place of completion of the process of overcoming self. A place of bliss. Hence, by extension, the ultimate place of bliss.

object The thing to which one gives attention. The mind is conditioned by its object. The term object here is technical and may be a thing, an idea, a person, or whatever we give attention to, whether it is real or imaginary.

object-related, object relation An important area of Buddhist theory relating to the role of objects in conditioning the mind. Object-related work involves deliberately focusing attention on the object in order to evoke responses that can be explored.

other-centered　An approach to psychological work that takes the focus away from the client on to other parties. This is particularly used by Buddhist psychology to break the pattern of self-grasping. It may involve work on imaginatively entering another's world.

other-perspective　Seeing the situation from the position of another person.

other-power　Buddhist approaches or schools that focus on faith, recognizing the pitfalls in trying to gain spiritual achievements through our own efforts, and our limited ability to achieve spiritual advances on our own.

prajna　Wisdom.

pratyaya　Conditions (verb).

precepts　The ethical code. Different levels of precepts are taken by lay people and monastics. Five lay precepts are common to most traditions as the basis for the committed lay life. Precepts are seen as an aid to training and a description of a wholesome life rather than as rules or commandments.

primal longing or vow　A deep, altruistic longing.

Pure Land　(1) A land as seen by a Buddha. (2) A mythical land, where enlightenment is easy to attain, created by Amida Buddha, who is the manifestation of the Buddha's teaching continuing in the world. (3) An other-power approach to Buddhism whose practice is based on the practice of *nembutsu*, which is the chanting of Amida Buddha's name, and faith in rebirth in Amida's Pure Land.

rebirth　Coming to a new life (literally or symbolically).

refuge　Taking refuge means placing complete faith in something. Traditionally Buddhists take refuge in the three jewels of Buddha, Dharma and Sangha.

rupa　Form; a phenomenon, an apparition; the thing perceived from our own frame of reference.

samadhi The state of single-pointedness, tranquil absorption achieved in meditation, concentration.

samjna Entrancement, association (commonly translated as perceptions).

samsara The cyclical world experienced by the deluded mind.

samskara Mental formations, confections and elaborations created by the mind.

samudaya Things that arise. Our response to affliction (the second of the Four Noble Truths).

sangha The Buddhist community, often specifically the ordained community.

self-power Buddhist practices that rely upon one's own efforts.

shadayatanas Literally, the uncontrollables. A term used for the six senses.

shunyata Empty of self.

sila Ethics.

skandhas Commonly known as the five aggregates. Five elements that make up the person. Five stages in the process of self-creation, which form a cycle.

smriti Mindfulness, having a positive object in mind. Having the mind full of Buddha.

sparsha Contact.

special objectivity Seeing one's own experience as other. Having awareness of one's thoughts, feelings and reactions without feeling identified with them.

tantra, tantric A path of Buddhist practice that involves transforming everything into an opportunity for spiritual development, even if those things are commonly thought of as harmful or negative.

Three Signs of Being A teaching that states that all constructed things (samskaras) are afflictive, all phenomena are impermanent, and all things (dharmas) are non-self.

trishna Craving, thirst.

upadana Clinging, ungenerosity.

vedana Reaction, having three valences: positive, negative and neutral (often translated as feeling); knowingness, prejudice.

vidya Clear seeing, enlightened vision.

vijnana Self-orientated consciousness (often simply translated as consciousness). The prefix vi- suggests either divided or observer consciousness. The unenlightened mentality.

vinaya The full set of precepts kept by ordained bhikshus and bhikshunis.

Western Terminology

anchor An object, idea, phrase, or image that can be used to mark a positive feeling psychologically to aid its recall at a later date.

bracketing A term from phenomenological theory, describing the setting aside of one's preconceptions so that one can see a situation freshly (i.e., putting one's perspective in brackets). Can also be described as creating an epoche.

congruence One of the three core conditions identified by Dr. Carl Rogers as necessary for psychological improvement. Congruence means being authentic and genuine in one's responses.

contagion The process whereby one person "catches" a psychological state from another.

core conditions Conditions identified by Dr. Carl Rogers as necessary for psychological improvement. Often three conditions are identified. Sometimes the list is expanded to six.

empathy Appreciating how it is for another person. Experiencing their story as if standing in the other's shoes. Perceiving the world as if through the eyes of the other person, while remaining aware of the "as if" condition.

empiricism Reliance upon data that are susceptible to observation and experiment rather than theory alone.

epoche A technical term in phenomenology; see "bracketing."

grounding   Techniques for calming oneself through calming the body and particularly being aware of physical contact.

invested object   An object, person, image, etc. that has been given symbolic meaning.

natural attitude   A term from phenomenology describing the common viewpoint. The shared conventions and delusions of a culture.

person-centered approach   An approach to therapy developed by Dr. Carl Rogers based on offering the core conditions and trusting the client's own ability to develop psychologically.

phenomenology   A school of philosophy which uses descriptive method to explore areas of experience previously thought of as subjective and not open to investigation. Originated by Edmund Husserl.

positivism   A trend in Western philosophy that asserts the achievement of progress through empiricism, established by Auguste Comte.

protagonist   The actor, especially the person who becomes the central focus of a psychodrama, presenting a personal story for group exploration.

psychodrama   A group method, often therapeutic, developed by Jacob Moreno, which involves enactment.

role reversal   A psychodrama technique that involves stepping into another character's shoes.

transference   A term used in psychodynamic approaches to describe the phenomenon whereby expectations and reactions associated with one person (often a parent) are played out in relation to another person (often the therapist).

unconditional positive regard   Complete nonjudgmental acceptance. One of the core conditions proposed by Dr. Carl Rogers.

Bibliography and References

Texts

In this book you will find reference made to the original texts listed below. The first three groups of texts are from the Pali canon, the collection of texts written in the ancient Indian language of Pali. Pali texts are particularly associated with the Theravadin or southern tradition of Buddhism but are widely used by all schools. There is an equivalent set of texts in Chinese that are 80 percent identical to the Pali texts. These were originally in Sanskrit, another ancient Indian language. Theravada Buddhism places its emphasis on the life of practice and spiritual accomplishment. The Pali texts offer a particularly detailed resource for the study of psychological method, since many of them give practical advice on overcoming psychological obstacles and detailed descriptions of mental processes.

Of the other texts listed here, the Heart Sutra is recognized by the Mahayana or northern schools of Buddhism. It is a feature of Mahayana Buddhism that it diversified into new ways of presenting the Buddha's teachings and particularly developed the notion of the bodhisattva, who placed the saving of others before personal salvation. Most Mahayana texts were originally written in Sanskrit but survive as early translations in different languages. It has become common to use Sanskrit as standard for many technical terms. In this book, Sanskrit is generally used unless the context makes it imperative to do otherwise. Rennyo's letters are an example. They are Pure Land texts, written by the fifteenth-century Japanese priest. They reflect the Pure Land school's emphasis on faith and humility. Pure Land approaches represent a strand in Buddhist thought that can be traced back to the Indian traditions and flourished in the Far East, particularly in China and Japan, where they still represent one of the largest Buddhist traditions.

Pali Texts

Majjhima Nikaya

This is the volume of texts in the collection of sutras known as the Pali canon. The texts in the Majjhima Nikaya offer short accounts of particular occasions on which the Buddha or one or other of his close disciples gave teachings. A number of translations exist, for example Bhikkhu Bodhi, 1995, *The Middle Length Discourses of the Buddha*, Wisdom, Boston.

Samyutta Nikaya

The Samyutta Nikaya is the third major section of the Pali sutras. It contains a series of sutras linked by theme. See Bhikkhu Bodhi, 2000, *The Connected Discourses of the Buddha*, Wisdom, Boston.

Abhidharma

The Abhidharma is a collection of texts that offers a systematic analysis of teachings on the mind. The text consists largely of lists of factors. See Bhikkhu Bodhi, 1993, *A Comprehensive Manual of Abhidharma*, Buddhist Publication Society, Kandy, Sri Lanka. A full translation of the Pali Abhidharma is available from the Pali Text Society, 73 Lime Walk, Oxford OX3 7AD, UK.

Mahayana and Other Texts

The Heart Sutra

This is short text is very widely known in the Mahayana Buddhist world. Versions occur in Sanskrit as well as in Far Eastern languages. The text is thought to be a distillation of the Larger Prajnaparamita Sutra, a central text in these traditions.

The Summary of the Great Vehicle, by Bodhisattva Asanga

This is one of the earliest texts of the Yogacara school, a school that developed around the fourth century CE and was instrumental in developing Mahayana philosophy. Asanga, the writer of this particular text, was a principal thinker in this approach. The edition quoted in this book is a translation from Chinese of Paramartha by J. P. Keenan (Tanisho 31, 1593) published by the Numata Center, Berkeley, CA, 1992.

Rennyo's Letters

Rennyo was a Pure Land priest in medieval Japan. His letters, collected in five sections, or fascicles, were written to his followers during his travels around Japan. They are regarded as scripture by the Jodo Shinshu tradition. Translations of Rennyo's letters can be found in the book *Rennyo* (M. Rogers and A. Rogers, 1991) listed below.

Select Bibliography

Akong Rinpoche. 1987. *Taming the Tiger*. Dzalendara, Eskdalemuir, Scotland.

Batchelor, S. 1983. *Alone with Others: An Existential Approach to Buddhism*. Grove Press, New York.

Batchelor, S. 1994. *The Awakening of the West: The Encounter of Buddhism and Western Culture*, Parallax, Berkeley, CA.

Beech, C. and Brazier, D. 1996. "Empathy for a Real World," in R. Hutterer, G. Pawlowsky, P. Schmid and R. Stipsits (eds), *Client Centered and Experiential Psychotherapy: A Paradigm in Motion*. Peter Lang, Frankfurt am Main.

Berzin, A. 2000. *Relating to a Spiritual Teacher*. Snow Lion, New York.

Bollas, C. 1993. *Being a Character: Psychoanalysis and Self Experience*. Routledge, London.

Brazier, C. 1998. *Reflected Selves*. Unpublished M.Phil. thesis, University of Keele.

Brazier, D. 1993. *Beyond Carl Rogers*. Constable, London.

Brazier, D. 1995. *Zen Therapy*. Constable, London.

Brazier, D. 1997. *The Feeling Buddha*. Constable, London.

Brazier, D. 1999. Dharma talk given at retreat in Amsterdam.

Brazier, D. 2001. *The New Buddhism*. Constable, London.

Brooks, C. 1974. *Sensory Awareness*. Ross Erikson, Santa Barbara, CA.

Chardin, T. 1964. *Le Milieu Divin: an essay on the interior life*, English edn. Fontana, London. (First publ. in French, 1957.)

Crook, J. and Fontyana, D. 1990. *Space in Mind: East–West Psychology and Contemporary Buddhism*. Element Books, Shaftesbury, UK.

Dalai Lama. 1997. *Sleeping, Dreaming and Dying: An Exploration of Consciousness*, ed. F. Varela. Wisdom, Boston.

Epstein, M. 1996. *Thoughts without a Thinker*. Duckworth, London.

Friedman, L. and Moon, S. 1997. *Being Bodies: Buddhist Women on the Paradox of Embodiment*. Shambala, Boston.

Jeffers, S. 1987. *Feel the Fear and Do It Anyway*. Century Hutchinson, London.

Jung, C. 1959, *The Archetypes and the Collective Unconscious*. Routledge & Kegan Paul, London.

Gendlin, E. T. 1981. *Focusing*. Bantam, London and New York.

Govinda, A. 1976. *Creative Meditation and Multi-dimensional Consciousness*. Quest Books, Theosophical Publishing House, Wheaton, Illinois.

Hanh, N. 1974. *Zen Keys*, Anchor Press, New York.

Hanh, N. 1990. *Present Moment, Wonderful Moment*. Parallax, Berkeley, CA.

Hanh, N. 1992. *Touching Peace: Practicing the Art of Mindful Living*. Paralax, Berkeley CA.

Hanh, N. 1993a. *For a Future to be Possible: Commentaries on the Five Wonderful Precepts*. Parallax, Berkeley, CA.

Hanh, N. 1993b. *Thundering Silence: Sutra on Knowing the Better Way to Catch a Snake*. Parallax, Berkeley, CA.

Jodo Shinshu Service Book. Honpa Hongwanji Mission of Hawaii.

Keown, D. 2001. *The Nature of Buddhist Ethics*. Palgrave, Basingstoke and New York.

McConnell, J. A. 1995. *Mindful Mediation*. Buddhist Research Institute, Bangkok, Thailand.

Macy, J. 1993. *World As Lover, World As Self*. Parallax, Berkeley, CA.

Manne, J. 1997. *Soul Therapy*. North Atlantic Books, Berkeley, CA.

Maslow, A. 1954. *Motivation and Personality*. Harper & Brothers, New York.

Mollon, P. 1993. *The Fragile Self: The Structure of Narcissistic Disturbance*, Whurr, London.

Murcott, S. 1991. *The First Buddhist Women*. Parallax, Berkeley, CA.

Queen, C. 2000. *Engaged Buddhism in the West*. Wisdom, Boston.

Reat, N. R. 1951. *Origins of Indian Psychology*. Asian Humanities Press, Berkeley, CA.

Reat, N. R. 1994. *Buddhism: A History*. Asian Humanities Press, Berkeley, CA.

Reynolds, D. 1980. *The Quiet Therapies*. University of Hawaii, Honolulu.

Reynolds, D. 1989. *Flowing Bridges, Quiet Waters*. Albany, NY: State University of New York Press.

Rhys Davids, C. and Norman, K. 1997. *Poems of the Early Buddhist Nuns*. Pali Text Society, Oxford.

Rogers, C. R. 1951. *Client-Centered Therapy*. Constable, London.

Rogers, C. R. 1961. *On Becoming a Person*. Constable, London.

Rogers, C. R. 1983. *Freedom to Learn*. Merrill, New York.

Rogers, M. and Rogers, A. 1991. *Rennyo*. Asian Humanities Press, Berkeley, CA.

Spinelli, E. 1989. *The Interpreted World*. Sage, London.

Suzuki, S. 1970. *Zen Mind, Beginner's Mind*. Weatherhill, New York.

Trungpa, C. 1973. *Cutting through Spiritual Materialism*. Shambala, Boston.

Trungpa, C. 1991. *Meditation in Action*. Shambala, Boston.

Worden, J. W. 1987. *Grief Counselling and Grief Therapy*. Routledge, London.

Xu-Yun. 1988. *Empty Cloud, the Autobiography of the Chinese Zen Master*, trans. C. Luk. Element, Shaftesbury, UK.

Index

Other Books by Ulysses Press/Seastone

BUDDHA IN YOUR BACKPACK: EVERYDAY BUDDHISM FOR TEENS
Franz Metcalf, $12.95
Buddha in Your Backpack is a guide for navigating the teen years like a Buddha. It's ideal for teenagers who want to learn more about Buddhism or for those who simply want a better way to understand what's going on inside themselves and in the world around them.

HOW MEDITATION HEALS: A SCIENTIFIC EXPLANATION
Eric Harrison, $12.95
Combining Eastern wisdom with medical and scientific evidence, this book explains how and why meditation improved the functioning of all systems of the body.

JESUS AND BUDDHA: THE PARALLEL SAYINGS
Marcus Borg, Editor   Introduction by Jack Kornfield, $14.00
Traces the life stories and beliefs of Jesus and Buddha, then presents a comprehensive collection of their remarkably similar teachings on facing pages.

WHAT WOULD BUDDHA DO?: 101 ANSWERS TO LIFE'S DAILY DILEMMAS
Franz Metcalf, $9.95
Much as the "WWJD?" books help Christians live better lives by drawing on the wisdom of Jesus, this "WWBD?" book provides advice on improving your life by following the wisdom of another great teacher—Buddha.

YOU DON'T HAVE TO SIT ON THE FLOOR: MAKING BUDDHISM PART OF YOUR EVERYDAY LIFE
Jim Pym, $12.95
Explains Buddha's teachings in easy-to-understand terms and shows how to practice Buddhism while retaining other religious beliefs.

To order these books call 800-377-2542 or 510-601-8301, fax 510-601-8307, e-mail ulysses@ulyssespress.com, or write to Ulysses Press, P.O. Box 3440, Berkeley, CA 94703. All retail orders are shipped free of charge. California residents must include sales tax. Allow two to three weeks for delivery.

About the Author

Caroline Brazier is a member of an engaged Buddhist order and a practicing psychotherapist for fifteen years. With her husband, David Brazier, the author of *Zen Therapy*, *The New Buddhism* and *The Feeling Buddha*, she has been developing the teaching of Buddhist Psychology in the context of the modern therapeutic relationship since 1995. Together they lead full-length training programs in applied Buddhist psychology and psychotherapy in Great Britain and regularly run events in Europe and North America. Details can be found through the website at www.buddhistpsychology.info or by contacting Amida Trust at The Buddhist House, 12 Coventry Road, Narborough LE19 2GR, UK.